Perpetua's Passion

Perpetua's Passion

The Death and Memory
of a Young Roman Woman

Joyce E. Salisbury

ROUTLEDGE

New York and London

Published in 1997 by
Routledge
29 West 35th Street
New York, NY 10001

Published in Great Britain in 1997 by
Routledge
11 New Fetter Lane
London EC4P 4EE

Library of Congress Cataloging-in-Publication Data

Salisbury, Joyce E.
    Perpetua's passion : the death and memory of a young Roman woman /
by Joyce E. Salisbury
        p.   cm.
Includes bibliographical references and index.
ISBN 0-415-91836-7 (hardcover). — ISBN (invalid) 0-415-91837-5 (pbk.)
    1. Perpetua, Saint, d. 203.   2. Passio SS. Perpetuae et Felicitatis.
3. Christian saints—Tunisia—Biography.   4. Christian martyrs—Tunisia—Biography.   5. Christian women saints—Tunisia—Biography.   I. Title.
BR1720. P42S25   1997
272'.1'092—dc21
[B]   97-21973
                                                                         CIP

To
Bob Balsley

Contents

Acknowledgments

As with all books, this one required me to learn about many new things. This task was forwarded and made even more enjoyable by the help of many people.

I could not have understood ancient Carthage so well without going there, or without the expertise of the archaelogists who have worked for decades slowly and painstakingly excavating the sites of that ancient city. JoAnn Freed, Colin Wells, and Susan Stevens were particularly generous with their hospitality and expertise in Tunisia.

Many other scholars, including Mary Ann Rossi and Thomas Heffernan, engaged in stimulating conversations that enriched this book. Gregory Aldrete brought the eye of a classicist to a careful reading of the manuscript. In spite of all this help, mistakes inevitably occur; they are all my own.

This book is enriched by the illustrations, which I needed lots of help to obtain. Bob Balsley, Margaret Alexander, Lynn Santure, and Lori Francis took photographs on site in Tunisia. Alicia Nowicki did the fine sketches. Lisa Quam prepared the maps with guidance from Professors William Niedzwiedz and William Laatsch. Jane Schulenburg provided the cover illustration. "The Passion of Perpetua," which is reprinted here, is from *The Acts of the Christian Martyrs*, translated by Herbert Musurillo (1972). Oxford University Press holds the copyright and has given permission to reprint the image here.

The Frankenthal family generously endowed the research fund that permitted me to cover the expenses of this scholarship. Finally, the book is dedicated to Bob Balsley, who shared the pleasures of travel in Tunisia and eased its rigors; who shared the burdens of reading seemingly endless drafts of this manuscript; and who will share with me all the memories this project generated.

Introduction

Eusebius, the fourth-century church historian, wrote in loving detail of many of the men and women who died for their faith. "Sometimes they were killed with the axe, ... sometimes their legs were broken.... Sometimes they were hung up by the feet head down over a slow fire ...; sometimes noses, ears, and hands were severed."[1] This fortitude by the martyrs was only half the story for Christians—the acts also had to be remembered. Eusebius wrote to "rekindle the memory of the martyrs,"[2] and similar recollections have continued among the faithful for more than a millennium. This book studies the interaction between martyrdom and memory, both the memory of martyrdom and the memories that the martyrs brought to the moment of their brave death. It is a story of the confrontation of ideas as well as people.

From the middle of the first century A.D. through the beginning of the fourth, Christians periodically experienced persecution. Sometimes individuals were arrested; sometimes groups. At times persecution was a response to some local incident, and by the fourth century it was a conscious policy of emperors who wanted to force Christians to renounce their new faith. In all these instances, pagans saw stubborn subjects, and Christians saw the hand of God. Further, instead of suppressing Christianity, pagans simply created more converts by their persecution.

Pagans and Christians may have seen martyrdom from dramatically different perspectives, but both agreed that it represented a visible clash of cultures and ideas. A question that has always troubled me as I have studied the past is simply "What were they thinking?" People's actions emerge from some understanding of the world; that is, actions are consistent with people's beliefs. I wanted to try to understand the mentality that would allow someone to walk confidently into an arena knowing that he or she would die violently. Of course, Christian texts said that such conviction was a miracle. That may be so, but it does not seem enough of an explanation. I decided to study the act of martyrdom and the conflict of ideas behind it by focusing on one martyr, Perpetua, who died eagerly when she had much to live for.

In A.D. 203, a young Roman matron, Perpetua, was arrested with four companions. She had been raised by a prosperous family who cared a great deal for her, and she was now married and nursing an infant son. In spite of her father's pleas, she insisted on proclaiming and living her Christian beliefs, and refused to sacrifice to the emperor. She was tried, sentenced to the beasts in the arena, and imprisoned. So far, her experience echoes that of many Christian martyrs. However, Perpetua was exceptional in that, while imprisoned, she kept a diary of her last days. In this diary, Perpetua recorded her feelings about her family, her son, and her identity. Further, she described four dreams that she believed were prophetic. It is in this intensely personal record of her thoughts that we can see the clash of ideas in the mind of one individual.

Perpetua's diary also includes an eyewitness account of the last days of the other martyrs arrested with her. The narrative allows us to follow in vivid detail their deaths in the arena. Within this book, I include the full text that has been preserved as the "Passion of Saints Perpetua and Felicity."

In this text (as in the phenomenon of martyrdom in general), the predominant cultural conflict was that between the power of Rome and the power of the faith of those adhering to a new loyalty. But other conflicts were also expressed. Families and family loyalties were tried and divided in these tests of faith. Perpetua wrote of her father's anguish and her rejection of her infant son. Gender roles and expectations became confused in the arena. For example, Perpetua dreamed that she appeared naked, transformed into a man. Furthermore, her experience raised other questions about gender, such as whether motherhood precluded martyrdom. There were even conflicts within the Christian communities, which were exacerbated as the faithful were tested. Finally, Perpetua's visions and her personal strength raised issues that subsequent Christians confronted even as they praised the model of her heroism. This book explores these and other intellectual and physical conflicts.

As people make decisions about their futures (as Perpetua was doing in the course of her arrest and trial), they draw from their experiences in the past. And their memory of an experience is more important than anything that might actually have happened. The conflicting ideas that met in the arena of Carthage represented cultural memories that Perpetua took for granted. Therefore, I explore the intellectual heritage, the memories that came together in Perpetua's narrative and in her dreams. I show how one young woman used and reinterpreted what she had learned to come to a well-integrated decision to follow the path to martyrdom. Of course, the fact that the decision is comprehensible makes it no less miraculous.

The structure of my book is the study of the prevailing ideas in ever-narrowing circles until they finally collide in the person of Perpetua as she faces the beasts in the arena. Perpetua was a citizen of the Roman Empire, and as such, she had a particular upbringing, education, and family life. This book, then, begins with Rome, but of course it is not an exhaustive picture of Roman thought and culture in the late second century. Instead, I focus on the particular aspects of Roman culture that probably had a direct impact on Perpetua's martyrdom. These aspects include her family life, religious sensibilities that grounded the gods in particular spaces, and a consideration of the emperor in whose honor Perpetua was killed.

The events took place in Carthage, North Africa. This cosmopolitan city had a long history and a separate tradition from that of Rome. Perpetua inherited cultural memories that were particular to that region, and her martyrdom cannot be understood outside the spaces and values of Carthage. Thus, chapter 2 locates the physical and intellectual background of this city that rivaled Rome in wealth and grandeur, and studies the sensibilities and traditions of sacrifice that in part guided Perpetua's ideas and actions.

The martyr's pagan past in some ways affected her choices, but obviously the most significant influence was what she learned in the Christian community. In chapter 3, I consider the origins and practices of the Carthaginian congregation. Perhaps most important, I explore the appeal of the young church. Christians like Perpetua and others were convinced that God was present in these communities, and they were attracted to the proximity of the divine. Perpetua brought these ideas to her prison and to the arena. My retelling and study of the text of the "Passion of Perpetua" itself begins in this chapter as the young community confronted the power of Rome with the arrest of the small group of martyrs.

The next two chapters, "Prison" and "The Arena," continue the account of Perpetua's martyrdom. Through her diary and an analysis of related texts, these chapters explore the meaning of her dreams and show how her mind drew from the memories of her experiences to shape a particular understanding of her future. I also explore her social identity as she finally gave up her son, renounced her father, and came to a new understanding of her role as a Christian woman. In "The Arena," I consider the expectations and experience of the spectators and the martyrs as they gathered in the space of the final confrontation where Rome intended to exert its power over the Christian community.

Although the arena ended with Perpetua's death, the story of Perpetua's passion did not end there. Her diary was read annually on the day of her martyrdom, so her memory influenced many subsequent generations. But just as she transformed her memories as she adjusted to the new circumstances of Christian martyrdom, the memory of her passion was reinterpreted to suit a changed Christian world. The last chapter summarizes the fortunes of Rome, Carthage, and the Christian community after Perpetua's death, and looks at the use and reinterpretation of her text over time.

There are a number of good and accessible translations of the text of the "Passion of Perpetua and Felicity." I have chosen to cite the version that has the most accessible Latin edition of the text in conjunction with a translation. I have for the most part kept Musurillo's translation, changing only those parts that I believed could be made more accurate or understandable to modern readers.

Things are never simple when paradigms shift and ideologies conflict. Martyrdom represents perhaps the most vivid moment in such a clash of cultures. During the early centuries of Christianity, individuals were willing to die, and die horribly, to bear witness to a new idea that was displacing an old one. This book explores this conflict of ideas in the life of one individual. It further considers the power of the idea of this young woman whom we have remembered for so long.

one

Rome

Vibia Perpetua "came of a good family: she was well brought up and a respectably married woman." This is all that we are directly told about Perpetua's life before she came into conflict with the authorities of Rome. Figure 1.1 shows a statue of a young second-century Roman matron from Carthage. Perpetua would have looked very much like this modest young woman who was roughly her contemporary. Although the description of Perpetua's background is brief, it allows us to understand a great deal about her upbringing, and what ideas she absorbed in her youth. As a traditional Roman girl, she learned early that the center of her world was family, home, and the spirits who guarded them.

HOME AND HEARTH

Perpetua's family name, Vibius, suggests that the family had been Roman citizens for many generations. Her father was likely of some high rank in the municipal province, perhaps of the decurial class, although some speculate that he might have been as highly placed as senatorial rank.[1] In either case, the family must have been influential in the community, and must have benefited from its association with the power and history of Rome.

When Perpetua was born, she would have been placed at her father's feet. Her father picked her up, accepting her into the family over which he was the undisputed head.[2] In traditional Roman families, the power of the father (*patria potestas*) was complete and lasted as long as he lived, even after the child reached adulthood. Yet, the relationship that

Fig. 1.1 Roman matron. Bardo Museum, Tunis. Photograph by Bob Balsley.

developed between father and daughter was frequently close and sometimes affectionate. Among upper-class Romans, the father-daughter tie was important.[3] Obedient daughters forged political and social ties for the *pater familias,* and their obedience was often rewarded with paternal love. Some Roman texts describe the great affection that existed between fathers and daughters. In a famous example, Pliny the Younger described a father's grief over the death of his thirteen-year-old daughter: He recalled how the child would "cling to her father's neck," and at her death, the father "cast off all his other virtues and is wholly absorbed by his love for his child."[4] We cannot know whether Pliny's example was typical, but as we shall see in Perpetua's account of her father's reaction to her arrest, his deep grief revealed the close father-daughter bond that was possible in Roman families. The elder *pater fa-*

milias surely had looked forward to his daughter's comforting and gratifying him in his old age, an expectation that was to be scorned by Christian writers and Christian daughters.[5]

The authority of the father extended to all those within his household. Perpetua's immediate family included her mother and two living brothers (a third brother had died in childhood). The full household that came under the control of her father included slaves and freedpeople. In fact, the very term *"familia"* included these people not tied by blood but linked by law.[6] When Perpetua was arrested along with two of the household slaves, more than the favored daughter were flouting the authority of the beleaguered head of this house.

Under the absolute and affectionate guidance of her father, Perpetua received a good education. The use of language in Perpetua's diary reveals her to be well educated, and there is no reason to think she was an exception among Roman daughters. There is a great deal of evidence that Roman families valued education for their daughters. Fathers were probably more involved in the education of their daughters than that of their sons because sons were more likely to have tutors.[7] Romans believed educated women would be best able to pass on to their sons the values of Rome. For example, the first-century writer Quintilian wrote: "As for parents, I should like them to be as well educated as possible, and I am not speaking just of fathers." He continued to give credit to educated mothers, like Cornelia, mother of the Gracchi brothers, for their ability to instill eloquence into their sons.[8] Or, one can see the example of an epigram set up by a woman named Eurydice, who was an approximate contemporary of Perpetua. Her inscription read: "Eurydice of Hierapolis set up this tablet, when she had satisfied her desire to become learned; for she worked hard to learn letters, the repository of speech, because she was a mother of growing sons."[9]

As these examples show, even a favored daughter's education was designed to help her fulfill her role as a good mother. Marriages in the Roman tradition were arranged to provide suitable alliances between families. Among upper-class Romans, women married very young (by our standards), between the ages of eleven and sixteen or seventeen.[10] The laws of Caesar Augustus did not begin to penalize a young girl for nonmarriage until she was twenty,[11] so we may assume this to be the outer limit for a respectable girl to marry. Perpetua married in the upper limits of this age range: the account of her martyrdom says she was "newly married" and "about twenty-two years old"[12] (although this means she was twenty-one by our counting system). Perhaps her fond father was unwilling to arrange for her marriage, or there may have been other causes for the delay.

The issue of Perpetua's marriage raises one of the questions that has puzzled scholars of this text: Where was her husband during the proceedings? The account of the trial and the full diary make no mention of her husband, except to say she was a respectably married woman, thus implying the presence of a husband. However, the lack of the husband's appearance at the trial or even a mention of him in Perpetua's diary has raised much speculation. Several explanations have been offered for the husband's absence from the text. Perpetua herself may not have thought it significant to mention him. He may have been edited out of the text by subsequent redactors, perhaps to reduce the sexual implications of the presence of a husband.[13] Perhaps the husband had so disapproved of her conversion to Christianity that he renounced her and separated himself from the proceedings.[14] Maybe he was just out of town.[15]

At the very least, the omission of the husband likely signals the form of marriage contract that Perpetua had entered into. Under Roman law, women could enter into a *manus* marriage, in which case the woman moved from the control of her father to the control of her husband. However, that was not the only marriage possibility. By the late Republic (two centuries before Perpetua's marriage), most marriages were contracted so that married women remained in their father's power. It seems certain that this was the case with Perpetua's marriage, or her father would not have been the one to come to the trial and plead with his daughter.[16]

We will never be certain of the reasons for the omission of the husband, but his absence may at least serve to further demonstrate the importance of the father-daughter tie in Roman society. Perpetua may have seen her role as daughter as the most important bond to discuss and ultimately break, and the Roman audience in the third century would not have found the emphasis on her father inappropriate. Furthermore, the emphasis on her father rather than her husband shows the importance of a vertical continuity between generations—a continuity from her father to future generations. Perpetua was the dutiful daughter fulfilling the expectations of that role even though she was married.

Perpetua was to fulfill the family's expectation by bearing children to continue the family line. She discharged this duty; when she confronted the authority of Rome, she was nursing an infant son. As a Roman matron, she was raised to transmit the values of Rome to the next generation.[17] It was for this vital role as preserver and transmitter of Roman culture that Perpetua had been carefully educated and carefully guarded by her loving father.

This description of Perpetua's family life and situation satisfies our modern sociological curiosity, but it does not do justice to the Roman mind. Perpetua's position in the family and in the home was carefully ritualized by religious feelings and practices, most of which had been established with the founding of the city itself.

Early Romans attributed the greatness of Rome and the Roman character largely to their piety. Polybius, a perceptive Greek commentator, in about 150 B.C. said that the one thing that set Romans over Greeks was "the nature of their religious convictions."[18] A century later, Cicero articulated the same position more fully: "Moreover, if we care to compare our national characteristics with those of foreign peoples, we shall find that, while in all other respects we are only the equals or even the inferiors of others, yet in the sense of religion, that is, in reverence for the gods, we are far superior."[19] Such references could be multiplied, and they all give a clear sense that the Romans perceived their religious sensibilities to be very pious and different from other peoples'. The question for us is "different how?"

The first thing that strikes a student of Roman religion is the sheer number of deities. The fourth-century Christian bishop Augustine included in his massive work, *The City of God*, a disdainful discussion of the Roman gods, and this discussion by a man raised in the Roman religion gives an excellent idea of the ubiquitous presence of the divine that marked the serious, pious, traditional Romans. As a general summary, Augustine wrote, "The Romans assigned particular gods to particular spheres and to almost every single moment."[20] Although the bishop listed many of the deities, even he admitted he could not list all of them. As he said, "The Romans had difficulty in getting them into the massive volumes in which they assigned particular functions and special responsibilities to the various divine powers." For example, the goddess Rusina was in charge of the rural countryside, Collatina the hills, Vallonia the valleys. Augustine concluded that this proliferation of specialized deities indicated that the Romans worshiped inferior demons who did not have enough power to control anything beyond their tiny domains. They were "so clearly confined to their own particular departments that no general responsibility was entrusted to any one of them."[21]

When we remove Augustine's Christian bias, we get a picture of a people who saw divine power profoundly linked to the spaces they inhabited. Celsus, a second-century Roman (roughly contemporary with Perpetua) who was a pious pagan, expressed the important link between the gods and the spaces they inhabited more positively than did Augustine:

> [F]rom the beginning of the world, different parts of the earth
> were allotted to different guardians, and, its having been appor-
> tioned in this manner, things are done in such a way as pleases the
> guardians. For this reason, it is impious to abandon the customs
> which have existed in each locality from the beginning.[22]

Because Celsus had such an ingrained belief in the relationship between space and divine beings who inhabited it, he said Christians were
at the very least ungrateful for living on the earth (the space of the
pagan deities) and offering them no sacrifices. He equated it with using
someone's apartment and paying no rent.[23]

A pious second-century Carthaginian noted almost in passing the
Roman care for observing the sacred nature of some spaces: "It is the
usual practice of wayfarers with a religious disposition, when they
come upon a sacred grove or holy place by the roadside, to utter a
prayer, to offer an apple, and pause for a moment from their journey-
ing."[24]

Florence Dupont has given the best summary of the association of
Roman religiosity with the spaces it inhabits: "The Romans thus spent
their lives moving between one religious space and the next, switching
god and appropriate behavior as they went. This was the form assumed
by polytheism in Rome: a proliferation of religious spaces."[25] In modern Western traditions, we take for granted a transcendent God who
can be addressed from wherever we are, and who we believe can keep
track of falling sparrows everywhere. It is a little hard to imagine a situation in which each space was guarded and guided by a different
deity, and that to be safe one needed to give the appropriate respect to
the guardian of every particular space. When Cicero complimented
the Romans on their extreme piety, he could well have been noting the
vigilance (touched with fear) that marked their awareness of sacred
spaces.

Of course the most important space of the Roman gods and goddesses was the eternal city of Rome itself. From the hills to the field of
Mars, the many divinities watched over the spaces and were attuned to
the public actions that took place there. The fourth-century pagan
writer Symmachus pleaded for the maintenance of pagan temples in
the face of Christian opposition. He recalled how the city itself was
visibly sacred to anyone walking through it: "Through all the streets of
the eternal city he followed the happy Senate and looked with blessed
eyes upon the temples, read the names of the gods on the gables, described the foundations of the sanctuaries, marveled at the founders."
He summarized his argument briefly: "[H]eavenly Providence has as-

signed the cities to various guardians."[26] Livy recorded a speech in which a Roman urged his compatriots not to move from Rome: "Your courage you can take with you and go elsewhere, but the fortune of this place [*fortuna loci*] surely cannot be transferred elsewhere."[27] This expresses strongly the Roman belief in the relationship between the gods and the public spaces they guarded.

But there were as many deities guarding the private space of the home. We have seen that the father was the center of the home, and this status was surrounded with religious ritual as well as legal authority. The father was charged with preserving the communal rituals that had served to preserve his family. He presided over the private rituals that emphasized family, home, responsibility, and duty—all the things that would ensure continuity of family and tradition. If the family continued under his stewardship, upon his death he would be venerated and used as a model for the behavior of subsequent family heads. There was no room in this system for individual longings. As Perpetua grew up in the home of a pious Roman family, she venerated the ancestors who were worshipped as having preserved her line. Her father could expect Perpetua's infant son to grow up and venerate him as he continued to preserve the heritage of the Vibii.

In addition to being guarded by the family ancestors, the home was in the care of many gods and goddesses, from Vesta of the hearth to many more too numerous to count. Augustine, again, might serve to give an example of the many household deities when he scornfully noted that the Romans needed three gods to guard the door: Forculus to guard the door; Cardea the hinges; Limentinus the threshold.[28] However, for a people so conscious of the importance of space, three gods at a door would not have been excessive.

When we recognize the importance the Romans placed on space and their need to identify the divine guardians of that space, we have only half the story of the traditional Roman religion. Knowing the right god or goddess is a beginning, but the Romans then believed one needed to recognize the divinity with appropriate ritual. Celsus said, "[W]e ought to give thanks to the gods who control earthly things, to render them the firstfruits and prayers, so that they will befriend us while we live."[29] Here we have the core of pagan religion: first one had to recognize the divinity linked to one space, then one had to offer the necessary cult ritual to that deity.

Rituals allow men and women both to appease the guardian of the space and to make the divine power of that space accessible for help. In Cicero's praise of Roman piety which I quoted above, the English translation says that Romans excelled in "reverence" for the gods.

However, the Latin word used was *"cultus,"* and this includes much more than the English word *reverence.* It also emphasizes right *action,* that is, the repeated performance of the right ritual acts. The respect for religious actions (that is, rituals) led to as much proliferation of ritual as there was of deities. Romans were so religiously conservative, or perhaps we should say careful, they were unwilling to abandon any religious rituals.[30]

Although many of the rituals were ancient and surrounded by extensive tradition, at heart Roman rituals that were practiced to appease the gods all shared a basic premise: the favor of the gods could perhaps be purchased by an offer of sacrifice. Depending on the circumstances, a sacrifice could be as simple as a few drops of wine offered on the family altar, or as grand as three hundred white oxen to be killed on the altar of Jupiter to keep Rome safe from the invasion of Hannibal in 217 B.C.[31] Whatever was sacrificed became the property of the gods, a gift from humans.

In human society, when one accepts a gift from someone, the donor and receiver are bound together in mutual obligation, and this principle was thought to apply to heavenly society as well. If the gods accepted the gift of sacrifice, people hoped they would respond favorably. And most Romans believed it worked. As late as the fourth century, on the eve of the victory of Christianity, Symmachus urged his compatriots not to abandon the old rituals that had kept Rome safe and prosperous: "[T]hese sacrifices drove away Hannibal from before my walls, and forced back the Gauls from the Capitol."[32]

The world of the ancient Romans was filled with religion. There were divinities too numerous to name, leaving hardly any space unsanctified. All demanded sacrifice to permit their spaces to be safe for humans, and Romans spent a great deal of time attempting to read omens and other signs to tell if their sacrifices had worked. Perpetua grew up in this crowded environment, and participated in the rituals that were the responsibility of the women of the family. Had Perpetua followed the traditional path of a highborn Roman woman, her life, like her mother's, would have been framed by a multiplicity of religious rituals.

Most of the many cults the Romans developed for women were designed to uphold ideals of female conduct.[33] In addition to behavior, cults preserved the carefully ordered Roman hierarchy. There were cults for respectable women and noble women, and others for lower-class women and slaves. There were cults for virgins, wives, women who had been married only once *(univira)*, and widows. Perpetua's life as a Roman woman was structured and defined by the cults that had been developed to preserve the social order.

When Perpetua was a girl, she probably observed her mother participating in the cults that dignified the role of Roman matrons. If her mother had been married only once, she could participate in the worship at temples reserved for *univirae*. She could touch a veiled statue in the temple of the cult of Patrician Chastity or participate in the worship of Womanly Fortune (Fortuna Mulieribris).[34] By reserving the most prestigious cults for women who had carnally known only one man, Roman families were advocating and attempting to preserve the strong family ties that seemed to have generated Rome's greatness.

In addition, Perpetua's mother would have participated in the cult of the Good Mother (Mater Matuta). This cult expressed a class exclusivity by permitting access only to Roman matrons, and having a ritual in which they physically abused and evicted a slave woman.[35] Tertullian, a contemporary of Perpetua's, claimed that this rite was also limited to *univirae*,[36] so we can probably conclude that this was likely the case at least in Carthage during Perpetua's life. The Roman religion (and the society that it mirrored) was not one of equality. When Perpetua and her slave Felicity were equal in martyrdom, they made a dramatic statement that Christianity transcended social structure instead of preserving it.

The Good Mother cult not only defined and reinforced group solidarity by excluding slaves but forged family bonds beyond those of the direct nuclear family. The rites of the Good Mother included particular rituals in which women prayed for the children of their siblings (or only their sisters—the sources are unclear).[37] Perpetua may have joined her mother at these rituals and forged close ritual ties with her mother's sister. At her trial, when Perpetua's father urged her to think of her aunt and not continue her headstrong path to martyrdom, he might have been calling on ties that had been ritually made at the rites of the Good Mother.

When Perpetua reached puberty (at about fourteen years old),[38] she would have come under the protection of Fortuna Virginalis, or Virgo, the goddess in the form of patroness of young girls. Perpetua would have dedicated her girlhood toga to the goddess, and after this dedication, she would have put on the *stola*, the dress of the respectable matron[39] (see Figure 1.1).

When Perpetua married, she then moved her devotions from Virgo to Fortuna Primigenia of Praeneste. In this form, the goddess was the patroness of mothers and childbirth. Perpetua's family no doubt saw in Perpetua's bearing of a healthy son the blessings of this goddess.

This general account of the rituals linked to a woman's life leaves out an important dimension of the religious experience of Roman women, the spiritual or emotional element. If the cults only reinforced social status, they would not have been satisfying or as popular as they were. In their rituals, Romans felt themselves in touch with the divine, connected in a mystic way. There had to be some religious coin of the realm that demonstrated that the gods and goddesses were indeed listening. The Romans saw this proof in the many dreams and omens which they spent a great deal of time interpreting. The women's cults particularly (especially that of the Good Mother) were associated with prophecy and ecstatic experiences.[40] A ritual in which someone felt herself ecstatically inhabited by the goddesses was a successful one indeed.

Of course, Perpetua did not emulate her mother and follow the stages of a woman's life through the worship at the altars of the goddess in her various incarnations. At some point she learned of Christianity and took a different path, but we'll follow this direction in a subsequent chapter. However, when people adhere to a new idea (a religion or philosophy), they do not start with a blank slate. They bring some of the old ideas that have become so much a part of their being that they do not even know they are there. This is what happened with Perpetua. She was a young Roman matron, connected to her family, bound by ritual understandings of the world that made the space she inhabited sacred to divine beings. Further, she expected these divine beings to be sometimes accessible to humans. They sent dreams, omens, and prophetic wisdom to those specially chosen to bridge the gap between the human and the divine. She kept these underlying assumptions of traditional Roman life as she worked to create a new understanding that would allow her to walk bravely into the arena.

As with all traditional Roman families, the core of the beliefs of the Vibii rested with home, hearth, and family. These ideas had been formed in the early settlement times of the Republic and had been preserved by the carefully conservative Romans. However, for two centuries before Perpetua's birth, these ideas were no longer sufficient to explain the Roman situation. Rome, so carefully linked to space, no longer simply occupied the space of the seven hills of the city. Rome had conquered other lands, lands guarded by other gods and goddesses. Their understanding of the sacred had to include much larger spaces, and this larger space was presided over by the godlike figure of the emperor.

EMPIRE AND EMPEROR

By the second century, when people said "Rome," more often than not they meant not only the city but the empire that covered much more territory. By then Rome encompassed the whole of the Mediterranean world, and the rituals developed by the traditional society to propitiate the gods and goddesses of the space around the city somehow no longer were adequate. For example, in 202 B.C., during the Punic Wars, an oracle had promised that the Great Mother, Cybele, would bring victory to the Romans. It was not sufficient to pray to Cybele for victory; the goddess (in the form of a large black meteorite) had to be brought to Rome and installed in the city.[41] Once placed there, she could guard that space and join the many deities who watched out for imperial Rome. In the same year, Scipio defeated Hannibal, so the oracle was right. As effective as this remedy seemed to be, it was impractical to think that Rome could move all the deities that guarded all the territory to the city itself.

The empire needed a god (or gods) who could transcend the individual spaces of the many cities that were guarded by their own divinities. From the time of Caesar Augustus, that god was the emperor. A decree issued circa 9 B.C. by a league of Greek cities in Asia expresses the veneration accorded Augustus and many of the subsequent emperors: "Whereas the providence which divinely ordered our lives created ... the most perfect good for our lives by producing Augustus and filling him with virtue for the benefaction of mankind, blessing us and those after us with a savior who put an end to war and established peace."[42] The most famous praise of Augustus as savior appeared in Virgil's *Aeneid*, when Aeneas is told of the glory that was to be Rome: "Here is Caesar and all the line of Iülus that will come beneath the mighty curve of heaven. This, this is the man you heard so often promised—Augustus Caesar, son of a god, who will renew a golden age in Latium."[43]

One might dismiss Virgil's poetry as politically inspired hyperbole, but there is some evidence that people *did* see the emperor as a form of divinity who could bestow blessings directly on them. We have many surviving petitions in which people appealed directly to emperors for favors. In these petitions, people addressed themselves to "your divinity" or "you, greatest and most divine of Emperors."[44] Inscriptions and literature show the degree to which people generally believed they depended upon the emperor to bring safety and prosperity to society.

Public welfare depended upon the well-being of the emperor, so it was appropriate that public religion focused on prayers for him.[45] This attitude was not so far removed from that of the reliance on the *pater familias* to preserve the family and keep it safe. The emperor became the father of the extended family of the empire. The family worship of Augustus became a public cult,[46] and ancestor worship became adapted to the new circumstances of empire.

Augustus accepted the responsibility of presiding over the cultic life of the empire by assuming the position of *pontifex maximus*, the chief priest of the empire. This effectively linked religious with political power in a way that had not existed in Rome under the Republic.[47] This link established the logic for subsequent deification of the emperors, first the dead then the living.

One of the religious sensibilities that most profoundly separates us from the ancients is the notion of "worshipping as a god" a living man. Paul Veyne makes this ancient feeling accessible to us as he explains that the ancients knew the emperor was not a god. (You don't declare a person a god if he actually is one.) However, the deification of the emperor was a decision to "award him 'honours equal to those of the gods' . . . , meaning sacrifices and altars, the external signs of the respect due to the gods." When cities deified a living emperor, they "recognized that he had a divine nature, as the sacramental formula put it."[48] So people venerated emperors because, by virtue of their office, they were perceived to have (or perhaps hoped to have) the kind of "genius" that could keep the state safe in the same way that an ancestor's genius kept a family intact.

Peace and prosperity of the empire was something that people all over the region could pray for. Offering sacrifices for the safety of the emperor could draw people together in a common hope.[49] This was a hope that transcended the many spaces that were guarded by the many separate territorial gods and goddesses who protected their favored cities and regions. In the second century, the North African proconsul who sentenced some early Christians to death (before Perpetua's trial) said: "We too are a religious people, and our religion is a simple one: we swear by the genius of our lord the emperor and we offer prayers for his health—as you also ought to do."[50] There could not be a more concise explanation of the cult of emperor. Pared down to its essence, it consisted of people praying and offering sacrifices for his well-being in order to receive well-being in return. In this way, Romans could continue many of their traditional attachments while accommodating the new, changed circumstance of an empire.

The importance of the imperial cult as a unifying principle was perhaps most visible in the provinces, which tended to suffer from the centripetal forces of local deities guarding local spaces. In North Africa, for example, there were many dedications made to many local deities "on behalf of the emperor's health."[51] In addition to such private prayers, Carthage had official priests who presided over the imperial cult, and priests of individual deified emperors, such as Augustus, Vespasian, Titus, Nerva Antoninus Pious, and later, Septimius Severus.

Furthermore, these priests were charged with presiding over a good number of ritual occasions throughout the year. The birthdays of deified emperors remained in the calendar indefinitely, and celebrations of other kinds took place during the life of an emperor. These rituals included blood sacrifices and lesser sacrifices of wine and incense along with presentations of games. By the middle of the third century, there were about twenty sacrifices a year in honor of deceased emperors and other imperial figures.[52] This scale of celebrations made the imperial cult highly visible in the Roman world, and for Romans used to cultic activities bringing prosperity, these sacrifices were an important part of the ritual year. The significance of these rituals perhaps will help us understand the great offense the Christians gave when they refused to participate.

In A.D. 146, about thirty-five years before Perpetua was born, the man who would become the first African emperor, Lucius Septimius Severus,[53] was born in Leptis Magna, a city in the North African province of Tripolitania on the shore south and east of Carthage. Like many privileged Romans living in the provinces (indeed like the Vibii), he received a good education, although it never quite erased his provincial background. For example, in spite of his Latin studies, he never lost his North African accent. After he was emperor, he was embarrassed when his sister visited Rome from Leptis, for she could hardly speak Latin at all.[54] It may be that his provincial roots led him to marry women from the provinces rather than from Rome itself.

Like many provincial young men, in 164 Septimius went to Rome to continue his studies and to begin the course of public life that was expected of an aristocratic Roman youth. The course of his career was certainly helped by a wealthy uncle, who lived in Rome and who could give him the necessary introductions. Under Marcus Aurelius, he served in Italy, Spain, Gaul, and Syria, rising consistently through the ranks. Septimius's chance to reach for the imperial purple came with imperial instability following the death of Marcus Aurelius. Marcus's son, Commodus, was unlike his Stoic father and was murdered in 192. The next emperor, Pertinax, was killed the following year. Septimius had himself declared emperor by his troops and marched to Rome to depose Emperor Julianus, whom Septimius declared to be a usurper. In the unstable times after the murder of Pertinax, the praetorian guard had offered the purple to the highest bidder, so Septimius had an opportunity to undo what had appeared to have been done so casually. By 197, Septimius had defeated his rivals and entered Rome in triumph to take over the rule that would last until his death in 211.

As emperor, Septimius never forgot that his rise to power was due to the affection of his troops. He was to the last a military emperor, always more comfortable in the field surrounded by his troops than in Rome surrounded by courtiers. The description given by one of his biographers reveals his Spartan nature:

> His clothing was of the plainest; indeed, even his tunic had scarcely any purple on it, while he covered his shoulders with a shaggy cloak. He was very sparing in his diet, was fond of his native beans, liked wine at times, and often went without meat. In person he was large and handsome. His beard was long; his hair was gray and curly, his face was such as to inspire respect.[55]

Septimius spent much of his reign fighting wars in the East and finally in Britain. Yet, even a military emperor like Septimius could not ignore a domestic side. As a Roman, he showed as much concern for his family as Perpetua's father did. Septimius was not only an emperor, he was *pater familias* of his household, and that proved to be as difficult a job as running an empire.

When Septimius was about twenty-five years old, his father died. He had to return to Africa at that time to set his affairs in order and take his place as the new *pater familias*. Three years later, he married a North African woman, Marcia, about whom little is known. They had two daughters, but Marcia died about ten years later. Septimius was not to remain a widower, and he seems already to have had imperial aspirations. He wanted a second wife suitable to the purple. He found her not in his provincial home of North Africa nor in the city of Rome. Instead, he turned to the East for his next bride.[56]

In about A.D. 180, Septimius led the legions in Syria. While there, he visited the temple of Baal (a god also venerated in North Africa). He came to know the priest, Julius Bassianus, who was well connected as a Roman and must have seemed well connected spiritually to the superstitious African.[57] The younger daughter of Julius, Julia Domna, was unmarried, and she had an auspicious horoscope: it showed that she should be the wife of a king.[58] In 187, when the widower sought a new wife, he turned to the beautiful Syrian woman. Julia Domna and Septimius were married probably in summer of 187. Septimius's attitude toward her horoscope was typically Roman: with an omen, the cause and effect could be reversed. The horoscope did not necessarily predict his rise to the imperial throne; it could just as easily cause his rise. Septimius was clearly playing the omens as best he could.

Julia bore him a son the following year.[59] He was named first Bassianus, then Antoninus, but history remembers him as Caracalla, the nickname that derived from the kind of hooded cloak he favored.[60]

The following year, a second son was born, Geta. This completed the imperial family. Consistent with his role as *pater familias*, Septimius had to provide for his progeny. He arranged good marriages for his two daughters by his first wife; they were married in Rome to men who would help their father consolidate his position as emperor. He tried to prepare his sons to take his place. He had Caracalla named Caesar as early as 197, when he first took the title of emperor, and he consistently tried to prepare both his sons to rule. However, as we shall see in the last chapter, the hatred the two boys had for each other overcame any hopes the father may have had for them.

Because he was emperor as well as *pater familias*, Septimius had many more ritual obligations than did other fathers. In addition to domestic rituals, Septimius was charged with care of the public good. He was both the focus of the imperial cult that served to join the empire together and, as a divine being, he was to bring the blessings of the gods to the empire and its people. He was in the peculiar position of being object of worship and responsible for worship. We can follow his efforts in both these related activities.

Septimius's first responsibility was to bring divine blessings to the empire. By the second century, one of the principal ritual acts of the emperors was to sponsor games in the arenas of Rome and the provinces. Septimius fulfilled this obligation in lavish ways. The ancient historian Herodian described the impressive sacrificial games that the emperor offered to the Roman people. He said Septimius put on "continuous shows of all kinds and slaughtered hundreds of wild animals from all over the world. . . . He also gave victory games, to which he summoned from every quarter performers of musical acts and mock battles." Herodian goes on to describe the many lavish simultaneous theater performances the emperor arranged. For the grand games of 202, heralds called people from all over to come to games "the likes of which they had never seen before and would not see again."[61]

The account of the family's involvement in the games of 202 shows the intimate relationship between the imperial family, sacrifices, and the prosperity of the empire. Septimius himself sacrificed nine cakes and other sacrificial foods with the formula "[B]y virtue of this may every good fortune come to the Roman people." The sacrifice made by his son, Geta, was even more impressive. He sacrificed a pregnant sow as a whole burnt offering with the same prayer offered by his father. Both concluded their prayers with the request that the "Latins [may] be ever obedient."[62] The sacrifices performed the traditional function of Roman religion: offer the gods something in hopes of a direct return in prosperity and peace (identified as obedience among the Latins).

Ritual acts were only half the story for religious Romans. The other half was proof of the efficacy of the sacrifices. In part, proof was the preservation of the emperor and empire (no mean feat with the Roman history of political assassination and civil war). A second part of the proof of divine involvement was the presence of omens and dreams. Dio Cassius gives a fine (if gruesome) example of the relationship between sacrifice and omens. He described how Septimius's predecessor, Julianus had "killed many boys as a magic rite, believing that he could avert some future misfortunes if he learned of them beforehand."[63] Julianus attempted by means of a sacrifice to call forth an omen that would give him foreknowledge.

The historians of Septimius's reign included frequent descriptions of dreams and omens as implicit proof that Septimius was connected to divinity. Not surprisingly, the greatest number of the omens pointed to Septimius's qualifications to be emperor. The implied message in the Julianus anecdote was that his sacrifice was not effective because the gods had not meant him to rule; he was a usurper. In Septimius's case, the omens pointed to his fitness to rule. For example, as a young man Septimius arrived at an imperial banquet inappropriately dressed. He was then lent a toga that belonged to the reigning emperor. He saw this as an omen predicting his rise to the throne.[64] It is not surprising that most of the omens were of this sort, because Septimius's divinity was based on his holding the imperial office; therefore, demonstrations of divine approval of that fact were essential in supporting the imperial cult.

In addition to performing rituals for the good of the state, Septimius was also a guardian of the imperial cult itself. One of his first acts as emperor was to create a public ceremony to deify the murdered emperor Pertinax, whom he claimed to be vindicating. He had a wax figure of the dead emperor made and arranged for it to lie in state in the Roman Forum. With much ceremony the figure was praised and mourned. Then, the wax effigy was burned, and at the same moment an eagle was released. The eagle's flight was to mark the deification, or apotheosis, of Pertinax.[65] By visibly emphasizing the deification of Pertinax, Septimius surrounded himself, as Pertinax's successor, with an aura of divinity.

Septimius further enhanced his imperial cult by associating himself with the Egyptian god Serapis. It was not unusual for emperors to claim a special relationship with one of the gods, indeed to imply that they were an incarnate god. The sources all indicate that when Septimius traveled to Egypt in 201 he was much influenced by the worship of Serapis.[66] From this time onward, Septimius was portrayed wearing his hair and beard in the style of Serapis (Figure 1.2 shows a bust of

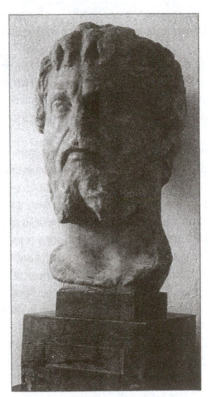

Fig. 1.2. **Septimius Severus.** Bardo Museum, Tunis. Photograph by Lynn Santure. Drawing by Alicia Nowicki.

Septimius with the forked beard and forehead curls that linked him with Serapis).[67] When Septimius built the great arch in his own honor in his hometown, Leptis, he was portrayed as Serapis, and his wife, Julia Domna, was depicted as Isis, the Egyptian goddess.[68]

Septimius's choice of Serapis as his associated divinity made a good deal of sense, and illustrates again the profound link in the Roman mind between divinity and space. In the first place, although Septimius was a Roman emperor, he associated with a deity from his native Africa. Yet, because the imperial cult was to transcend limited space, Septimius's choice of Serapis was also suitable.

The traditional Egyptian gods did not include the god Serapis; instead, the important pair was Isis and her brother/husband Osiris. Although the cult of Isis spread throughout the Mediterranean world, Osiris was a god particularly associated with the Nile.[69] In the Hellenistic period, as many of the Egyptian deities were assimilated into the Greek pantheon, Osiris was changed into Serapis. As Plutarch explained in the early second century, "It is better to identify . . . Serapis with Osiris, who received this appellation at the time when he changed his nature. For this reason Serapis is a god of all peoples in common."[70] In his new form as Serapis, the old god Osiris left his traditional space of the Nile and brought healing, salvation, and protection to wide areas of the empire. Thus, Serapis was an appropriate incarnation for a North African emperor whose imperial cult was to tie the empire together.

There was one more way Septimius seems to have tried to strengthen the imperial cult, and this act would have the greatest impact on the fortunes of Perpetua and her family. In 202, he issued an edict that forbade conversion to either Judaism or Christianity.[71] We have no way to be certain what made him decide to issue the edict. Perhaps it was his desire to encourage the cult of Serapis/Septimius that made him try to discourage competing conversions.[72] Perhaps the reason was political: Jews and Christians were becoming influential in the East, and Septimius, who had just returned from there, may have been trying to reduce their power.[73] Whatever the precise motivation for the edict, it had some results. The imperial cult might have been strengthened a bit in some localities by the reduction of competition, and Christians died for their beliefs. Eusebius, the great fourth-century chronicler of church history, said that the Severan persecution fell hardest in Alexandria, where many Christians died (including the father of the famous church father Origen).[74] The strength of the persecution in Alexandria makes sense because Septimius had just been to Egypt, and his association with the Egyptian god Serapis gave him a good deal of support among Alexandrian pagans. The persecution was not limited to Egypt but spread westward in North Africa. A small group of Romans in Carthage who were studying to convert to Christianity came into direct conflict with the emperor's edict. Perpetua and her companions would violate the edict and be offered as sacrifices for the well-being of the emperor's son Geta.

LONGING FOR THE DIVINE

The system of Roman religion which I have outlined should have taken care of people's spiritual needs. The spaces of the home and city were guarded and the guardians ritually appeased. The political entity of the empire was cared for in the name of the imperial cult. The only problem with the system was that it did not work. In texts of the period, along with the careful descriptions of rituals and deities, there appears a growing sense of uncertainty. The uncertainty seems to have begun with the expansion of the empire at the end of the first century B.C.,[75] when Rome moved beyond the spaces carefully circumscribed by their traditional rituals. Historians who have written about the subsequent centuries note this spiritual longing in different ways. For example, in a classic work, E. R. Dodds writes of the second and third centuries as an "age of anxiety."[76] A modern biographer of the emperor Septimius Severus saw his reign as the "beginning of a period of considerable moral, intellectual, and spiritual ferment."[77] The spiritual ferment is evident in the number of inscriptions dedicated to various gods of the empire. During the reign of Septimius there are dramatically more inscriptions surviving than from any other period of the empire.[78] Frequency of inscriptions can testify as easily to prosperity as to spiritual longing, but nevertheless it does show that people were trying to communicate with their deities. These examples can be multiplied but should be enough to suggest that something was going on in the spiritual life of the empire.

The problem that seems to have been experienced by many in the Roman Empire was a spatial one: the divine world appeared to have moved further away from the human one. Dodds recognized that the texts showed an increased emphasis on the "antithesis between the celestial world and the territorial one."[79] This distance caused some to question the efficacy of traditional rituals, like the sacrifices offered to the deities. Lucian of Samasota in the second century wrote a scathing satire of sacrifices, imagining gods opening their mouths to eat the smoke and drink the blood spilled on the altars.[80] He concludes with dismissal of the sacred rituals that were at the heart of the Roman religion: "In view of what the dolts do at their sacrifices and their feasts and processions in honour of the gods, what they pray for and vow, and what opinions they hold about the gods, I doubt if anyone is so gloomy and woe-begone that he will not laugh to see the idiocy of their actions."[81]

It was the rare Roman who achieved the level of cynicism expressed by Lucian. Most tried to solve the problem by bringing divinity and humanity more closely together. Plutarch, who wrote in the early second century, expressed this struggle succinctly: "The effort to arrive at the Truth, and especially the truth about the gods, is a longing for the divine."[82] This longing for the divine formed as much a part of Perpetua's (and Septimius's) mental universe as the rituals and beliefs that were so carefully preserved as part of the traditional Roman religion. Perpetua ultimately joined the divine and the human in Christian martyrdom in the arena, but that was not the only possibility for a second-century searcher.

One way to bring heaven a little closer to earth was through astrol-ogy and magic.[83] These are related in that they attempt to understand the secrets of the universe through reading the heavens. This under-standing was supposed to allow one to manipulate the future through this foreknowledge. Magic was an attempt to use celestial power to manipulate events on earth. Both express a longing for humans to have more access to divinity. There was little provision for (or practice of) magic and astrology in traditional Roman religion developed in the close-knit spaces of the early Republic. By the first and second cen-turies A.D., however, the practice of both was growing exponentially.[84]

We have seen the degree to which Septimius himself depended upon the practice of astrology. He selected his second wife by this means to try to manipulate the future, and this was not an isolated in-stance. His biographer wrote that the emperor consulted horoscopes frequently, for this was "a study in which like most Africans he was very proficient."[85] This phrase not only shows the emperor's affinity for the art but suggests how extensively it was practiced in North Africa, where Perpetua and her comrades were exposed to it.

Magic, too, was widely practiced. We can read many of the magical spells that everyday people wrote down and buried in an attempt to use the supernatural to control the mundane. One example of a magical at-tempt to influence events may be seen in an inscription in Rome that tried to conjure up demons to ensure that a charioteer would lose:

> May he not leave the barriers well; may he not be quick in the con-test; may he not outstrip anyone; may he not make the turns well; may he not win any prizes . . . ; may he meet with an accident; may he be bound; may he be broken; may he be dragged along by your power, in the morning and afternoon races.[86]

Magic was also used by those who were highly educated and cul-tured. A famous North African from the second century, Apuleius, is a perfect example of a man who was driven by a longing for the divine, and who pursued his quest through many paths, including the study of magic.[87] He was a well-known citizen in Carthage; he had even been accorded the honor of being appointed as the chief priest of that city.[88] He wrote prolifically, and Perpetua, a generation later, would have known about this famous man, for his statue had been erected in Carthage. This was a high honor for which Apuleius had thanked his fellow citizens.[89] Apuleius was honored as a scholar, philosopher, and man wise in the ways of divinity. Two centuries later, the great North African Augustine further honored Apuleius by quoting him exten-sively and discussing his philosophy in *The City of God*.[90] Apuleius makes a wonderful case study of a second-century Roman who tried to access divinity by many different paths, and I shall follow his spiritual quest as I look at the various outlets for Romans' spiritual longings.

Apuleius was certainly interested in magic. His work, *Metamorphosis, or The Golden Ass* was based on the premise of a widespread curiosity about magic. He had firsthand knowledge of the subject and problems related to it because he was put on trial for practicing magic. In his "Apology," we have his defense, and this educated, articulate tract gives us a fine lens through which to see ancient understandings of magic beyond the spells that survive in inscriptions and texts.

Although Apuleius denied that he was guilty of the charges brought against him, he did not deny the existence or efficacy of magic, nor did he hide his knowledge of it. The charges brought against Apuleius were several: (1) He purchased a fish for magical purposes; (2) he used a mirror; (3) he kept "secret things" wrapped in linen on his household altar; (4) he burnt birds for magical purposes; (5) he had a statue made of rare wood, and (6) he used a love charm to win his wealthy wife. Many of these charges show the fine line between accepted traditional religion and forbidden magic. After all, Roman religion allowed reverence for statues of gods, and indeed Apuleius produced the statue of "rare wood" and showed it to be a statue of Mercury, and thus a legitimate cult object.[91] Further, burning animals on altars as sacrifice was central to traditional Roman religion. The charges show more about people's insecurities concerning the supernatural (and about Apuleius's enemies) than they do about any new rituals.

In denying these charges, Apuleius did reveal a great deal of knowledge about magic. For example, when he dismissed the fish charge, he said that things other than fish are sought by sorcerers: soft garlands, rich herbs, "male incense," "brittle laurel," "clay to be hardened," "wax to be melted in the fire."[92]

What he revealed as the essence of his "apology" was that he had studied a great deal of esoteric knowledge in his search for the divine, but that it was a legitimate quest. He quoted philosophers and physicians in his defense,[93] showing what a fine line there was between magic and the pursuit of knowledge. He called philosophers the "high priests of every god,"[94] and he surely numbered himself among them.

As Apuleius rightly noted, the pursuit of philosophy for the ancients was another way of trying to have access to the divine. Dio Cassius tells us that Septimius's wife, Julia Domna, studied philosophy and surrounded herself with sophists. Dio surmised that she did this because she was excluded from political involvement by one of Septimius's advisers.[95] However, the history of Septimius and his wife reveals a consistent pattern of searching for divine truth by all means possible, and Julia Domna's exploration of philosophy was perfectly consistent with this search.

The most popular Hellenistic philosophies, Epicureanism, Stoicism, and Platonism, all in some form or another attempted through reason and rationalism to bring humans a bit closer to the divine. Epicureans urged people to live lives of "calm beatitude" like that of the gods.[96] In emulation, heaven and earth were joined. Philosophers did not simply offer wisdom in large matters, such as how one is to live one's life; they also offered reflection about smaller matters, frequently of interest to those attracted to magic. For example, Apuleius quoted from Epicurus in his consideration of the use of mirrors for magical purposes, wondering if indeed "images proceed forth from us, as it were a kind of slough that continually streams from our bodies?"[97] By offering explanations of the natural world, philosophy shed light on the supernatural. However, philosophy as an enterprise generally scorned magic as unworthy of the rational thought that was leading up to knowledge of God. The second-century pagan philosopher Celsus, for example, dismissed the magic/miracles that drew Christians: "[T]hose who have had anything to do with philosophy . . . are above such trickery."[98]

Stoicism offered a clear ethical system that emphasized personal dignity in a world controlled by fate.[99] But it also offered a way of bringing the supernatural world in touch with the human one, for by focusing on personal behavior, it located God within. The great stoic Seneca wrote: "God is near you, he is with you, he is within you. . . . [A] holy spirit indwells within us, one who marks our good and bad deeds, and is our guardian."[100]

The most important philosophic movement that established a system of bringing heaven and earth together was Platonism. Apuleius proudly quoted Plato and the philosopher's "glorious work, the *Timaeus*" and showed how Plato explained the "constitution of the whole universe."[101] Apuleius's work was so imbued with Platonism that Augustine identified Apuleius as a Platonist.[102] Celsus is another fine example of the pagan pursuit of philosophy as a spiritual choice in competition with Christianity. In *On the True Doctrine*, he ridiculed Christianity and advocated following traditional Roman ritual enhanced with Platonic understanding. He contrasted the teachings of Plato with those of Christ and found the latter wanting.[103] He urged all spiritual seekers to "follow reason as a guide."[104]

These (and other, similar) second-century Platonists set the stage for the great Neoplatonic synthesis of the third century. Then, philosophers like Plotinus and his student Porphyry created a complex system that offered an explanation for how the divine and the human were linked together, both in life and after it. Plotinus argued that the existence of the soul in humans marked the presence of the divine, and this presence closed the gap between humans and the deity: "The Soul once seen to be thus precious, thus divine, you may hold the faith that by its possession you are already nearing God: in the strength of this power make upwards towards Him: at no great distance you must attain: there is not much between."[105] At his death, Plotinus is reputed to have expressed his deeply held belief in the possibility of reunion of the soul with its creator by saying he could now try "to make that which is divine in me rise up to that which is divine in the universe."[106] The space that separated humans from God became insignificant in the Neoplatonic system.

Plotinus and his followers in the third century shaped Platonism into a form that was readily absorbed by Christian thinkers. By the fourth century, Christians like Augustine saw no incompatibility between Neoplatonism and Christian wisdom. In the second century, however, that was not yet so. In the writings of Celsus and others, Platonism was one of the many options selected by people longing for the divine. Christianity was another.

Philosophy had a somewhat limited appeal. Its practitioners needed leisure and education, and the income that both of those require. More people tried to satisfy their spiritual desires through one or more of the mystery cults that were extremely popular in the second century. Apuleius, in his eclectic search, was also an initiate of mystery religions. During his trial for magic, he acknowledged that he kept "secret" items wrapped in linen, but he again argued these were legitimate religious items. He claimed to have been initiated into a number of mystery religions: "I, . . . moved by my religious fervor and my desire to know the truth, have learned mysteries of many a kind, rites in great number, and diverse ceremonies." And he kept at home "certain talismans associated with these ceremonies."[107] Apuleius was one of many who looked to the mystery religions for the special knowledge of divinity, and these cults formed a major element in shaping the thought of the second century.

Septimius Severus shared an interest in sacred mysteries with his subjects. When he traveled into Egypt, his biographer wrote, "He inquired into everything including things that were carefully hidden; for he was the kind of person to leave nothing, either human or divine uninvestigated."[108] Septimius's identification with Serapis was a way of joining himself with the deity in a sacred, mystical mystery. Furthermore, Herodian described Septimius's continued interest in the mysteries, and his desire to incorporate the mystery cults into the public imperial cult. Septimius frequently arranged "all-night religious ceremonies in imitation of the mysteries."[109] These efforts to encompass individual longing for the divine into the imperial cult did not work. There was a profound opposition between the individualism implicit in the mystery religions and the public cult of the emperor that would not be resolved until more than a century later, when the emperors converted to Christianity. During the second century, people were drawn directly to various mystery cults to satisfy their religious longings; they did not want to go through the emperor.

There were many mystery religions in the second century: Eleusinian rites, cults of Dionysius, Mithras, Isis, and others. All shared some general characteristics that gave them a great deal of appeal for people searching for Plutarch's divine truth. Unlike the public cults that were fully open to everyone, mystery religions had secrets available only to the specially chosen, and the final initiation served to link the believer with the deity.[110] This mystic union eliminated the space between the natural and supernatural that represented the heart of the second-century religious dilemma. Furthermore, mystic union generally offered the initiate a hope for life after death. Apuleius recorded that Isis spoke to him, saying, "[I]t is within my power to prolong your life beyond the limits set to it by Fate."[111] This salvation was offered to any who would receive the secret initiation. Through such initiations, common people might hope to share the divinity, the apotheosis, experienced by emperors.

These general elements that the mystery religions shared formed a religious experience that shaped people's consciousness of the holy. This was even more so because only the final initiation was secret. Other elements of the cult worship were public and highly visible, offering tantalizing proof to observers that some special people had been able to bridge the gap between heaven and earth. It is worth looking in some detail at these elements of worship because they influenced, indeed defined, Perpetua's understanding of the sequence of progress to the holy. As we shall see, her martyrdom had many elements of an initiation into a sacred mystery.

People desiring initiation began with a ritual purification, which could take various forms, and which made the initiate worthy of entering the next stage, or the procession. The procession was a public phase of the mysteries, in which people moved from the profane to the sacred. The procession moved with music and dance from the public arena to the sacred precincts of the cult deity. Dancing, and music in general, offered a way to seek and celebrate individual ecstatic experiences, one characteristic of mystery religions. Finally, those who had been selected for initiation moved to the most sacred space where they could encounter the manifest deity during initiation.[112]

In the second century, one of the most popular of the mystery cults was the cult of Isis. This was the cult that drew Emperor Septimius and his wife, Julia Domna. Further, it was a visible cult in North Africa and one that appealed strongly to women. It would have been one possible outlet for Perpetua's spiritual longings had she not turned to Christianity. Perpetua's countryman Apuleius, whose spiritual quest we have been following, was an initiate and priest of Isis. The spiritual environment that shaped the martyr and the emperor was strongly influenced by the cult of the North African deity.

Isis had been a goddess of ancient Egypt for more than two millennia before her worship spread to the rest of the Hellenistic world. In the mythology of the goddess, Isis was said to have lived through the experiences that confronted many ordinary women during their lives. Isis loved her brother/husband Osiris (later transformed into the more universal Serapis). Osiris was killed by his jealous brother Set, so Isis suffered the deep loss of her beloved. She searched for him, and spent some time as a prostitute during this period of trial. Finally, she collected his dismembered body, and bore a child by him before he was brought back to life. She was often portrayed as a good mother nursing the infant Horus. As this brief summary may show, Isis offered compassionate understanding to women, mothers, sons, lovers, and those driven by adversity to lives that traditional Roman religion scorned. Isis was no *univira* who carefully tended conservative and tranquil homes.[113]

For all Isis's association with women's experience, her powers were not limited to women's spheres. She was the creator goddess: she divided heaven from earth, she assigned languages to nations and invented alphabets and astronomy. She controlled lightning, thunder, and winds.[114] She was both omnipotent and loving, and she claimed a universality that contrasted with the local deities. The goddess expressed her omnipresence to Apuleius, saying: "I, whose single godhead is venerated all over the earth under manifold forms . . ."[115] Her appeal was wide and included both men and women in her priesthood and her followers.

One of the best descriptions of the cult of Isis was written by Apuleius, whom we have seen as an omnivorous seeker of spiritual truth and an initiate into her mysteries. In his witty book *The Golden Ass*, Apuleius writes of an inquisitive young man, Lucius, who dabbles in magic and accidentally is turned into a donkey. The novel is about his adventures as he searches for a way to resume his human form. At the end, Lucius sees Isis appearing to him in a vision; he is called to conversion and resumes his human form. The new Lucius, however, is different from the old. He is no longer drawn to magic as a way of understanding and controlling the world. Instead, he becomes a priest of all-knowing Isis, and receives true knowledge, that of mystic spirituality. In this amusing yet poignant tale, we can see the longing of individuals in the second-century empire for personal meaning, for visions, and for individual salvation. The many followers of Isis were less articulate than Apuleius but bear silent testimony to the inadequacy of traditional Roman religious expressions to satisfy their spiritual longings.

Perpetua would have been frequently exposed to the cult of Isis through public observances visible to everyone. Worship of Isis included a number of public festivals. Daily rituals to the goddess included prayers at the beginning of the day and in the afternoon at her numerous shrines. During midday, the shrines were open for individual private prayer and meditation.[116]

In addition to these daily celebrations, there were two major annual celebrations of her cult. One was the Festival of Search and Discovery that took place in the fall and recalled the search of Isis for her husband.[117] The second celebration took place in the spring and revealed and celebrated the goddess's ties to the sea. This celebration recalled Isis's searching the waters of the Nile for Osiris's dismembered body and noted the spring's calming of the rough waters.[118] Because of this link to the sea, it is not surprising that Isis was a patroness of navigation and commerce. Therefore, port cities were particularly receptive to her worship. On March 5 of every year, magnificent processions proceeded to the sea to inaugurate the shipping season.[119] Apuleius described one such procession that included musicians, priests, priestesses, and worshipers marching joyously to the sea to greet the goddess.[120]

Perpetua must have grown up witnessing the public worship of the goddess and watching the annual processions that helped mark the seasonal cycles. The presence of the Isis cult in Carthage is perhaps strangely relevant to the young matron's imminent martyrdom. Rodney Stark, in an excellent analysis of the growth of Christianity, shows that there is a highly significant correlation "between the expansion of Isis and the expansion of Christianity. Where Isis went, Christianity followed."[121] The longing for the divine that drew some followers to the Egyptian goddess drew others to Christ. And Perpetua's memory of the sacred processions seems to have shaped her descriptions of her progress to martyrdom.

All these various quests for spiritual connection with the divine, from magic through philosophy through mystery religions, shared one major characteristic with the traditional Roman religions that they were supplementing. People trying these paths wanted to know they worked. In traditional Roman cults, people wanted to know their sacrifices had been accepted by some response from the deity. This response could take the form of an omen or a dream. Practitioners of these other forms of religion were at least as strong in their desire to see the proof of the efficacy of their rituals. The proof that the divinity was imminent involved visible signs of that imminence.

The best sign of divine presence was thought to be prophecy, through which one could know the future. Apuleius said that the "prize of magical incantations" was "divination and prophecy,"[122] and by this he meant that the goal of magic was prophetic utterance. Prophetic sayings usually accompanied an ecstatic condition. Apuleius, revealing his Platonism, explained that human souls could be lulled into a kind of trance so that consciousness of the body would fade, leaving the soul to recall its divine origins. In this condition, the soul could predict the future.[123] Plotinus was said to have achieved divine union in an ecstatic trance several times during his life,[124] so even pure philosophy sometimes demonstrated its validity in the Roman spiritual coin of prophecy.

Ecstasy and prophecy were at the heart of the mystery religions as well. Livy described the bacchanalian rituals: "Men, as if insane, with fanatical tossings of their bodies, would utter prophecies."[125] Seneca described with horror the frenzy in the worship of Cybele, when men in an ecstatic passion castrated themselves.[126] The priests of Isis were supposed to be particularly adept at prophecy,[127] and dream instruction assumed a central place in the cult of Serapis.[128] In describing his own initiation in the cult of Isis, Apuleius remembered how he was called to the cult through a dream.[129]

Dreams were not separate from prophecies uttered in ecstasy because they, too, could be prophetic. Just as in ecstasy, when the soul was believed to be communing with the divine, in dreams the soul was free to probe divinity. So, dream messages were looked on as part of the proof of divine intervention. As an incarnation of Serapis, Septimius Severus gave a great deal of credence to dreams, as did his wife, who the chronicler said was "skilled in dreams."[130]

In a world longing to experience the divine, prophetic utterances of all kinds were given a great deal of weight. Of course, the search for prophets led to misunderstandings and bred outright charlatans. In Apuleius's trial, he explained that a boy in his company was not in an ecstatic trance; he was experiencing an epileptic seizure. It was a medical problem, not a religious expression.[131] The second-century religious skeptic Lucius offered a detailed and delightful description of a false prophet who capitalized impressively on people's desire to be in the presence of the divine.

Lucian wrote how a particularly fine-looking young man decided to take advantage of people's desire for prophecies. This young man, Alexander, would found a prophetic shrine so he would become rich. He succeeded beyond his expectations, and Lucian carefully exposed how Alexander wrapped a large serpent around himself and held a fake serpent's head in his hand. The head of the serpent seemed to speak, uttering prophecies.[132] The cult was structured as a mystery religion with all the appropriate ceremony, and it was also self-consciously established as an alternative to competing spiritual movements. Lucian wrote how Alexander led the crowds in shouting, "Out with the Christians!" and "Out with the Epicureans."[133] The cult was extraordinarily popular because it appealed to the religious hopes that were so pervasive in the second century.

As a daughter of Rome growing up in the late second century, Perpetua would have been exposed to all the ideas I have outlined here. She was raised in the closely guarded spaces of the family and the home, where sacrifices were offered to household deities, and where her father carefully guarded the destiny of his family. Further, Perpetua grew up knowing that the welfare of Rome was secured through the prosperity of the emperor and *his* family. In traditional fashion, Perpetua had watched and participated in sacrifices at the altars for the well-being of the imperial family. Finally, Perpetua could not help but see the spiritual longing that dominated the age. Magicians and astrologers were everywhere; processions for mystery religions were dramatically visible; and philosophers like Apuleius spoke in the forum and won great renown for their intellectual searches.

Perpetua shared this spiritual longing or she would not have been drawn away from the more traditional Roman path that her father had expected her to take. We know she sought after the prophetic dreams and visions that marked divine presence or she would not have recorded her own dreams so carefully. Other young daughters of Rome with such spiritual longings followed the cult of Isis. Perpetua sought out the mysteries of the risen Jesus.

two

Carthage

Perpetua was not purely a daughter of Rome. Her experiences and her interpretations of those experiences were shaped by her life in Carthage, the provincial capital of North Africa (see figure 2.1). Carthage was the wealthiest and most cosmopolitan city of the empire after Rome itself. Here one could see people and goods from all over the empire. Merchants (much as today) sold their wares in crowded stalls in the forum. The city hummed with the sounds of many languages. Perpetua, like Emperor Septimius Severus, could speak Punic, a Semitic language that had been brought to North Africa by the first founders of the city. Her preservation of the old language is one suggestion that we must look to her Carthaginian heritage as well as to her Roman one to understand her martyrdom.

THE CITY

According to legend (which we have no particular reason to disbelieve) Carthage was founded in about 800 B.C. by a Phoenician princess, Elissa, known more popularly as Queen Dido. Dido left Tyre in a dispute with her brother and sailed westward through the Mediterranean seeking a new region for settlement. Dido and her crew were not charting unknown waters; for centuries Phoenician vessels had sailed the western Mediterranean as far as Spain looking for raw materials (especially metals) for trade. As with all ships in antiquity, Phoenician vessels hugged the shore as they traveled during the day, and anchored every night. By the time Dido sailed, there were probably anchorages and

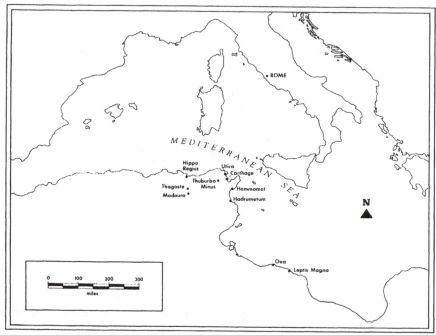

Fig. 2.1 Mediterranean. Map by Lisa Qualm.

some small settlements for Phoenicians about every thirty miles along the North African coast.[1]

Dido stopped at a promising harbor. The local tribesmen objected to the settlement, but legend tells us that they were persuaded to give her as much land as could be covered by one ox hide. She began to shave the hide so thinly that they relented and let her have the settlement she wanted for fear that her skill with the ox hide might let her claim all of North Africa. The dominant feature of Carthage (ancient and modern) is the Byrsa hill, which overlooks the port. The word "Byrsa" seems to have been derived from the term "ox hide" in recollection of the founding legend.

Queen Dido is said to have committed suicide rather than marry a local chieftain. Virgil changed the tale a bit to have Dido commit suicide at the departure of her beloved Aeneas, who went on to found Rome. However she died, the city Dido founded grew and prospered. Carthage is perfectly situated for a commercial center. The ports were improved by the Carthaginians to provide an interior, protected military harbor and an exterior one for the large merchant barges that ensured Carthage's wealth. The whole city covered about seven miles, with three sides protected by the sea (see figure 2.2). The remaining sides had more than twenty-one miles of walls with parapets and towers.[2] The center of

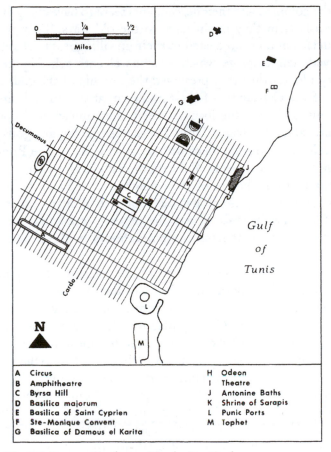

Fig. 2.2 Roman Carthage. Map by Lisa Qualm

the city, with its forum and grid of streets, was built near the ports at the foot of the Byrsa hill. The hill itself was capped with a strong fortification that guarded the city.

The cosmopolitan residents of ancient Carthage lived in attractive multistory stone houses that had courtyards equipped with even sinks and bathtubs. Excavations of these homes have revealed the earliest examples of true mosaic technique in the Mediterranean world.[3] Perhaps the Carthaginians developed and exported the technique that Greeks and Romans would turn into the magnificent works of art that would so lavishly decorate the floors of the houses Perpetua lived in and visited.

At the height of its power, the population of Phoenician Carthage probably approached 400,000, of whom probably no more than 100,000 were of fairly pure Phoenician heritage.[4] In response to this ratio, the colonists and their descendants seem to have clung even more tenaciously than they might have to the old ways. They outdid the Phoenicians in their homeland in their unwillingness to change. They preserved their language, which became well entrenched in the city and countryside. Further, they preserved the worship of the gods and goddesses of the Canaanites of their home country. Although there were many minor deities, the focus of their worship centered upon Baal-Hammon and his consort, Tanit. These were demanding gods, and the Carthaginians appeased them with sacrifices, just as the Romans and other Mediterranean people did with their gods. However, the Phoenicians (much to the horror of their neighbors) retained the practice of human sacrifice long after it had died out even in their homeland in the East. This cultural tenacity was one of their strengths, but it would lead to estrangement from their neighbors in the Mediterranean world.[5]

One of the earliest descriptions of the ancient Carthaginians was quite positive. Herodotus, the Greek historian who wrote in the late fifth century B.C., praised their commercial integrity, relating an incident that shows the Carthaginian merchants as honest traders. The Carthaginians had sailed out of the Mediterranean to trade along the coast of Africa. Unloading their cargo, they returned to their boats and sent up smoke signals to summon the local tribesmen to trade. The natives approached and laid out what they thought would be an appropriate amount of gold for the goods, then withdrew without taking the items. Herodotus wrote with praise of these negotiations: "They say that thus neither party is ill-used; for the Carthaginians do not take the gold until they have the worth of their merchandise, nor do the natives touch the merchandise until the Carthaginians have taken the gold."[6]

This kind of description of honest traders disappeared from the primarily Roman sources after Carthage began to confront the power of Rome about two hunderd years after Herodotus. The Roman sources were neither particularly objective nor flattering. Nevertheless, we can at least get a sense of how their neighbors perceived the prosperous Carthaginians. Polybius, who wrote circa 200 B.C. during one of the Punic wars between Carthage and Rome, accused the Carthaginians of being too materialistic:

> At Carthage nothing that results in gain is looked upon as disgraceful; at Rome nothing is more shameful than to accept bribes or seek a profit by improper means. A proof of this is the fact that at Carthage candidates obtain public offices by openly presenting gifts, whereas at Rome the penalty for this is death.[7]

Livy, too, in describing the losses suffered by the Romans during the war, added a sarcastic reference to Carthaginian morality. The Carthaginian general had agreed to let the Romans go if they surrendered. "This pledge Hannibal observed with true Punic reverence and threw them all into chains."[8]

Plutarch, writing four hundred years later, was even more harsh in his assessment of the Carthaginian character: "It is bitter, sullen, subservient to their magistrates, harsh to their subjects, most abject when afraid, most savage when enraged, stubborn in adhering to its decisions, disagreeable and hard in its attitude towards playfulness and urbanity."[9]

Archaeological finds of beautiful jewelry, vials for perfume, and the comfortable houses belie Plutarch's dismissal of Carthaginian appreciation for "playfulness and urbanity." However, a conservative (stubborn?) clinging to tradition and a fear of change certainly marked their approach to life. These characteristics continued through the time of Perpetua, and shaped the Carthaginian view of the world.

Probably the characteristic that most marked the descendants of Dido's settlement was success. The city prospered and came into conflict with the other emerging power in the Mediterranean, Rome. Between 264 and 146 B.C., Rome and Carthage fought three devastating wars, known as the Punic Wars. ("Punic" referred to Phoenicia, looking back to Carthage's initial settlement.) These long wars were fought at sea, in Spain, Sicily, Italy, and North Africa. They included the famous invasion of Italy by Hannibal as he crossed the Alps with his elephants and succeeded in laying siege to the city of Rome itself. At times the two great cities fought themselves to exhaustion and signed treaties that temporarily stopped the warfare. However, the third, and last, Punic war ended with the destruction of Carthage.

Plutarch recorded the Roman statesman Cato's speech in 150 B.C. as he tried to spur his countrymen, after the second Punic War, to resume the fighting against Carthage, reminding the Senate that Carthage was "only three day's sail from Rome."[10] Cato was expressing the truth that there was no room in the western Mediterranean for two great maritime powers, and he ended all his speeches with "Carthage must be destroyed."[11] The inflammatory language worked, and the Third Punic War was begun. This time there would be no treaty to settle the dispute. Rome insisted that the city of Carthage be moved ten miles from the coast. The Carthaginians, whose history and power were linked to the sea, could not agree.

In 149 B.C., the Roman army led by Scipio Aemilianus blockaded the city of Carthage and approached from a three-hundred-foot-wide sandbar in front of the commercial harbor (see figure 2.2). Only a single wall protected the city at this spot, and by using the sandbar, Scipio was able to break through the barrier.[12] After easily taking the forum near the ports, Scipio had to confront the fortress on the Byrsa hill. More than fifty thousand people had retreated behind its walls,[13] but thousands more tried to protect their houses along the slopes. Polybius, the Roman historian who witnessed the events, described vividly how the troops fought six days and nights on the hill, both at street level and on the rooftops of the buildings, some of which were six stories high. Scipio had his troops burn the neighborhoods of the hill that had represented the prosperous suburb of the old city. Finally, the stronghold itself could not hold. The Carthaginian general, Hasdrubal, surrendered; the Punic Wars were finally over.[14] Rome was the undisputed master of the Mediterranean.

The victorious general, Scipio, recognized the loss of a great civilization:

> Scipio, beholding this city, which had flourished 700 years from its foundation and had ruled over so many lands, islands, and seas, as rich in arms and fleets, elephants, and money as the mightiest empires, but far surpassing them in hardihood and high spirit . . . now come to its end in total destruction . . . shed tears and publicly lamented the fortune of the enemy.[15]

The victor of such a long war did not remain unchanged. Even during the war, Rome departed from its usual customs, particularly during the desperate times when Hannibal threatened the city. At that time, Romans resorted to human sacrifice, burying four foreigners alive in the Cattle Market. Even the Roman historian Livy said this sacrifice was "wholly alien to the Roman spirit."[16] The modification of Rome did not end with the war itself. The Roman religion did not readily accommodate to empire, and after the Punic Wars, Rome had an empire that included much of the Mediterranean world. Some Romans lamented the price Rome had paid for the destruction of Carthage. One said that with the removal of Rome's rival, the city's "passage from virtue to vice was not a gradual process but a headlong rush."[17] The transformation of Roman values was even more poignantly mourned by Silius Italicus: "[I]f it was fated that the Roman character should change when Carthage fell, would that Carthage was still standing."[18] Carthage would not be left standing: Scipio was ordered to destroy the city completely and allow no one to remain there.[19] He did so, and the famous city was abandoned for a century. Contrary to modern legend, the land surrounding Carthage was not salted to keep it from producing.[20]

The newly acquired province of Africa was governed from Utica, an old city just north of Carthage that had supported Rome in the last Punic War, in the person of a proconsul, who was to be of a noble family and a member of the Senate of Rome. It was always Roman practice to let native communities govern themselves, keeping their traditional forms and worshipping their traditional deities. This was true in Africa, so the Carthaginian system of governance by representatives called "suffetes" continued,[21] and Baal-Hammon and Tanit continued to receive their customary veneration.

The port city founded by Dido was too valuable a location to remain ignored by the Romans. Caesar Augustus in about 40 B.C. recolonized the city by sending (according to Appian) three thousand colonists from Rome, and offering land there to others.[22] Augustus also reorganized the African provinces into one that was now known as Africa Proconsularis, with the capital at Carthage.[23]

When the Romans rebuilt the city, they kept the valuable ports and used the old Punic city grid by the shore. However, they centered the town on the top of the Byrsa hill. The area was not large enough to lay out a suitable forum, so they increased its size by building large columns over the rubble of the Punic houses to support the ground of the new forum.[24] The new forum was huge—more than 98,000 square feet—with temples and a porticoed plaza.[25] Then they laid out a new urban grid centered on the forum.

For their provincial cities, Romans used the same grid system that they used to set up their military camps for the night. The main road running from left to right was the Cardo Maximus, and the main road running top to bottom was the Decumanus Maximus. All the other left-right roads are cardines; all other top-bottom roads are decumani. To indicate decumani to the left and right of the Decumanus Maximus, surveyors used the terms "left" (*sinistra*) and right (*dextra*). Similarly, to indicate cardines above and below the Cardo Maximus, they used *ultra* ("on the farther side") and *citra* ("on the nearer side"). For example: the intersection of the second road to the right of the Decumanus and the first road above the Cardo was indicated with the notation DD2UC1 (Dextra Decumanus 2, Ultra Cardo 1) (see figure 2.2).[26]

The grid provided the order that structured the growth of the city. By the second century, the city had returned to and even exceeded the prosperity it had known before its conquest. Under emperors Hadrian and Antoninus Pious further building took place that created what became an intellectual center of the West for the next two centuries—the city that shaped Perpetua's experience in her youth.

Figure 2.2 shows the layout of Carthage after the constructions of

Antoninus Pious. The forum on the Byrsa hill remained the center of urban activity; people walked, prayed, and spoke together there. The great library that Apuleius praised in his speeches to the second-century Carthaginians probably stood there,[27] as did the bookstores and schools that drew a young Augustine in the fourth century. The forum was also the location of the trials of the Christians that were to draw as many curious crowds as the speeches of great orators.

The Byrsa remained the center of urban life, but the urban grid also contained the other great structures that were the hallmarks of a Roman city. The large amphitheater on the northwest edge of the town was second only to that in Rome itself. The circus for chariot races on the western edge of the grid was also one of the largest in the empire.[28] On the opposite side of the city, Carthaginians went to one of the two theaters. The first was built by Hadrian in the middle of the second century. This theater captivated the young Augustine as much as the crowds had in the forum. Hadrian's theater has been restored and its fine acoustics have made it the site of annual music festivals. The second theater, a covered theater, or *odeon*, was built during the second century, and, as a good Roman city, Carthage had many baths. The impressive Antonine Baths, near the sea, had a magnificent view (see figure 2.2). They enclosed an area of about 58,500 square feet, larger than any in the empire except those in Rome that had been constructed under Nero.[29]

Second-century Carthage was a great city. It was founded and grew in the Roman fashion and was second only to Rome itself in the immensity of its public buildings and the wealth of its citizens. Maps and monuments can be misleading, however. Carthage was not simply a copy of Rome; the city and its inhabitants kept their distinctive heritage. North Africans, even to the imperial family of Septimius Severus, continued to speak Punic. Yet language was not the only measure of North African ethnic identity.

There is a predictable rhythm to cultural identity in relation to colonization. At first, new colonists make a point consciously to preserve the culture they brought with them. The early Roman colonists to Carthage rebuilt their city and structured their lives modeled on Rome. In time, however, as colonists seem to feel more secure that they will not lose that which they brought, they seem more ready to embrace local customs.[30] Over the course of the second century, it became fashionable for the upper classes of Carthage to claim some African origin, even if their background was purely Roman.[31] This was visible not only in the preservation of the Punic language but also in the worship of Saturn and Caelestis, seen as the Roman equivalents of Baal-Hammon and Tanit. Roman North Africans also gave their children names that were typically African, like Datus, Fortunatus, Saturninus.[32] In the second century, Tertullian described the traditional Carthaginian robes and asserted that these were the ceremonial robes worn by priests of Aesculapius.[33]

When Perpetua dreamed, she included in her dreams the priests of Saturn and the spaces of Carthage. Like so many provincial Romans, she was a product of Rome but also of the province that formed the backdrop of her life. The backdrop included the spaces and history of Carthage but also the daily life that was particularly North African, and the intellectual life that made Carthage famous for centuries.

LIFE AND CULTURE

The prosperity of Punic Carthage depended primarily on trade supplemented with olive oil and wine production; under the Romans the potential of the North African lands was more fully exploited. When Caesar Augustus founded the colony, Rome needed wheat to feed the many who lived in the capital, and the lands of the new colony were devoted to the growing of wheat. In the middle of the first century, North Africa, particularly the land surrounding Carthage, became the breadbasket of Rome. African wheat was especially praised for its quality, and Pliny reported extraordinary yields of 150 to 1.[34] The numbers were likely an exaggeration in the ancient world, where yields as low as 4.5 to 1 were common,[35] but they express a reality of awe for the productivity of the North African soil. They also show the wealth that was generated by agricultural riches in an empire whose demand for food was insatiable.

By the late first century, Rome's grain supply seemed secure and African agriculture was permitted to diversify. Great groves of olive trees were planted in the hills surrounding the grain fields, and vineyards were restored to the North African land.[36] Olive trees were (and still are) particularly suited to this climate since, they require remarkably little moisture, efficiently taking advantage of the morning dew. Once planted, they take almost ten years to bear fruit, but they require little labor and produce for decades. Great presses were built throughout the countryside to extract the precious oil. The dry air itself was (and still is) rich with the aroma of ripe olives.

Pliny, in his work on natural history, praised the oil that was so essential to Mediterranean life: "Olive oil has the property of imparting warmth to the body and protecting it against cold, and also that of cooling the head when heated."[37] Olive oil was also burned in the many small oil lamps that archaeologists now excavate by the hundreds. These lamps have an opening for a wick to be submerged into the oil but are covered to keep mice from drinking it. The liquid that brought light to homes and warmth to bodies also brought wealth to purses, for it was easy to transport and in great demand.

To exploit these productive agricultural resources, the land was organized in large estates cultivated by slaves or peasants who reaped little benefit from the production. The Romano-African owners lived very well, some in manor houses on their estates but more often in houses in town so they could participate in the urban life that so defined the Roman culture. Just as the wealthy in Rome would go to their country estates periodically, so did the North African elite, but in the second and early third centuries, the good life was defined as urban life.

By the early third century, there were about two hundred cities in the farmlands that surrounded Carthage, some only six or eight miles apart.[38] The townhouses in the cities were small, yet comfortable. Most were laid out with rooms around a courtyard, and excavations show that the wealthy surrounded themselves with beauty. The courtyards had running water for fountains and flowers. The floors of many of the houses were decorated with beautiful mosaics, which have served as valuable sources relative not only to their owners' artistic sensibilities but also to their daily lives.

The Punic Carthaginians may have developed the technique for mosaic floors, but the Roman Carthaginians transformed it into a high art. At least by the second century, there was a busy mosaic workshop in Carthage. At that time, by far the principal patrons commissioning mosaics were individuals decorating their homes. Public mosaics (particularly in the public baths) would not become popular until later. North African designers developed images that influenced other regions in the Mediterranean.[39]

Some mosaics showed garden scenes and recounted mythological stories, but the North Africans seemed to favor more concrete images—representations of events in their daily lives. In the time of Septimius Severus, the most popular image was a hunting scene.[40] Figure 2.3 shows one such scene: a man riding to the hunt following his hunting dogs, whose names, Ederaturs and Mustela, were immortalized in the mosaic. Another kind of image popular in the mosaics is less appealing to modern tastes: these depict shows that patrons sponsored in the arenas of the cities. Figure 2.4 is of two boxers, with the realistic detail of blood gushing from the head of the loser. To see beauty and fame in blood shed publicly was a characteristic of Rome in general

Fig. 2.3 Hunting scene (mosaic). Bardo Museum, Tunis.
Photograph by Bob Balsley.

Fig. 2.4 Boxer (mosaic). Bardo Museum, Tunis. Photograph by Bob Balsley.

and North Africa in particular. The mosaics that graced the floors of families like Perpetua's both reflected and shaped the way they looked at the world.

As Romans moved their urban style to North Africa and as they relied on the great farms to provide grain for export, they confronted a fundamental reality of life in North Africa: scarcity of water. The ways of Roman agriculture demanded a great deal of water, and the Roman engineers built dams, reservoirs, and gigantic cisterns.[41] But the cities' "thirst" seemed almost unquenchable. The fountains in the private houses, the latrines, and most of all the great baths required that water be brought from springs in the mountains down to the cities.

The great aqueduct of Carthage was built in the early second century under Emperor Hadrian, who reacted to a drought and the suffering of Carthaginians by commissioning an aqueduct that would be one of the longest in the Roman world. It brought water from thirty-five miles south of Carthage, meandering for about seventy-five miles before its water flowed into the city at a remarkable rate of almost eighty gallons a second.[42] Great cisterns were also built on the outskirts of Carthage near the amphitheater to supplement the supply.

Other provincial towns also built aqueducts and cisterns and dug wells to try to maintain the comfortable way of life that marked Roman North African civilization. In the late second century, these efforts were successful; the province was marked by cities and prosperity, and dominated by the great center, Carthage.

Perpetua was born into the wealthy class that lived so graciously in the province, but we are not certain exactly where she lived. The original account of her martyrdom was Latin, and it gave no information about the location of the family's home. Shortly after this account was written, it was translated into Greek, but the Greek version adds information that was missing from the original. The Greek version says that the group was arrested in Thuburbo Minus (modern Tébourba), about thirty-three miles on the Bagrada River to the west of Carthage[43] (see figure 2.1). Because the Greek version is not the original, this information must be used with caution. The translator either had independent knowledge of the events and added the location accurately or inserted inaccurate information for reasons we cannot know.[44]

If the family did live in Thuburbo Minus or own property there, its members lived the life of the wealthy rural landowners described above. Thuburbo was in the prosperous agricultural region that served as Rome's breadbasket. The town itself had been founded as an early colony for veterans of the Roman army[45] and offered the full range of amenities for the urban-dwelling rural elite. Whether the family came from Thuburbo Minus or lived in Carthage itself, which is the assumption scholars have drawn from the Latin version of the martyrdom, the capital of the province would have nevertheless dominated its experience. The trial and execution very likely took place in Carthage. Well before that, the family would have traveled to the city to take advantage of the cultural life there, and Perpetua's brothers would probably have been sent there to complete their educations. Throughout its existence, Carthage drew the wealthy and promising from provincial towns much further away than Thuburbo Minus.

One such promising youth was Apuleius, the famous philosopher discussed in the previous chapter. Like Perpetua, Apuleius came from a provincial town, Madaura, but he went to Carthage to complete his education.[46] Two centuries later, another provincial young man made his mark by studying in the intellectual center of the province: the Christian saint Augustine. Augustine began his education in his hometown Thagaste, then traveled to Madaura to study literature and public speaking, but his education culminated in Carthage.[47] Between the times of these two great men who had been educated at Carthage, Perpetua and her family, too, would have been drawn to the city. The intellectual life there shaped Perpetua's experiences just as it shaped the intellectual growth of men like Apuleius and Augustine.

The public world of Carthage was known for its intellectual vibrancy.[48] When Apuleius spoke to the cosmopolitan audience, he praised the city for "possessing so many friends of learning among her citizens."[49] Elsewhere, he praised the city even more extravagantly: "Carthage is the venerable instructress of our province, Carthage is the heavenly muse of Africa. Carthage is the fount whence all the Roman world draws draughts of inspiration."[50] Even allowing for Apuleius's rhetorical flourishes, his assessment of the city as a cultural capital was shared by many.

The intellectual life of Carthage included private conversations in the crowded forum and public orations of the kind Apuleius gave in the forum or in the theater. It also included an array of performances in the theater built by Hadrian. Among them were comedies by the Roman playwrights Terence and Plautus; these often told of comic situations, usually involving love trysts, that explored a full range of human emotion while playing out rather frivolous plots. Performances also included mimes and pantomimes with slapstick comedy, and shows ranging from comedy to tragedy to ropewalkers to jugglers and dancers.[51] Augustine was fascinated with the theater because, he asserted, he could encounter along with the audience all kinds of human emotions that might normally not be part of his experience.[52] People's intellectual and cultural life in second-century Carthage was enhanced by their participation in theater and art, just as it is in today's cultural centers.

Perpetua and her family would have attended these performances, and as they walked through the town they would have learned from the formal and informal speakers. They also would have seen the praise of learning that was marked by such things as the statue of Apuleius that had been erected less than fifty years before. We can make general statements like these, but to translate them into specific intellectual influences that had an impact on Perpetua's choices as she moved toward martyrdom is more difficult. However, it is possible to trace a few specific aspects of Carthage's cultural life that seem to have made a direct difference to the young Roman matron: the languages of North Africa, the literature, and the very diversity of the place that exposed her to many new ideas, including those of the Christian community.

During the second and third centuries, the intellectual life of Carthage was expressed in both Latin and Greek. (By Augustine's time, Greek had fallen into disuse.) Apuleius claimed that he gave speeches in both languages to satisfy the cosmopolitan audience.[53] Perpetua's family was at least trilingual, speaking Latin, Greek, and Punic. That Greek was a significant part of her family's experience is strongly suggested by the fact that Perpetua's young deceased brother's name was Dinocrates, a Greek name. The prevalence of Greek in North Africa means that Greek literature was accessible and part of the intellectual heritage of Carthage, and hence of Perpetua herself.

One form of literature that likely influenced Perpetua's view of the world was the Hellenistic novel. Julia Domna (Septimius Severus's wife) probably included at least one of these novelists in her literary circle,[54] which suggests how popular they had become by the reign of Septimius (and in the lifetime of Perpetua). These novels increasingly are studied as revealing of the thought of the Hellenistic world.[55]

Most of the novels were written in Greek, although Apuleius wrote an influential one in Latin, *The Golden Ass* or *Metamorphosis*. Apuleius's work was influenced by earlier Greek novels, showing their availability in North Africa. Perpetua certainly read *The Golden Ass*,[56] and likely read, or at least heard about, other such novels. We know that at least one of the novels, *Metiochos and Parthenope*, was regularly performed in the theater,[57] and it seems implausible that so famous a theater as that in Carthage would not have featured this popular play. This body of literature is important because the novels share characteristics that in some way mirror Perpetua's actions.

The basic story of most of the novels involves a pair of (very) young

lovers who fall in love (usually at first sight). The two are then separated, and each undergoes adventures and trials before they are reunited to live happily ever after. Within this general plot summary, it is
worth considering what lessons Perpetua might have taken from these
Hellenistic novels.

First, there appears a praise of youth. The novel fragment *Ninos* describes a speech in which a young man argues that a girl of fourteen is
plenty old enough to marry and bear children, and in fact the couple
should seize the day to achieve their desires because the future is always
uncertain anyway.[58] Although Roman society advocated youthful marriages, these were conducted under the guidance of the *pater familias*,
not initiated by youthful lovers. These novels praised the idea of young
people—teenagers—standing up for what they wanted. This was not
Roman, but it was what the young Perpetua did when she defied her
family to follow Christ.

A second characteristic of the novels is that they portray strong,
independent female characters. This is in striking contrast to appropriate female roles as articulated in traditional Roman society. Heroines
like Parthenope, Antheia, and Sinonis are resourceful and outspoken.[59]
Some, like Chariclea in *The Ethiopian Story*, get captured by bandits or
confront other dangers and comport themselves with bravery and wit.[60]
A remarkable heroine in *Ninos* dresses in gender-ambiguous clothing
and leads a band of Assyrians to capture a fortified city. Although
wounded, she makes a brave escape while elephants are trampling her
men.[61]

The heroines and heroes withstand all kinds of tests and trials
during their adventures before they are restored to each other. These
trials often took place in the center of Roman power, the amphitheater.
One youth was tested in the arena to prove his worthiness.[62] Another
had to wrestle a gigantic Ethiopian in the games as his final test. As
these two examples show, the many private struggles that they experienced frequently culminated in a public trial that proved their mettle.
The sequence mirrors the experiences of Christian martyrs who began
with a search within their consciences and ended with a public confrontation with Roman power.

Finally, the novels promised a happy ending for the worthy (and, of
course, the heroes and heroines who withstood all the trials the evil
world threw at them were worthy). In part, the happy endings offer
what we have come to expect from modern romances: lovers reunited
to live happily ever after. However, the Hellenistic novels frequently
offer a spiritual dimension to their happy endings. After wrestling the
Ethiopian, the hero of the tale claims to have earned the ability to

prophesy,[63] which was the mark of spirituality in the ancient world. In this tale the two lovers end up not only being married but being invested into the priesthood.[64]

The moral of these stories is that if you are young, brave, and persistent, you will achieve your earthly desires. You will also be rewarded by the gods with spiritual benefits. In the *Golden Ass*, Apuleius creates a perfect example of this integration of adventure story with a spiritual result. At the center of the novel, Apuleius tells an enchanting tale of Cupid and Psyche. Psyche is a beautiful young woman who captures the heart of the God of Love himself. The two live and love happily in a handsome, hidden palace. Because of Psyche's jealous sisters and her own tragic curiosity, the lovers are separated. The God of Love seems lost to the young woman. However, she is determined to seek him out, and withstands a number of trials in that search: the wrath of Venus; having to perform seemingly impossible tasks; and facing death by going into the underworld. Her efforts make her worthy in the eyes of the gods, and Jupiter brings her to heaven. She drinks a cup of ambrosia to make her immortal, and she and Cupid have a celestial wedding and produce a child, Joy.[65]

On the one hand, this tale fits exactly the formula of lovers separated and finally rejoined after adventures and trials. On the other hand, by having the God of Love himself be one of the lovers, the story takes on an allegorical tone and becomes a longing of the soul (Psyche) for God. In this allegorical form, the tale was popular among pagans filled with spiritual longing and later with Christians searching for God.[66] The close connection between spiritual quests and the romantic Hellenistic novels is further confirmed by Apuleius's ending of *The Golden Ass*. In a novel that clearly drew on the Greek romances, Apuleius ended not with the marriage of a happy couple but with an autobiographical religious experience of the cult of Isis, the culmination of his own soul's longing for the divine.

We can see how Apuleius was led from romantic novel to spiritual quest because he wrote his own novel depicting that transition. When we turn to Perpetua, we cannot be so certain about this kind of influence. We do know she read Apuleius, and it is highly likely that she read or saw theatrical depictions of other romantic novels. I suggest (without being able to prove it exactly) that the novels may have influenced Perpetua by offering a particular kind of role model that might have made it easier for her to proceed so proudly to martyrdom. I think it is difficult (if not impossible) for us to act if we cannot imagine ourselves doing so first. This is the modern argument for the influence of science fiction literature, for example. Once we imagine in fiction the creation of certain technological advances, we can proceed to invent them. In the same way, the fiction adventure stories may have helped Perpetua imagine herself as an active young heroine who could withstand trials in the expectation of a happy and spiritual ending. We cannot know for sure the exact nature of this literature's influence on the intelligent young woman, but we can say that it formed part of the cultural heritage that shaped her world in Carthage.

When the narrator of the Passion of Perpetua wrote briefly that she was well educated, the phrase implied full participation in the rich cultural life of Carthage. Perpetua grew up not only shaped by the Roman values that her family firmly advocated but shaped by the diversity that was Carthage. This included a variety of language and of literature, and it included a range of ideas—Roman, Greek, African, and of course Christian. Carthage in the second century was marked by diversity as well as by prosperity and a vibrant intellectual life. All those things shaped Perpetua's experience, and one would imagine that such a setting would have led to a positive view of life. However, that was not so.

Although the literary sources praise the dynamic urban life of Carthage, we should remember that, from a modern perspective, ancient cities were remarkably crowded, filthy, and dangerous because of both crime and disease.[67] Life was exciting but fragile. The Carthaginians seem to have confronted this fact perhaps more than most. Perpetua grew up exposed to a profound anxiety that had always marked the people of Carthage, and that led them to emphasize the importance of personal sacrifice as a way of preserving their prosperity.

SACRIFICE AND SUICIDE

Throughout the ancient world, offering sacrifices to the gods was the central form of worship. Romans offered animals, cakes, and wine at the many altars both public and private. They hoped the gods would respond favorably and offer benefits or at least withhold destruction. It would not take much of a leap for people who held this worldview to decide that the greatest sacrifice would bring the greatest benefit, and the greatest sacrifice was human blood. Aline Rouselle captures the power that such a sacrifice held for people: "Paradoxically, the spilling of blood, . . . symbolized the respect in which life was held by all. Everyone was insistent on the necessity of spilling blood, as it was the price that had to be paid for the survival of the community and for the salvation of each individual."[68]

Although it is difficult to get precise information about so distant a time, it seems that the Semitic world in the ninth century B.C., where Dido and her crew originated, included the practice of human sacrifice. The Bible describes a king of Moab who was losing a battle against Israel. The king then took his eldest son and "offered him for a burnt offering upon the wall." The sacrifice worked and Israel withdrew.[69] More generally, the Bible describes people who "offer up their sons and daughters in fire to their gods."[70] Israel itself was not exempt from at least the possibility of offering an ultimate sacrifice. The Book of Exodus relates God's command "You shall give Me the first-born among your sons,"[71] and the Bible further tells of Abraham's willingness to follow this command by sacrificing his beloved Isaac. That Isaac was saved at the last minute by an angel's intervention does not change the fact that human sacrifice was seen as a requirement that the Hebrew God might ask of his people.[72]

There were many connections between the ancient Phoenicians who were Dido's ancestors and the Hebrews who recorded the command for human sacrifice. Jezebel, daughter of the Phoenician king of Tyre, married the king of Israel and brought Phoenician idolatry to Israel.[73] Hiram, the king of Tyre, provided lumber and workers for the building of the Temple of Solomon. Further, there were many similarities between these two Semitic languages.[74]

In the seventh century B.C., the Hebrew prophets began to oppose the sacrifice of eldest sons.[75] Jeremiah vehemently separated the people of Israel from their Phoenician neighbors as he cried out against the practice of human sacrifice: "[t]hey have filled this place with the blood of innocents, and have built the high places of Baal to burn their sons in the fire as burnt offerings to Baal. . . . [T]his place shall no more be called Topheth or the valley of the son of Hinnom but the valley of Slaughter."[76]

After the seventh century, there is no more real evidence of human sacrifice among the Hebrews or the Phoenicians of the eastern Mediterranean.[77] Long before that, however, Queen Dido and her crew had left the East. When they came to settle Carthage, they brought with them both the ancient gods and their hunger for human blood. With the zeal of new colonists, they preserved the ancient ways long after those ways had died away in their homeland.

Archaeologists of Carthage have excavated a cemetery that would have been on the edge of the ancient city near the ports (see Figure 2.2). It contained only urns and stelae of children and animals that had been sacrificed to Baal-Hammon and Tanit. Archaeologists have called this the "tophet," after the biblical reference in Jeremiah to the spot where children were sacrificed. Almost all the stelae record that the sacrifices were given in fulfillment of a vow or in response to some divine favor.[78] This still sad space, which is filled with layers of rubble, vividly expresses the fears of ancient parents who responded to their deep anxiety about the future by sacrificing their children. What is perhaps most impressive about the site is the sheer number of urns buried there. Between 400 and 200 B.C., during the height of Carthaginian power, as many as twenty thousand urns may have been deposited: an average of one hundred deposits a year or slightly fewer than one every three days.[79] Such numbers mean either that this was an everyday feature of Carthaginian life or, more likely, that many children were sacrificed at once in times of perceived danger. Most probably the large numbers of urns came from a combination of parents satisfying individual vows by sacrificing a single child and an occasional public need demanding a sacrifice of a goodly number of children. The archaeological evidence to date indicates that the majority of the sacrifices involved one to three burials at a time.[80]

The remains in the tophet show both child and animal bones, but both children and animals were sacrificed throughout the period of its use; there was not a progression from human to animal offerings.[81] Instead, apparently at times an animal could substitute for a promised child, just as Abraham could substitute a ram for his beloved son Isaac. An inscription on a stone in rural North Africa describes this practice. A family sacrificed a sheep to Saturn (the Roman name for Baal-Hammon) in thanks for the cure of their daughter. The parents, like the biblical Abraham, claimed to have received permission for the substitution in the form of a "vision and a vow," and thus the sheep offered "breath for breath, life for life,"[82] and the child was spared. The presence of animal bones in the place of human sacrifice simply testified to the occasional kindness of the Punic gods who at times suspended their harsh contract—Carthaginian prosperity in exchange for the lives of an astonishing number of their children.

The excavations in the tophet bear silent witness to the truth of the written sources that tell of the Carthaginian practice of child sacrifice. Christian writers as late as the fourth century A.D. recalled in horror the practice of sacrificing children. Eusebius of Caesarea wrote that rulers had to give up the most beloved of their children in times of "great crises or danger."[83] Augustine wrote that Carthaginians sacrificed their children because humans were the most valuable sacrifice of all. Of course, Augustine used this information as a contrast with the more benign practices of the Christian God, but the memory of the sacrifice was powerful.[84]

The most detailed description of the sacrifice came from the ancient author Diodorus of Sicily, who wrote an account of the Punic wars with Rome. Diodorus wrote that during the dark days of the First Punic War, the Carthaginians tried to understand how they seemed to have lost the favor of their gods. They looked to their traditional rituals to see if any had been neglected. Diodorus tells us they selected two hundred of the noblest children for sacrifice, and another one hundred voluntarily were sacrificed. Then the author described the way the children were burnt: "There was in their city a bronze image of Cronus [Baal-Hammon, known as Saturn or Cronus], extending its hands, palms up and sloping toward the ground, so that each of the children when placed thereon rolled down and fell into a sort of gaping pit filled with fire."[85] Although Diodorus did not say what happened next, archaeological evidence shows the burnt bones were gathered and placed in urns and buried under a commemorative stele.

It seems that the children were killed before they were placed in the arms of the god. Plutarch described the sacrifice: "They themselves offered up their own children, and those who had no children would buy little ones from poor people and cut their throats as if they were so many lambs or young birds."[86] This sacrifice also required that the children and the parents offer it willingly. Tertullian explained that youth helped in the children's complicity. Describing the worship of Saturn in the "Apology," Tertullian wrote that children must be selected who are too young to understand death so they would laugh at the knife; further, compliant parents fondled their children to make them laugh at the moment of death.[87] Minucius Felix also described the importance of parental involvement in the sacrifice: "Infants are sacrificed to him [Saturn] by their parents, who stifle their squalling by caresses and kisses to prevent the sacrifice of a tearful victim."[88]

Plutarch's description suggests that the parents' complicity did not come easily. He says if mothers shed a "single tear" the good effect of the sacrifice was nullified and the child would be sacrificed anyway. Furthermore, "[T]he whole area before the statue was filled with a loud noise of flutes and drums so that the cries of the wailing should not reach the ears of the people."[89] Of course, this makes sense. For a sacrifice to be efficacious, it must be difficult. The most difficult sacrifice of all would be for parents joyfully to hand their children to the knife and flame.

The Carthaginian tradition of sacrifice was made more influential by the fact that it was not limited to parents' willingness to deliver their children to the flames of Baal-Hammon. If this had been so, the inclination may have died out under Roman pressure to abandon the prac-

tice. However, Carthaginians also valued self-sacrifice, a sacrificial suicide that offered the most precious gift to the gods, themselves.

Suicide is a particularly troubling concept, for us and for the ancients who contemplated it. Some philosophers, like Plato and Aristo-
tle, disapproved of it; others like the Cynics and some Stoics approved
of it as an honorable option in a dishonorable world.[90] In many instances, an acceptable suicide is linked to powerlessness. We are accustomed to reading about heroes who by their strength or influence make
a dramatic impact on their societies. However, this does not mean that
only people who have strength or power care deeply about things
larger than themselves. How does an individual who has little to offer
make a contribution to his or her community? How do powerless people rise above that constraint to make a political or even a spiritual difference? Women frequently are in the position of lacking the power to
change their circumstances, so in the ancient texts, women at times sacrificed themselves in the hope that their deaths would make an impact.
These sacrifices became part of the cultural memory, a recognized contribution, and a model for other people who felt powerless to make
change.

This notion of sacrificial suicide is not limited to the ancient world,
nor is it limited to North Africa. However, it held particular appeal in
Carthage—both Punic and Roman. In a society that preserved the idea
of human sacrifice, self-sacrifice captured the imagination. The crucial
turning points in Carthaginian history were marked by a sacrificial suicide, usually of a woman.

North Africans remembered the suicide of Queen Dido mostly
through Virgil's telling. The poet described how the queen built her
own funeral pyre, climbed on it and killed herself with her sword.
Dido's sister held her bleeding body while the city mourned and honored the death of its queen.[91] This story formed the starting point for
the history of Carthage. It was used to explain the animosity between
Carthage (embodied by Dido) and Rome (in the person of her lover
Aeneas) that led to the destruction of Punic Carthage. However, it was
also a model of the supreme sacrifice that an individual could offer.

As late as the fourth century, the Christian Augustine wrote against
suicide[92] but nevertheless recalled that in his youth he had been profoundly drawn to this tale; he had cried for Dido who "died for love of
Aeneas" and who "surrendered her life to the sword."[93] Dido was only
the first of many Carthaginians who were remembered because they
sacrificed themselves.

The Carthaginian general Hamilcar Barca in 485 B.C. was fighting the Greeks in Sicily. The battle was going against him, and the historian Herodotus describes the Carthaginian account: "Hamilcar remained in camp, sacrificing and offering for favorable results whole bodies of victims on a great pyre. But when he saw the rout of his troops happening and he was at that moment pouring the libations on the victims, he threw himself headlong into the pyre." Herodotus goes on to say that the Carthaginians recalled his sacrifice as worthy, and "have made memorials to him in all the cities of the colonists, the greatest monument of all being in Carthage itself."[94] Hamilcar was remembered more for his sacrificial suicide than for his victories in battle.

As the history of Carthage continued, so did the tradition of suicide. At the end of the Third Punic War, the moment of Punic Carthage's destruction was framed and recalled with the death of a woman. After the Carthaginian general Hasdrubal surrendered, his wife reproached him for cowardice. In a final gesture, she cursed her husband, "Upon this Hasdrubal, betrayer of his country and her temples, of me and his children, may the gods of Carthage take vengeance." With these words, she killed their children, flung them into the fires that were consuming the city, and plunged in after them. Appian concluded his account of the incident with his own reproach of the husband: "With these words, . . . did the wife of Hasdrubal die, as Hasdrubal should have died himself."[95]

With the reestablishment of Carthage under Roman rule, the nature of worship of the old gods changed. Baal-Hammon became known as Saturn and Tanit became Caelestis. The nature of the sacrifice to these deities changed as well. In Rome human sacrifice had been banned as early as 97 B.C., but it took much longer than that for the prohibition to take full effect. Hadrian in the mid second century A.D. extended the ban throughout the empire, but it was not until the third century A.D. that the practice of human sacrifice was virtually eliminated in the Roman world.[96] Christian apologists like Minucius Felix would repeatedly point to the continuation of human sacrifice in the Roman world as evidence of Roman spiritual decadence.[97]

It is difficult to trace the practice of child sacrifice specifically in North Africa, for the sources are ambiguous and the practice tenacious. Tertullian in the late second century said that the public sacrifice of children was banned in the "proconsulate of Tiberius." Tertullian offers as witness to this ban the testimony of members of the army who killed the priests who performed the sacrifice.[98] This passage has generated controversy because we do not know whether he refers to Emperor Tiberius in the first century A.D., or to a proconsul of North

Africa in the second half of the second century.[99] Tertullian's text citing contemporary witnesses suggests the later date.

Christian authors asserted that child sacrifice continued in private even after its public banning. This may be supported by excavations of regular cemeteries (not the tophet, which ceased to be used during Roman times). These cemeteries had an unduly high percentage of child burials, which some experts suggest supports the continued occasional practice of child sacrifice in response to some vow.[100]

Whatever was going on in private, the Romans vigorously banned public human sacrifice on the altars of the gods. However, they preserved a particular form of human sacrifice: gladiatorial combat, which Tertullian tells us arose from the practice of human sacrifice. The contests came from the "belief that the souls of the dead are propitiated by human blood," so captives or slaves were sacrificed at funerals.[101] Later, gladiators were condemned men who were trained to die fighting in the arena. They swore a deep and terrible oath to be "burnt, to be chained up, and to be killed by an iron weapon,"[102] and ultimately to bare their necks unflinchingly to the killing blade. While banning human sacrifice in one form, the Romans kept it in another. The games in the arena where humans and animals were killed in a ritual fashion were immediately popular in North Africa. They were perfectly consistent with the sensibility of sacrifice and suicidal sacrifice that was so deeply ingrained in the people's consciousness.

The mosaics that graced the North African homes and showed scenes from the arena like the boxers shown in figure 2.4 show visually the Carthaginian attachment to blood sacrifice. Illustrations in chapter 5 show even more shocking mosaic scenes from the arena. The praise of sacrifice surrounded the prosperous North Africans.

Rome changed the space and expression of human sacrifice from the arms of Baal-Hammon to the arena but did not change the ideal of sacrifice and of sacrificial suicide. Nor did it change the Carthaginian tradition of marking important points of its history with a mythology of sacrifice. For example, such a legend arose to explain the building of the all-important aqueduct of Carthage. The story says that a Roman soldier fell in love with a native princess. She scorned his attentions and established what seemed to be an impossible condition to his winning her hand: she would not marry him until the waters of the Zaghouan flowed to Carthage. The enterprising Roman built the impressive aqueduct and went to claim his bride. Like Dido and General Hasdrubal's wife, the princess killed herself rather than submit, throwing herself from the top of the newly built aqueduct.[103] By adding this legend to the founding of the aqueduct, the wary Carthaginians could rely on sacrificial blood to ensure the continuation of the water supply to the city.

Such stories continued to mark the history of Carthage until its conquest by the Arabs. At that turning point, a daughter of the defeated Christian general committed suicide by throwing herself off a camel rather than be taken captive.[104] (I admit the height of a camel does not seem lethal, but the significant fact here is the importance placed on the suicide even though the mechanism at hand seems fairly improbable—unless we assume that the camel was walking along the edge of a mountain cliff.)

Even the novels that circulated during that time contained praise for the willingness to die rather than compromise one's principles. In the novel *Babyloniaka*, the heroine is ready to kill herself rather than marry against her will.[105] In the *Golden Ass*, Apuleius tells a tale of a woman who committed suicide at the tomb of her dead husband after brutally avenging his killers. [106]

Perpetua grew up hearing the stories of sacrifice and sacrificial suicide. For a Carthaginian, the opportunity to die for a cause was a deeply ingrained value. During her imprisonment, Perpetua's compatriot Tertullian reminded the group of the long tradition of people who died willingly. He wrote to the imprisoned Christians listing pagans who threw themselves into a volcano or onto a funeral pyre. He continued his chronicle of suicides, writing "even women have despised the flames." He mentions Dido and the wife of General Hasdrubal, both of whom were part of the Carthaginian mythology. He continues cataloguing other men and women who died bravely and concludes that these examples should make it easier for Perpetua and her companions to face death in the arena:

> Therefore, if earthly glory accruing from strength of body and soul is valued so highly that one despises sword, fire, piercing with nails, wild beasts and tortures for the reward of human praise, then I may say the sufferings you endure are but trifling in comparison with the heavenly glory and divine reward.[107]

Tertullian's use of pagan examples to stir Christian resolve points up one of the ironies we confront when we study the ways memories are used. In some tracts, Tertullian is fierce in his condemnation of pagan rituals, in particular rituals calling for sacrificial blood. In his tract "Spectacles," he succinctly articulates the Christian position: "Do you have desire for blood. . . ? You have the blood of Christ."[108] Christ's blood was the sufficient sacrifice that replaced all others. Yet, Tertullian lived and thought in a time and place that valued sacrifice and sacrificial suicide. He drew from this tradition to bring people's actions to a Christian purpose.

Like her contemporary Tertullian, Perpetua brought the sum of her education and experience—all her memories—to her decision to die for her faith. These experiences included the strong tradition of Rome that made it so difficult for her to withstand the pressure of her family and her obligations. However, her ideas were also strongly shaped by her experience in North Africa. As a Carthaginian she was prepared for self-sacrifice. She was also exposed to the many ideas that circulated in the cosmopolitan region. These ideas included literature that advocated far more feminine initiative than her traditional Roman upbringing might have permitted.

Her intellectual heritage from both second-century Rome and North Africa included a spiritual longing. This longing fueled a search for new truths on the part of educated North Africans like Apuleius and Tertullian and many others. Perpetua must have been included in that group. Her writings and her dreams show that she drew from her rich background in her spiritual quest. However, there remains the most significant influence in her intellectual progress. Among the diverse ideas that she heard about in the cosmopolitan region was the story of the risen Christ. The ideas Perpetua learned in the Christian community in Carthage formed the third great intellectual thread that wove the pattern for the martyr's brief life.

three

Christian Community

ORIGINS

Of all the diverse views that Perpetua and her family encountered in Carthage, why was she drawn to the beliefs of the Christian community? There is not enough information to answer that question for Perpetua personally; one can only look generally at why Romans converted to the apostolic church. The answer begins with how Perpetua came to be exposed to the ideas at all. That is, how did Christianity come to Carthage? Unfortunately, this is another question on which the sources are largely silent.

Tertullian (Perpetua's contemporary) did not write about the origins of the Carthaginian church, so we may well assume that the church began early enough to be beyond his memory.[1] In light of the organizational structure and some of the practices of the early North African church, the Christian community was probably founded by travelers from the eastern Mediterranean (rather than from Rome).[2]

The most plausible (although by no means certain) explanation for the founding of the African church is that during the first- and second-century wars in Judea, a number of Jews came to Carthage. For example, legend tells us that a synagogue was founded on the nearby Island of Jerba by Jews who fled Palestine with the destruction of the Temple in A.D. 70. Roman sources say Titus brought thousands of Jewish slaves and settlers to Carthage after his victory.[3] It seems plausible that many of the Jews displaced in the first century and early second came either willingly or as slaves to this prosperous port city. Among all these Jews might well have been followers of the Jesus movement.

We do know that by the second and third centuries there was a fairly extensive Jewish community in Carthage. A large Jewish cemetery on the coast about three miles north of the center of the city has been partially excavated.[4] Its size suggests a Jewish community in the second century of at least three hundred to five hundred people, which means there would have been more than one synagogue in Carthage.[5] It seems probable that we may find the origins of the Christian mission in this Jewish community.[6]

When studying the history of Christianity, many authors have undervalued the role of first-century Jews in the missionary efforts of the Christians. The texts from the writings of Paul onward emphasize the animosity of the Jews to the followers of Jesus. Paul is known as the apostle to the gentiles precisely because he reduced the Old Testament purity and legal requirements and made it easier for gentiles to convert. This has led some scholars to argue for a hypothesis that the Christian church radically departed from its Jewish roots in the late second century.[7] Certainly in the accounts of the third-century martyrs, Jews are mentioned as some of the most vocal opponents to the Christians.[8] However, the extreme animosity attributed to the two groups may well have grown out of the need to define as separate groups that had originally been close. Indeed, "the argument between Judaism and Christianity was at the beginning largely a family affair."[9]

Recent scholarship has emphasized the importance of the Jewish communities as the location of most of the converts to Christianity in the early generations.[10] In fact, the success of the Christian expansion was in part due to its use of diaspora Judaism.[11] As we apply this understanding to North Africa, we may assume that followers of Jesus located in the northern suburbs of Carthage slowly spread their beliefs. Rodney Stark has shown convincingly that "attachments lie at the heart of conversion," so conversions extended along social networks.[12] Believers spoke to their friends and families, and when those people were urban and sophisticated as well as somewhat religiously discontented, conversions occurred.[13]

Hellenistic Jewish communities throughout the empire also provided a mechanism for spreading the Christian message to gentiles. In many of the cities, there were gentiles who supported the diaspora synagogues. These people were apparently not organized in any particular way but were religious, known as "God-fearers" who attended services and contributed money to the synagogues. Some moved toward conversion to Judaism, but others simply supported a pious community in their midst.[14] Jews (unlike Christians) did not claim an exclusive right to salvation. They believed that gentiles could share the blessings of God based on good works.[15] No doubt these God-fearers were people longing to share the divine blessings that seemed to be in the Jewish community. At the same time they kept their allegiance and association with their own pagan families and friends.

When the apostles traveled to synagogues to tell of the risen Christ, their words were most readily received by the God-fearers,[16] who kept connections in both the Jewish and Greek communities. Timothy, the recipient of Paul's letters, was of mixed Jewish and Greek background, educated in the Scriptures but uncircumcised.[17] Timothy and the many other God-fearing men and women mentioned in the Bible might serve as typical converts in the equally cosmopolitan city of Carthage.

By the beginning of the third century, when Perpetua lived, the Christian population throughout the empire was small but visible. Stark estimates the total number of Christians as about 217,000, or less than 0.5 percent of the total population.[18] This is a small percentage but not an insignificant absolute number, particularly when the greatest concentrations would have been in the major cities. The situation in Carthage paralleled that of the empire as a whole.

Tertullian in 212 wrote to the governor of the province urging him to end the persecution of Christians. One of his arguments was that a serious persecution would decimate a large portion of the population of Carthage.[19] Tertullian certainly exaggerated the percentage of people that might be affected by a serious persecution, but he was right that the number would be noticeable. If we take Stark's rough estimate of Christians throughout the empire and apply it to Carthage, we might project about 2,000 Christians in a city of about 500,000.[20] The actual number of Christians might be a bit higher, since there had been a serious plague throughout the empire in 165, and non-Christians probably died at a greater rate than Christians because of the superior care of their own sick by the Christians.[21] So, when Tertullian sarcastically asked the governor, "What will you do with so many thousands of human beings?" he could have been close to accurate. Tertullian was certainly accurate when he described the degree to which Christians permeated Carthaginian society: "Every man will recognize his own relatives and companions among [those arrested] ... men of your own rank among them, noble ladies, and all the outstanding persons of the city, and the relatives or friends of your own friends."[22]

The networks of conversion had spread enough so that when Christians gathered in the house-churches of the more affluent, there were people from all social classes and from many different families. A new community had formed by the beginnings of the third century. It had acquired an identity that transcended both the Hellenized Jewish community that had spawned it and the cosmopolitan pagan community that increasingly embraced it. When Tertullian explained that Christians were called a "third race" after Jews and Greeks (pagans), he recognized that a new identity had emerged.[23] Like many other families in Carthage and elsewhere, Perpetua's family was divided by loyalty and religious belief. Perpetua's father was a traditional Roman *pater familias*. Yet, within his own household his daughter, one of his sons, and some slaves were catechumens (studying to prepare for baptism).

This brief narrative of the origins of Christianity in Carthage can give us some information about how the movement began and how it spread. We can imagine networks of converts meeting and talking. But beginning to understand how a movement spread does not address the more vexing question of why. Even allowing for enough religious dissatisfaction to cause households to split in their longing for the divine, why did people choose to follow Christ? The empire had plenty of competing cults and philosophies that promised fulfillment and that had many more adherents. Perpetua, her friends, and many like her chose a more difficult way. To try to understand their choice, we must look within the house-churches at the small assemblies of the faithful who were convinced that God was in their midst.

PRESENCE OF THE DIVINE

Conversions most likely took place at the services during which Christians assembled. People may have heard from their friends about the Christian community and attended a service, just as the God-fearers attended Jewish services at the synagogue. Historians have offered a number of hypotheses to explain conversions. Some suggest that people converted because of the strong Christian community in which people cared for one another.[24] Others suggest that people followed Christ for the afterlife that was offered,[25] or out of fear for the damnation that was threatened.[26] In the late fourth century, the North African Bishop Augustine claimed that some people converted out of fear and others out of desire to please some highly placed person.[27]

None of these answers is wholly convincing. The first presupposes that the converts did not already have a strong community. This was not the case with many, including Perpetua, who had to separate from family and community to follow Christ. The strong Christian communities were important in preserving the religion and supporting the converts, but community spirit alone could not have caused the conversions. Augustine's suggestion that people were anxious to please fits the more prosperous church of the late third century, not the besieged congregations of the late second. People might well change religions for a nicer afterlife or out of fear of punishment in the hereafter, but first they would have to believe in that afterlife. Here is the heart of the matter for the second-century seeker of divinity: Was God present at the assemblies of the Christians?

How would someone know that God was present? We have seen that the religious coin of the realm in the empire included miraculous healings, magic, and, perhaps most important, prophecy. If Christians were going to convince pagans of the truth of their message, they would have to be seen to possess the divine presence in ways convincing to their audience. And, indeed, Christians from the earliest decades through the second century in Carthage repeatedly demonstrated to their satisfaction the presence of the divine.

Eusebius, the fourth-century church historian, described the miraculous gifts that were manifested in the early communities: "Some have foreknowledge of the future, visions, and prophetic utterances; others, by the laying on of hands, heal the sick and restore them to health; and before now, . . . dead men have actually been raised and have remained with us for years."[28] The first three of these gifts have much in common; it was hard to distinguish among prophecy, foreknowledge, and visions. Visions, for example, might be powerful for the person experiencing them, but when they were described to the community, they became a form of prophecy.

Christians did not have a monopoly on prophecy; among pagans, it had always been a significant mark of divinity.[29] In the ancient world sometimes a god would speak directly through a medium and sometimes divinities would respond to specific questions through their prophets.[30] Judaism also had a tradition of charismatic prophecy.[31] Speaking of the Christian communities, Eusebius said the prophets would expose "men's secret thoughts" and "expound the mysteries of God."[32] These prophetic goals were as central to the Jesus movement as they were to the cults that permeated the Hellenistic world.

Prophetic utterances are just as subject to disbelief as any points of theology. Skeptics needed proof that the prophet indeed was guided by the Spirit. From the point of view of the observer, the most dramatic forms of divine presence were ecstatic experiences in which believers seemed transported, even possessed by divinity. The apostle Peter, for example, fell into a trance when he saw a vision,[33] and it is likely that the visible sign of the trance increased the credibility of the vision. There has been much written on the nature of ecstatic experiences, trances, and prophecies, but here I will take a general definition of an altered state of consciousness that is visible to witnesses to characterize all these experiences.[34] More detailed studies may well want to distinguish among the various kinds of altered states, but for my purposes it is enough that witnesses could recognize the existence of a transcendent state.

Christians shared with pagans the capacity to experience trances and prophesy in altered states, but from the earliest years, Christians exhibited an impressive and highly visible new form of ecstatic prophecy: speaking in tongues (glossolalia). Eusebius said, "[W]e hear of many members of the Church who have prophetic gifts and by the Spirit speak with all kinds of tongues."[35] Glossolalia was a significant feature of the earliest Christian communities, and it continued to be important through the time of Perpetua. It was one of the more frequent manifestations of the divine in the communities,[36] and as such it was probably a significant factor in conversions.

The beginnings of the Christian mission may be traced to the events that occurred on Pentecost. One hundred twenty followers of Jesus were gathered together when they experienced a collective vision: They all heard the sound of a mighty wind and saw tongues of fire "resting on each one of them. And they were all filled with the Holy Spirit and began to speak in other tongues, as the Spirit gave them utterance." Some people heard in these words their own languages but others, "mocking" them, said, "They are filled with new wine,"[37] implying that they were drunk and speaking unintelligibly.

Whether they were speaking in foreign languages or glossolalia, ecstatic speech marked the presence of the Spirit from the beginning, and it continued to hold a central position throughout the account of expansion described in Acts. For example, when Peter was preaching to gentiles, the "gift of the Holy Spirit had been poured out" on them. "For they heard them speaking in tongues and extolling God." Peter said that this proved their worthiness for baptism, because they "received the Holy Spirit just as we have."[38] When Paul preached to the congregation in Corinth and laid his hands upon them, they, too, began to speak in tongues.[39] In these instances, the Apostles linked glossolalia with their own experience at Pentecost, and made it one of the defining elements in becoming a Christian.[40]

As the church expanded, the visible presence of the Spirit in prophecy and specifically in speaking in tongues continued. Paul, in his letter to the Corinthians, accepted the presence of glossolalia in the community; indeed he claimed to speak in tongues more than anyone else.[41] He explained that when one speaks in tongues, one speaks to God, "for no one understands him but he utters mysteries in the Spirit."[42]

Glossolalia is a particularly visible manifestation of the seeming presence of the divine within a person and a community. However, it is not the only expression. Glossolalia lies on a spectrum of ecstatic experiences that range from visions and prophecy to speaking in tongues. The apostle Paul seems to have separated prophecy from glossolalia where previously there had been less clear division.[43] In his letter to the quarreling Corinthians, he distinguished the various gifts from tongues to prophecy to interpretation of tongues. He established the paradigm of a spectrum of gifts of the Spirit that would allow future congregations to be convinced of the presence of the divine whether its prophets were speaking in tongues or not.

Modern sociological studies of ecstatic expression and in particular glossolalia offer some insights on what the people in these early congregations experienced. One of the findings is that glossolalia tends to fade over time. After initial outbursts, manifestations are fewer and less intense.[44] By making glossolalia simply one form of ecstatic expression, not the defining one, as it had been for the faithful present at Pentecost, Paul provided a means for testing the presence of the divine even after the initial enthusiastic glossolalia faded. For the next two centuries after the death of Paul, various forms of ecstatic expression remained the hallmark of the Christian communities.

The Christian texts describe a continuous expression of ecstatic prophecy through the first few centuries after Christ. Most of these texts were not as careful as Paul to distinguish the form of the spiritual gifts, so we cannot always tell whether prophets were speaking in tongues or expressing other kinds of visions. However, the very ambiguity of the texts on this point is testimony to the fact that all these forms of ecstatic prophecy existed on a continuum. What was important was that the Spirit was believed to be firmly and visibly present in the congregations.

Justin Martyr in the beginning of the second century wrote that prophetic gifts were a conspicuous feature of the church right up to his own time.[45] Irenaeus in the late second century criticized a Gnostic example of ecstatic prophecy. He described how the heretic Marcus elicited a prophecy from a wealthy woman. Marcus "excited" the woman who then "impudently utters some nonsense as it happens to occur to her."[46] In spite of his criticism, ecstatic prophecy was not limited to heretics. Tertullian praised prophetic and ecstatic gifts.[47] A pagan contemporary of Tertullian wrote scathingly of contemporary Christian emphasis on prophecy, of which he claimed to have "firsthand knowledge." He said he had seen many who "make a show of being 'inspired' to utter their predictions."[48] Fifty years later, Cyprian described ecstasy as a peculiarly Christian state.[49] The bishop wrote of children who saw visions while in an ecstatic state, and in another letter he described people led astray by a woman who appeared to be in an ecstatic state but who actually was a false prophet.[50] All these and similar witnesses span the centuries that frame Perpetua's conversion. These many texts show the extent to which prophecy remained central to the Christian experience.

The emphasis on charismatic presence of the Spirit had a number of implications for the structure of the services and for the leadership within the community. Community worship was probably characterized by exuberance and joy, with spontaneous singing and prophecy. Some of the singing and prophecy was certainly glossolalic.[51] In these early charismatic communities, the leaders were those who seemed most filled with the Spirit; authority in the primitive church was primarily charismatic.[52] Paul placed prophets above administrators in what little hierarchy the communities possessed,[53] and when prophetic gifts were the measure of rank, women had access to community leadership.

There has been a great deal of controversy over the role of women as leaders in the early Christian communities.[54] Without attempting to resolve this thorny issue, I can offer a few general observations. Women certainly served as leaders of some sort in the early communities. Some held authority because of their prophetic gifts; for example, women in Paul's community in Corinth were praying and prophesying in public and deriving recognition for those activities.[55] Others exerted leadership because they had money and owned the houses in which the communities met. Still others served their communities in more formal roles as deacons.[56]

Although it is difficult to say much more about women in general as community leaders, we can say with certainty that Perpetua exerted some leadership in her congregation.[57] She acted as a leader in prison and in the arena. Her qualifications for leadership were clearly her dreams and visions, which were believed to be prophetic. Just as Paul put prophets above priests and deacons, Perpetua and her fellow martyr Saturus placed prophetic martyrs over more official figures. Prophecy was alive in Perpetua's community at Carthage. As Mary Ann Rossi summarizes so well, Perpetua's "personal contact with the divine generated a charismatic power that was diffused over the group as a whole."[58] Perpetua's role in her community was typical of charismatic leadership in the early church, and points to the close relationship between spiritual gifts and community.

Again, modern sociological studies shed some light on the association between community and ecstatic expression.[59] Glossolalia, for example, is most readily experienced in community. As people speak in tongues, it seems to infect others. This may be true whether someone is a believer or not, or whether they seek the experience or not. This is also true of other visible forms of ecstatic expression. Therefore, the community itself was essential to the presence of the Spirit, and as individuals were seeking proof of the imminence of the divine, they would learn that prophecy and ecstasy were tied to community.[60]

Ecstatic expressions are linked intricately to community, but there is a built-in paradox. The experience of the Spirit on the part of individuals also can lead to divisiveness in the very communities that stimulated the experience. Paul's letters show that this problem emerged among the earliest converts. In First Corinthians, when Paul separated glossolalia from other kinds of ecstatic expression, he noted that although glossolalia was a manifestation of the Spirit, it did not enhance the community the way prophecy did. Glossolalia could serve the community only if someone were present with the gift to interpret the tongues: "He who prophesies is greater than he who speaks in tongues, unless someone interprets, so that the church may be edified."[61]

By establishing this hierarchy, he kept charismatic gifts as the mark of the community, and he urged their continuance.[62] However, he established one measure by which the gifts could be tested, and a means for controlling them: if they contributed to the benefit and solidarity of the community they were true; if not, they were false. Paul posited an ideal community in which all members would have gifts of the Spirit in different forms and in different measures. Some would prophesy, some would speak in tongues, others interpret, others teach, and others heal and perform miracles. The combination of the gifts would form a corporate community.[63]

Paul's vision of a charismatic corporate community seems to have coexisted with a more formal organization derived from the synagogue in which the community was preserved from division by obedience to priests and deacons, leaders of the church by virtue of their office rather than by virtue of their charisma.[64] Already by the composition of the letters to Timothy (falsely attributed to Paul), charismata had become a power of office that an individual received by virtue of his ordination, rather than a visible descent of the Spirit.[65] By Perpetua's time, Tertullian described her community as being led by elders of high moral character,[66] and presided over by an hierarchy of deacons, presbyters, and bishops.[67] At the same time, Tertullian was vehement in preserving the prophetic character of the community. The rise of Christian organization was marked by the tension between these impulses that we see in Tertullian's writings.[68]

Beyond the tension between authority of office and authority by charisma, two main problems emerged as predominant in the charismatic communities. The first was how to tell true prophets from false. The second was the divisive individualism that Paul first identified as sometimes coexisting with the gifts of the Spirit. In communities that gave a privileged position to people who possessed charismatic gifts, it was essential to distinguish between true and false prophecy. One of the most interesting early texts to discuss this problem is an early manual for Christians, the *Didache*, which probably dates from the middle of the first century.[69] This text describes a community in which prophets came and went regularly, and the faithful had to be vigilant lest the prophets disrupt or deceive them. The *Didache* is wonderfully direct and practical when dealing with prophecy. On the one hand it insists upon respect for those who have the gift of prophecy: charismatics are called the "high priests," and people are told not to question their words spoken in a trance. On the other hand, it offers specific tests for the veracity of a prophet: his deeds must correspond to his teaching; he must take no money and he must leave within three days of his arrival.[70]

The New Testament book Second Peter, which was probably written after the *Didache*, perhaps early in the second century, also addresses the problem of false prophets. It echoes the concern of the *Didache* by warning against the greed of false prophets, who presumably were trying to make a profit from their gift. It also points to the ultimate control of prophecy, by accusing false prophets of despising authority.[71]

The mid-second-century apocryphal visionary text *Shepherd of Hermas* addressed the same problem of false prophets, showing its continuation into the time of Perpetua. The *Shepherd* begins with the premise that the true prophet should not accept money. Furthermore, the community should test the prophet's life and teachings to see if they seemed consistent with community beliefs.[72] If they were, the faithful could accept the prophecy as true.

The test by community is a tricky one, as modern judges trying to use "community standards" as a test for pornography rulings have repeatedly discovered. The church would ultimately turn to a different authority to test the veracity of prophets: ordained church leaders rather than the collective community. Obedience to authority would become the way to control charismatics in the church, but that was not to be fully implemented until well after Perpetua's death. In her community there still existed the tension between prophecy and order, and the prophecies were tested by the scrutiny of the community as a whole. In bringing prophecies to the judgment of the faithful, the Carthaginians were following the recommendations in the biblical texts they read. Paul had urged the Corinthians to weigh the prophetic utterances that they heard to determine their veracity.[73] In Paul's letter to the Thessalonians, he urged the community to embrace prophecy but "test everything; hold fast what is good, abstain from every form of evil."[74] Perpetua wrote down her visions, her prophecies, for them to be taken to the community that would judge them. Without this public dimension, we may not have had Perpetua's text preserved, for the community obviously judged it and found it to be true.

The second major problem in the charismatic communities was discord. Divisiveness appeared in the earliest communities, and was the impetus for Paul's great letters to the Corinthians. He wrote, "It has been reported to me . . . that there is quarreling among you."[75] Paul urged the community to be bound by love and to put aside differences. He recognized quite rightly that prophecies pass and speaking with tongues would cease and all that would be left in the community was the love that joined them.[76] Paul's hope that love would transcend division was probably too optimistic. Subsequent thinkers offered other solutions.

In the texts that date from the late first century and early second, the authors strongly advocate leadership of the clergy as the solution to quarreling within the flock. Clement of Rome (circa A.D. 96) in a letter to the Corinthians, Paul's contentious community that was quarreling again, urged them to forget their differences and live amicably with their clergy.[77] The letter of Ignatius of Antioch to the Corinthians about a decade later is even stronger in directing the faithful to maintain their unity through the authority of their bishop.[78]

By essentially renouncing the leadership of charismatics in favor of hierarchical control, communities were to receive the certainty of unanimity, the preservation of communities. Ignatius praised this sort of ideal community in which "minds . . . are in unison, and affections . . . are in harmony." In fact, he envisioned the community as one body in which all would come to meetings "like one man, without a thought of disunity in your hearts."[79] Such a community would achieve salvation together as a collective unity.[80]

Perpetua had read the letters of Paul and probably some of the works of the apostolic fathers. When she converted in the Christian community of Carthage, she must have believed God was present in that community. She further believed that God's presence was manifested through prophecy and even glossolalia and that those things were connected to the solidarity of the community. Finally, she knew that the community, although essential to the preservation of the faith, was fragile. Her dreams and her diary reflect these beliefs, and are understandable only in the context of these communities balancing individual charisma with collective good.

At this point in our study of the mental forces that shaped Perpetua's life, it is time to introduce the account of her martyrdom. Perpetua's text includes an autobiographical diary of her experience that is framed by an editor. The anonymous editor/narrator, probably male, was an eyewitness to the martyrdom and received Perpetua's and Saturus's writings (Saturus was one of Perpetua's companions in prison), and included them in his account of the events.[81] It is unlikely that he was Tertullian himself, as some have suggested, but he certainly came from the Carthaginian community that included that church father.

The narrator/editor situates the Passion precisely at the intersection between individual prophetic gifts and the needs of the community, and places Perpetua's prophetic visions within the context of the prophets in the other early Christian texts we have been examining. Further, he offers the text to the community so that everyone can participate in the experience of the martyrs and be led to salvation with them:

> *The deeds recounted about the faith in ancient times were a proof of God's favor and helped the spiritual strengthening of men as well; and they were set forth in writing precisely to honor God and to comfort men by the recollection of the past through the written word. Should not then more recent examples be set down that contribute equally to both ends? For indeed these too will one day become ancient and necessary for the ages to come, even though in our own day they may enjoy less prestige because of the prior claim of antiquity.*
>
> *Therefore, let those who would restrict the power of the one Spirit to times and seasons look to this: the more recent events should be considered the greater, being later than those of old, and this is a consequence of the extraordinary graces promised for the last stage of time. For in the last days, God declares, "I will pour out my Spirit upon all flesh and their sons and daughters shall prophesy and on my manservant and my maidservants I will pour my Spirit, and the young men shall see visions and the old men shall dream dreams." So too we hold in honor and acknowledge not only new prophecies but new visions as well, according to the promise. And we consider all the other functions of the Holy Spirit as intended for the good of the Church; for the same Spirit has been sent to distribute all his gifts to all, as the Lord apportions to everyone. For this reason we deem it imperative to set them forth and to make them known through*

the word for the glory of God. Thus no one of weak or despairing faith may think that supernatural grace was present only among men of ancient times, either in the grace of martyrdom or of visions, for God always achieves what he promises, as a witness to the non-believer and a blessing to the faithful.

And so my brethren and little children, that which we have heard and have touched with our hands we proclaim also to you, so that those of you that were witnesses may recall the glory of the Lord and those that now learn of it through hearing may have fellowship with the holy martyrs and, through them, with the Lord Christ Jesus, to whom belong splendor and honor for all ages, Amen.[82]

The narrator/editor explicitly recognized the importance of historical memory to the community. He also believed the presence of the Spirit was not simply a historical memory but an ongoing blessing. He preserved Perpetua's text so the community could share it in its liturgical and educational practices. The text would then become part of the community's memory.

CHRISTIAN LIFE

It may have been that Perpetua and many like her were persuaded to convert to Christianity in large part because of the visible presence of the Spirit. However, conversion meant that they were joining a new community. As Wayne Meeks has shown, conversion to philosophy was a withdrawal from society, but conversion to Christianity meant a "resocialization into an alternative community."[83] One of the striking differences between this religious community and that of the pagans was that Christianity was not bound to a particular space. Augustine noted how Roman religion was linked to physical space but Christianity was not.[84] Just like the Jewish communities after the destruction of the Second Temple, the Christian religion was separated from a cult location; religious space was interior and primarily seen to exist in an afterlife.

In his "Apology" arguing for the acceptance of Christianity, Tertullian emphasized that Christians were part of the life of Carthage: "Are we not men who live right with you, men who follow the same way of life, the same manner of dressing, using the same provisions and the same necessities of life?" He continued to stress that Christians worked in all fields and lived in all areas.[85] In another second-century letter, a Christian wrote of the Christian community that it was not separate from the larger community in which its members lived but coexisted in space, yet he said Christians were foreigners because their home was heaven.[86] Justin Martyr tried to explain to the Romans: "When you hear that we look forward to a kingdom, you rashly assume that we speak of a human kingdom, whereas we mean a kingdom which is with God."[87] This rather convoluted explanation expresses the new spatial relationship the Christians were advocating: they both were and were not part of this world. This position that seemed ambiguous to the space-bound Romans would be one of the issues that would cause a confrontation with authority.

Christians also had to separate themselves from traditional family ties. Tertullian wrote of the difficulties faced by women who were married to pagans: "Who, finally, will without anxiety endure her absence all the night long at the pascal solemnities? . . . Who will suffer her to creep into prison to kiss a martyr's bonds? Nay, truly, to meet any one of the brethren to exchange the kiss?"[88] There was built-in rupture of the family fabric as members converted individually. Yet, the Christian communities offered fictive family ties that seemed as strong as any blood ties.

Paul had described the new bonds that were forged in terms of familial affection. Previous strangers became "brothers and sisters" of the Christian communities.[89] Leaders became "fathers," and the faithful were "children." Tertullian created a new genealogy in which all Christians were children of their father, God, and born "from the one womb of their common ignorance," and thus were all siblings.[90] Within these egalitarian "families," there was a familiar and comforting space for those who had to give up their own families. The narrative of Perpetua was dominated by family attachment to the new community that had become her family.[91]

Christians declared that members of this new family had to change all aspects of their lives.[92] This included living what they called a new morality, which was a new way of conceiving what behavior was fitting.[93] Much of the morality would have looked familiar to a conservative Roman, who took a strict morality from a study of philosophy. Tertullian listed the characteristics shared by Christians and virtuous pagans: "The philosophers . . . teach the same virtues, and they too, profess morality, justice, patience, moderation, and chastity."[94] In addition, Christians tried to achieve a peace of mind that rose above all the passions that might disrupt the mind. "Frenzy" was forbidden, as were anger and jealousy and bitterness and lust.[95] These similarities mattered less than the fact that the Christians defined their actions as different and superior.

There were, however, some moral innovations that the Christians could claim. Perhaps the most striking was a disdain for money and material things in general. In the empire, money was the necessary base from which prestige flowed. Justin Martyr wrote of the change that conversion brought: "We who loved above all else the ways of acquiring riches and possessions now hand over to a community fund what we possess."[96] Tertullian, too, said that Christians had no hesitation in sharing all they had, which may have contributed to the Christians' reputation of being "worthless in business."[97] The willingness of prosperous Christians to renounce much of their worldly gain allowed the communities to support their needy members in ways that were both more generous and more personal than Rome could achieve with its bread and circuses.

The list of the needy was long; Tertullian identified the poor, orphans, "aged men who are confined to the house," shipwrecked sailors, anyone in the mines or in prison.[98] Christians also cared for the sick, captives, or even strangers needing hospitality.[99] The scale of their charity by the middle of the third century was strikingly visible. By that date, the church in Rome alone, for example, was supporting more than fifteen hundred widows and other persons in distress.[100]

Another innovation in Christian morality that was mentioned repeatedly by Christian apologists was their ban on exposing infants. Christian infants were not laid at their father's feet, as Perpetua had been, to see if they would be raised or left to die.[101] This had the additional benefit of increasing the number of Christian children raised compared with pagan ones.[102] The concern for all members of the community, including the newborn, helped to solidify the congregations, which in turn helped contribute to the strong spirituality that grew out of those communities. Christian morality was particularly successful in preserving the community life that led to its ultimate victory.

A final, though more abstract, moral innovation of Christians was their value of love and peace. Christians were not only to care for members of their own community but even to try to love those who hated them. It is hard to know how many people achieved this feeling, but Christian writers described behaviors that at least were supposed to reflect feelings of loving one's enemy. Christians were "forbidden to return an injury, lest, through our action, we become wrong-doers like them."[103] In addition, many believed Christians should not wage war at all or exact any form of revenge.[104]

People who may have been drawn to Christianity for the spirituality had to be prepared to change their social lives in order to join the community. Furthermore, the community did not want members who were not fully committed to the total change in life that conversion implied.

By A.D. 200, there was a structured process for testing and training would-be converts: the discipline of the catechumenate. At the time of her arrest, Perpetua and one of her brothers were catechumens: they were involved in the formal education period that preceded baptism.

To become a catechumen, a believer was formally brought into the Christian community: he or she received an exorcism, was signed with the cross, and was regarded as a Christian. During this period, the emphasis was on the catechumen's character and conduct rather than on dogmatic instruction.[105] The believer had to prove he or she could live as a Christian before receiving full instruction into the mysteries. The length of the catechumenate varied, but it was probably extensive; by the fourth century, two to three years was recommended. We have no idea how long Perpetua had been a catechumen before her arrest, but certainly it had been long enough for her to identify strongly with the Christian community.

Catechumens were allowed to attend the services and participate in everything except the Eucharist itself. Thus, the weekly liturgical practices formed part of Perpetua's experience, as did ecclesiastical writings like Tertullian's "On Prayer," which was written in about 200 directly to catechumens like Perpetua.

At the center of Christian worship were the assemblies of community members. Some writers urged the congregations to meet frequently,[106] but at the least, they did so once a week. Sunday was chosen because "it is the first day when God created the world and when Christ arose from the dead."[107] Justin Martyr said that on that day, Christians from cities and the outlying districts assembled.[108] By requiring that people not approach the altars of God "without settling any controversy or quarrel we may have contracted with our brethren,"[109] Tertullian emphasized the degree to which these gatherings were essential for community solidarity.

At the gatherings, people took turns reading sacred and educational texts. Justin recommended "memoirs of the Apostles or the writings of the Prophets."[110] Written materials available in Perpetua's community were extensive. In addition to the writings of Paul, Perpetua knew the Pentateuch, the Book of Revelation, the *Apocalypse of Peter, Enoch*, the *Gospel of Thomas, Esdras*, and the *Shepherd of Hermas*.[111] In addition, Perpetua no doubt was familiar with many of the tracts written by Tertullian, her influential and prolific contemporary. The readings, listened to together, helped create a collective mythology for the community, and shaped many of the images in Perpetua's visions. Perpetua's diary, in turn, became one of the corpus of respected readings that was read in the Carthage communities for centuries.

At various points in the service, members of the congregation were invited to contribute. Tertullian wrote that "each one, according to his ability to do so, reads the Holy Scriptures or is invited into the center to sing a hymn to God."[112] This is consistent with Paul's description of a service in which he charges the congregation: "When you come together, each one has a hymn, a lesson, a revelation, a tongue, or an interpretation."[113] It is during this time that one might hope for a prophecy, either in tongues or in a trance, that would demonstrate the presence of the Spirit.

The service also consisted of a series of prayers, some set and recited by the leaders, and others spontaneous, offered by the congregation. Prayer was central to the practice of the community in Carthage. Tertullian's treatise on prayer is one of his more eloquent and moving articulations of belief in the strength of communal prayer. Tertullian forbade Christians to use the power of prayer to cause evil to come to their enemies, for that was pagan practice. (He certainly was aware of the busy traffic in curses and spells that pervaded North Africa.) Christian prayer had to be limited to good, but the list he gave showed the wide range of situations in which they believed prayer to be effective; prayer could aid the souls of the dead, heal the sick, exorcise demons, open prison doors, "loosen the chains of the innocent," remit sin, repel temptations, end persecution, increase courage, help travelers, "calm the waves," "stun robbers," and generally help the poor and rich alike[114]—everything from practical help in this world to spiritual help in the next. And the presence of the divine in the communities gave them a confidence that their prayers would be answered.

Tertullian further said that the faithful should prepare themselves properly for the power of prayer. They should not eat or bathe before prayer, and they should assume a proper mien: hands slightly raised, and with downcast eyes and a low voice. Tertullian also gives us a glimpse of the diversity in Christian practice, for he says that some groups do not kneel when they pray, but it was the custom in Carthage to kneel, except on Easter. Community members sealed their prayers by the "kiss of peace," which was given on the lips. Tertullian insisted that the prayer was incomplete without the "bond of a holy kiss" (except on Good Friday, when the kiss was omitted.)[115] The kiss that bound the community members together was a reminder once again of the importance of the collective to the spiritual health of each individual. It was this kiss that Tertullian had warned would offend pagan husbands of Christian wives.

After the prayers, the catechumens had to leave the service before the final mystery of the Eucharistic meal. However, there was no prohibition against describing the general sharing of the Body and Blood, so Perpetua would have known what to expect after her full acceptance into the community.

Tertullian tells us that the shared meal that linked the community to God was offered at the early morning service, in which the faithful received the sacrament from "the hand of none but the bishops."[116] The *Didache* describes the Eucharist service's emphasis on giving thanks for God's blessings. The cup of wine and broken pieces of bread were distributed to community members while they offered prayers of thanksgiving.[117] The service then ended with more prayers and parting blessings.

For Perpetua and the other catechumens to attend the Eucharist service, they would first have to participate in the central ritual of conversion: baptism. In our age of primarily infant baptism, it is possible to underestimate the power of this initiation rite. In the ancient world, however, this was a serious and highly visible ceremony in which the catechumen finally and fully renounced his or her old life in favor of a new one. The rituals of this important rite were correspondingly powerful.

Tertullian and the other early texts I have been discussing mention various aspects of the baptism ceremony. However, the fullest description of the ritual for this early period is in a text by Hippolytus of Rome probably written a decade or two after Perpetua's death. It likely reflects the baptism practices that the young North African catechumens would have anticipated.

On the night before their baptism, the catechumens were to fast to purify themselves. Then they came together and the bishop laid his hands on them to exorcise any demons, blew on their faces, and traced the sign of the cross on their forehead, ears, and nostrils.[118] On the morning of their baptism, "at the moment when the cock crows," the children, men, and women (in that order) assembled at the font. The water should be "living," that is, flowing, if at all possible.[119]

The catechumens were then stripped naked, which represented their complete renunciation of their old lives. They came naked to be newly born into the new community that watched and waited to receive them.[120] Standing naked before the Christian community had to be a profoundly intimate and embarrassingly powerful experience for modest Roman women. Although they were accustomed to seeing nudity in the arena and in the artwork that graced their cities, they were deeply modest in their private lives. At the time of Perpetua, men and women did not bathe together in the public baths; such a practice had been banned by emperors right before and right after Septimius Severus.[121]

In Latin, the word *nudus*, "naked," could also mean "rough, uncouth," which shows that Romans felt nudity among decent people was indecent.[122] Roman practice even insisted that a virtuous wife always keep one garment on in the marriage bed. Yet, on their day of baptism, women joined the community naked, with their hair unbound.

At the edge of the baptismal pool, the catechumen was anointed with oil from her head to the soles of her feet to purge any remaining demons. Next she entered the pool, where she was submerged three times while the bishop prayed. As she emerged, she was anointed again with holy oil.[123] Then she was wrapped in robes of white to symbolize the purity of her new state. Tertullian describes how the newly cleansed then received the sacrament of the Eucharist and were also given a taste of a mixture of milk and honey.[124] Milk is the food of the newly born,[125] so it may symbolize the reborn state of the baptized. The honey was to give the sweet taste of heaven.[126] From this moment on, the baptized were fully members of the Christian community and expected to share with that community the promised salvation.

Perpetua likely had been a catechumen long enough to know the rituals that she could expect. (Tertullian had recently written his tract "On Baptism," which certainly would have circulated in the community.) Her dreams are full of images drawn from the rituals of the Christian community. Perpetua and her brother looked forward to a clear progression in faith that many before her had followed. Instead, this progression was interrupted by a confrontation with the authority of Rome.

CONFRONTATION WITH AUTHORITY

The editor of Perpetua's diary described the arrest with a frustrating brevity, for he gives no information on the circumstances surrounding the confrontation:

> *A number of young catechumens were arrested, Revocatus and his fellow slave Felicitas, Saturninus and Secundulus, and with them Vibia Perpetua, a newly married woman of good family and upbringing. Her mother and father were still alive and one of her two brothers was a catechumen like herself. She was about twenty-two years old and had an infant son at the breast. (Now from this point on the entire account of her ordeal is her own, according to her own ideas and in the way that she herself wrote it down.)*

Why were they arrested? The periodic persecution of Christians has been a much-studied subject, yet the answer to this basic question remains tantalizingly out of reach. Certainly, this relatively new religion whose adherents were becoming visible, if not numerous, was much misunderstood. The North African apologist Minucius Felix (circa 240) listed many shocking charges made against Christians. They gathered together with "the lowest dregs of society, and credulous women." They met in the dark and despised the temples. They disdained present tortures, yet "dread those of an uncertain future." In loving one another as family, they committed incest, and cannibalism, and indulged in orgies after shocking love feasts. Finally, they threatened the whole world with destruction.[127] One can see hints of badly misunderstood reality within these accusations: There *were* Christian Eucharistic feasts at which "brothers and sisters" exchanged kisses of peace while expecting the destruction of the world. The Christian apologists quickly and universally denied all such charges.[128] Tertullian wrote with characteristic sarcasm: "Who has detected the traces of a bite in our blood-steeped loaf? Who has discovered, by a sudden light invading our darkness, any marks of impurity, I will not say of incest, (in our feasts)?"[129] None of the records of the martyr trials suggest that any Christian was charged with these crimes.

The exciting and titillating rumors may have led to community suspicion, and some animosity on the part of the neighbors of Christians. During the time of Tertullian, there was at least one building that was identified with Christian worship. Pagans knew the time and place of Christian assembly, and sometimes the worshippers were surrounded and assaulted, or detained.[130] This kind of malicious prejudice would not hold up in court in the form of charges, but it might lead neighbor to accuse neighbor of Christian worship. Such disturbances might also lead provincial governors to decide that the presence of Christians was a threat to peace and public order. This general charge of disturbing the peace more than any other probably brought Christians to be questioned.[131]

Not surprisingly, confrontation arose when Christians came to the attention of the authorities. There is a famous correspondence between Pliny the Younger and Trajan in 112 that came about when Pliny was a provincial governor who arrested some Christians who had been reported to him. Pliny wrote that he found nothing illegal in the life of these people who carefully avoided crime and met "before daybreak" to sing and worship God. However, they stubbornly refused to sacrifice to the Roman gods. Pliny asked the emperor how he should handle these people. Trajan's response was designed to avoid trouble, but it did not resolve the legal ambiguities. Pliny was told not to "seek out men of this kind," but when they were brought to court, they should be punished.

Tertullian described this letter with scorn, saying, "How unavoidably ambiguous was that decision! . . . So you condemn a man when he is brought into court, although no one wanted him to be sought out. He has earned punishment, I suppose, not on the ground that he is guilty, but because he was discovered for whom no search had to be made."[132] Although Tertullian described with well-deserved sarcasm the process that led to Christian martyrs, he described it accurately.

Christians were quite rightly perceived to be antisocial: they were creating their own society. They did not worship the gods of Rome, and to the religious Romans, this sacrilege was the definition of antisocial. The apologists could repeatedly point out that Christians were peaceful members of the community, but in Roman eyes, if they did not correctly observe at least the imperial cult, they were not good citizens. They were alienating the *pax deorum*, the peace that the gods brought to the empire.[133] The crime the Christians were charged with was an existential one: they *were* Christians. Tertullian summed up the matter: "The confession of the name of Christian, not an investigation of the charge determined guilt."[134] This was a capital status offense, and it made the trial records quite brief. All that needed to be determined was that the accused was a Christian.

Perpetua's community knew firsthand of the potential danger of its commitment. Twenty years earlier, within the memory of many, the first North African Christians were martyred. In the year 180, twelve Christians were arraigned in the governor's chambers at Carthage. The *Acts* of these martyrs record the proconsul's interrogation. The Christians denied they were criminals and reaffirmed that they were good citizens. They paid taxes and respected the emperor's laws. Yet, the proconsul found them guilty: "[They] have confessed that they have been living in accordance with the rites of the Christians, and whereas though given the opportunity to return to the usage of the Romans they have persevered in their obstinacy, they are hereby condemned to be executed by the sword."[135]

The martyrs were beheaded. The charge could hardly have been any more vague, and enforcement was highly idiosyncratic. Tertullian had rightly said there were thousands of Christians in Carthage, and many people knew who they were. Yet, before the late third century there was no systematic attempt to arrest those who claimed to be Christians. The single determining factor in these early martyrdoms was the inclination of the provincial governor.[136]

About a decade after Perpetua's martyrdom, Tertullian wrote to the North African governor urging him not to begin a new cycle of persecutions. In his letter, Tertullian gave examples of previous governors who exerted their authority in varying ways. One thought of a formula that would allow a Christian to answer in a way that he could be freed. Another freed a Christian without making him sacrifice. And another dismissed the case against a Christian because he perceived that the charge grew from neighborly malice.[137] Tertullian's interesting letter shows the wide range of discretionary powers that were available to the governors. The decision to prosecute or not was very much up to the individual governor and his assessment of what might be in his best interest.

Christians also had a range of responses to the periodic persecutions. The arbitrary nature of the executions contributed to the belief that martyrs were selected by God.[138] Martyrdom was a gift, and it was in God's hands to determine who was chosen. This would have been the early Christians' response to the question that most troubles me: Why were some arrested and others not? The solution of God's plan still did not address the question of how Christians should respond.

Tertullian did not think Christians should flee from the possible gift of martyrdom, but he did allow for the possibility of prudence: if it was too dangerous to gather together by day, worship at night; gather in smaller groups; or come to worship by different paths.[139] Some individuals and indeed whole congregations tried to solve the problem of persecution in the traditional Roman manner of bribery. Tertullian disapproved of this practice, but all were not as rigorous as he.[140] Tertullian believed that Christians should not flee from persecution, but neither should they seek it out. However, there is a fine line between those positions.

Church leaders repeatedly forbade people from directly challenging the authority of Rome, but that did not stop those who sought the crown of martyrdom. Even Tertullian bragged about those Christians who rushed voluntarily "to the contest, and we rejoice more when condemned than when acquitted."[141] A study of all the accounts of the martyrs suggests that more were martyred because they voluntarily stepped forward or even committed suicide than as a result of having been sought out.[142] Saturus, one of the martyrs executed with Perpetua's group, was not initially arrested with them; he voluntarily joined the group in prison so he could share their glorious death. Saturus was a leader of Perpetua's community, and he exemplified the practice of voluntary martyrdom.

In spite of the fact that the persecutions were sporadic, by the late second century, some Christian communities had experienced periodic persecutions resulting in martyrdoms. Sometimes denunciations came because conversions seemed to threaten the cohesiveness of family life.[143] At other times, neighbors turned in neighbors or servants denounced masters,[144] and sometimes persecutions just seemed the random hand of God. Nor did persecutions show gender bias. In fact, in North Africa women represented a high proportion of the martyrs.[145] These general experiences of persecution lingered in people's memories at the time Perpetua became a catechumen and was preparing for her baptism. We must now look at the specific events that preceded her arrest.

In spring and summer of 197, Carthage established an extraordinary festival season. Houses were decorated with laurel, great banquets were held, and sacrifices were made to the genius of the emperor. During the city's celebration, it became clear that every Carthaginian did not join in. Christians and Jews both believed these celebrations were idolatrous, and thus they were forbidden to celebrate. Their houses remained undecorated, and they stayed sober while others celebrated.[146] It is impossible to assess directly the impact of this highly visible separation of pagan from Christian and Jew, but it surely must have come to the attention of pious pagans.

A few years later, sometime after 201, Emperor Septimius Severus issued an edict forbidding conversion to Judaism and Christianity.[147] It was during this time that Septimius had identified himself with Serapis, and it may be that his edict against conversions was an attempt to encourage the cult of Serapis at the expense of other missionary religions.[148] The fourth-century church historian Eusebius blamed Septimius for "instigating persecution," and listed martyrs all over the empire who had been arrested after the edict.[149] However, it was the discretion of the local governors that determined when and where Christians would be persecuted. Without an eager prosecutor, Septimius's edict would have had little effect in Carthage.

As it happened, in 203 Carthage possessed just the sort of eager governor who would follow through on the edict against conversion. Perpetua tells us that the prosecutor of their case was the procurator Publius Aelius Hilarianus, who had taken office at the death of the previous proconsul. In a careful study of Hilarianus's earlier career in Spain, James Rives has demonstrated that the proconsul was a highly religious man who held a strongly conservative view of religion.[150] He had served Rome in Asia and Spain before being assigned to his high post in Africa. He was precisely the sort of man to have been offended by the Christians' seemingly sacrilegious behavior during the festival some years earlier. Tertullian also tells us there was some anti-Christian agitation during Hilarianus's governorship.[151] These circumstances would have made Hilarianus willing to make an example of Christians by enforcing Septimius's edict against conversion.

These circumstances do not explain why this particular small group of Christian catechumens were arrested at that particular time. We do know that they were sentenced to be executed on the occasion of the birthday of Septimius Severus's son Geta. I suggest that this was not a coincidence. The highly pious, ambitious Hilarianus may well have decided to offer a fitting sacrifice for the celebration and decided to enforce Septimius's edict to find some victims. We do not know how he settled on the household of the Vibii. The narrator/editor's description of the arrest seems to indicate that the first to be arrested were the household slaves who were catechumens. This would have been a way for Hilarianus to make his point, to find sacrificial victims for the arena and not to offend noble families by arresting influential people. However, it did not turn out that way. Arrested with them was the daughter of the house, Vibia Perpetua (although her brother, who was also a catechumen, was not arrested). It is likely that she stepped forward as the others were arrested, combining the notion of voluntary martyrdom with Carthage's tradition of sacrificial suicide. Whatever precipitated the arrest, the Rubicon had been crossed. Perpetua takes up the narrative in her own words.

> While we were still under arrest my father out of love for me was trying to persuade me and shake my resolution. "Father," said I, "do you see this vase here, for example, or water pot or whatever?"
> "Yes, I do," said he.
> And I told him: "Could it be called by any other name than what it is?"
> And he said: "No."
> "Well, so too I cannot be called anything other than what I am, a Christian."
> At this my father was so angered by the word "Christian" that he moved towards me as though he would pluck my eyes out. But he left it at that and departed, vanquished along with his diabolical arguments.

In this dialogue, we can see the importance attached to the status of "Christian." As a catechumen, Perpetua was already a Christian, and her dialogue shows that she already saw that as a state of being; her conversion was complete. Her father knew the ramifications of that identification. No further crime was needed, and his rage would shortly change to anguish for his stubborn daughter.

The group seems to have been kept under some sort of house arrest for a few days, during which Perpetua made her final conversion from catechumen to baptized Christian.

For a few days afterwards I gave thanks to the Lord that I was separated from my father, and I was comforted by his absence. During these few days I was baptized, and I was inspired by the Spirit not to ask for any other favor after the water but simply the perseverance of the flesh.[152]

We cannot know whether Perpetua was baptized with the full ritual of anointing and triple immersion that she could have looked forward to in the regular course of her conversion. But it hardly matters since full baptismal images appear transformed in her dreams. She felt herself fully introduced to the mysteries of the Christian community.

At her baptism, Perpetua records her first "prophecy," and she records it so nonchalantly that it seems that she has been in touch with the Spirit before this, but we cannot know for sure. In this instance, the Spirit foretells that her brief future on this earth will end with her martyrdom. There are repeated associations in the Christian texts between baptism and martyrdom. Both are seen as deaths of the old person and births of the new.[153] Tertullian called baptism in blood a second form of baptism.[154] It was to this second baptism that the Spirit called Perpetua. After their water baptism, the catechumens had fully violated the edict against conversion. They were moved from house arrest to prison.

four

Prison

PRISON AND TRIAL

Perpetua's baptism while she was under house arrest marked a turning point. She and her companions had directly violated Septimius's edict against conversion, which freed the proconsul to bring charges. A few days after the baptism, Revocatus, Felicitas, Saturninus, Secundus, and Perpetua were moved from house arrest to prison. The prison was probably next to the residence of the governor on the Byrsa hill in the center of Carthage.[1] The account of another martyr, Pionius, who was executed in Carthage at the end of the third century, describes the location of the prison in more detail. The account tells how the martyrs were arrested, led through the forum through the eastern entrance, and taken to the adjacent jail.[2]

The prison that was used for Perpetua may have been similarly located. The group was completed by Saturus, who had been a leader in the Christian community and who voluntarily joined the group in prison. Perpetua wrote of her fright at her imprisonment:

> I was terrified, as I had never before been in such a dark hole. What a difficult time it was! With the crowd the heat was stifling; then there was the extortion of the soldiers; and to crown all, I was tortured with worry for my baby there.[3]

Prisons in Roman Carthage were makeshift affairs, simply crude holding areas for prisoners until they were moved elsewhere. The most secure area of a temporary prison would likely be in an underground storage area, thus in the dark. Accounts of later Carthaginian martyrs draw the same kinds of pictures of the holding prison. When Montanus and his Christian companions were arrested and imprisoned in Carthage in A.D. 259, the prison was termed a "foul darkness" like the "pitch-black veil of night."[4] Another imprisoned Christian woman told of a vision that reveals more information about the temporary nature of the holding area. She said she saw the stone that was in the window miraculously removed so she could glimpse the heavens.[5] Her vision suggests ways prisoners were kept secure (by placing large stones in the windows) and also reveals the longing for light. Perpetua, too, feared the dark, crowded conditions of the prison space.

It was customary for prisoners or their friends and relatives to bribe the guards to get better treatment. The surrogate family that made up the Christian community in Carthage rallied to the help of the prisoners. Perpetua expressed her gratitude for their help:

> Tertius and Pomponius, those blessed deacons who tried to take care of us, bribed the soldiers to allow us to go to a better part of the prison to refresh ourselves for a few hours. Everyone then left that dungeon and shifted for himself.[6]

The support of the free Christians for the imprisoned confessors played a crucial role not only for prisoners but in shaping the image of the church itself. Tertullian referred to two kinds of help. One was institutional: resources of the church that were given to ease the prisoners' condition, which he called "the nourishment for the body which our Lady Mother the church [offers] from her breast." This is one of the earliest references to the church as Mother, and it clearly derives from the serious need for sustenance that martyrs like Perpetua experienced during the hardships of imprisonment. The second kind of help was the generosity of individual Christians who contributed from their private resources.[7]

Tertullian himself offered something for the group: words of encouragement. In his tract "To the Martyrs," he sent "some offering that will contribute to the sustenance of the spirit. For it is not good that the flesh be feasted while the spirit goes hungry."[8] There is some dispute about the date of Tertullian's tract, but the evidence seems strong that it was written to this small group imprisoned in March 203.[9] Even if the tract had been written earlier,[10] Perpetua and her companions would have known of it. In it, Tertullian reminded the group of people in the past who had sacrificed themselves in the Carthaginian tradition. He even referred specifically to imprisoned women (which further argues for its composition for Perpetua's group), urging them to be as brave as men, and as other brave Carthaginian women, like Dido.[11] Threads of Tertullian's letter weave through Perpetua's dream narrative; she seems to have taken his words to heart. The Christian community both as individuals and as a collective gathered to help the imprisoned members in their time of need. The strong community that formed part of the appeal of the early church was visible even in the darkest prison.

Once Perpetua had been released to a more comfortable place in the prison, her attention turned to her child. Perpetua's spiritual progress required her to break her filial ties with her father. Now she confronted her maternal ties with her son. Her immediate concern was to feed him: *"I nursed my baby, who was faint from hunger."* Then, as any young mother might, she consulted with her own mother. *"In my anxiety I spoke to my mother about the child, I tried to comfort my brother, and I gave the child into their charge."*[12]

Her family took the child and kept him for "many days," but this did not end Perpetua's concern for him. She requested and received permission to have the baby stay with her in prison. Her mind was eased once she had the child in her care: *"At once I recovered my health, relieved as I was of my worry and anxiety over the child. My prison had suddenly become a palace, so that I wanted to be there rather than anywhere else."*[13]

Perpetua's ambivalent position regarding her son reveals some potential ambiguity regarding the roles of mother and martyr. Did one have to renounce the maternal role in order to seek Christian spiritual perfection in the same way that Perpetua renounced her expected role as dutiful daughter? This ambivalence probably derived in part from the fact that the earliest example of martyrdom in the Judeo-Christian tradition centered on a mother who was martyred with her sons. This martyrdom was described in the *Book of the Maccabees* in the Old Testament Apocrypha, and Perpetua very likely knew this text.[14]

These Maccabean martyrs were tortured in the second century B.C. because they refused to break Jewish law and eat forbidden food. The longest account of this martyrdom is preserved in *4 Maccabees*, written probably in the first century A.D. In this account (which influenced many subsequent Christian heroics)[15] an aged mother was brought to the authorities with her seven sons. The author of *4 Maccabees* was careful to detail maternal love: "Observe how complex is a mother's love for her children, which draws everything toward an emotion felt in her inmost parts. . . . In seven pregnancies she had implanted in herself tender love toward them, and because of the many pains she suffered with each of them she had sympathy for them."[16] Yet, she did not try to save her sons, instead she "urged them on, each child singly and all together, to death for the sake of religion," and "they obeyed her even to death in keeping the ordinance."[17] The mother, too, was martyred after watching her sons die.

Although the author of *4 Maccabees* found the mother exceptionally brave ("she fired her woman's reasoning with a man's courage"),[18] he nevertheless seemed to find nothing structurally incongruous about a mother's becoming a martyr. Judaism in the Hellenistic world was a community-centered religion. Indeed, the central tenet of Judaism was precisely to preserve a separate community intact in spite of the strength of the surrounding culture. One of the ways societies traditionally had marked community was by eating together, and indeed family and community meals were frequently guided by the women of the households, the mothers. So in this traditional structure, mothers drew the community together through control of the food that the group shared. Jewish dietary laws, while satisfying Biblical injunctions of purity, served to mark the Jewish community as a community, remaining separate from the surrounding society.

Presumably, before her arrest the Maccabean mother cared for the integrity of the Jewish community and the family's place within it. As part of that care, she kept the dietary laws that marked her family as Jewish, and she made sure her sons kept the same laws. After their arrest, the mother fulfilled the same function. She urged her sons to keep the dietary laws that preserved the family as members of the Jewish community. This martyrdom was about preserving family identity and piety in the face of oppression. This family role was appropriate to a mother, especially a pious mother raising dutiful sons. The author of the text called her the "mother of the nation, vindicator of the law and champion of religion."[19] Religion was joined with nationality and law, providing a complete picture of what traditionally constituted community. Mothers served to continue that community.

A century after *4 Maccabees* was written, Christian martyrs looked back to this model of martyrdom, but the situation had changed. Christian communities were creating new social structures that called for individuals to leave their fathers and mothers, to break previous community ties and form new communities. Motherhood, with its emphasis on family, on creating and preserving future generations, would seem to be incompatible with personal salvation gained through martyrdom. The goal of Christian martyrdom was to follow the example of Christ and not let considerations of family, society, or cultural continuity get in the way. The martyrs took seriously Jesus's call to leave worldly concerns behind. Tertullian, in his letter to the imprisoned group, reminded them of this point succinctly: "The Christian . . . even when he is outside the prison, has renounced the world."[20]

When Perpetua happily had her son in prison with her, she may have at some level hoped to maintain both her roles, mother and martyr. Perhaps she imagined herself, like the Maccabean mother, dying with her son. However, Christian witness was more individual than Jewish community solidarity. She was not to have her son join her in martyrdom, but it would take more time in prison before Perpetua came to that realization.

A few days later, the prisoners heard they were to have a hearing to determine their fate. Perpetua's father, *"worn with worry,"* came to see her at the prison to try to persuade her to abandon this course. Any of us who has tried to persuade an intransigent twenty-year-old to renounce some course of action can surely react with compassion to Perpetua's father's desperation:

> *Daughter . . . have pity on my grey head—have pity on me your father, . . . if I have favored you above all your brothers, if I have raised you to reach this prime of your life. Do not abandon me to be the reproach of men. Think of your brothers, think of your mother and your aunt, think of your child, who will not be able to live once you are gone. Give up your pride! You will destroy all of us! None of us will ever be able to speak freely again if anything happens to you.*[21]

Perpetua's father tried to draw Perpetua back again into the family that formed the core of Roman society. He reminded her of her relatives, of the family honor in the community, and of the special ties between father and daughter. In his letter to the martyrs, Tertullian warned them that relatives would try to draw the martyrs back from their purpose,[22] and that was certainly Perpetua's father's desire. Tertullian need not have worried about the young woman; her resolve was strong. Perpetua wrote:

> *This was the way my father spoke out of love for me, kissing my hands and throwing himself down before me. With tears in his eyes he no longer addressed me as his daughter but as a woman. I was sorry for my father's sake, because he alone of all my kin would be unhappy to see me suffer.*
>
> *I tried to comfort him saying: "It will all happen in the prisoner's dock as God wills; for you may be sure that we are not left to ourselves but are all in his power."*
>
> *And he left me in great sorrow.*[23]

Romans who adhered to the values I described in the first chapter would have found this confrontation with the *pater familias* shocking. Perpetua had to forget or reject all her Roman upbringing to emerge victorious in this confrontation. Her rebellion and her father's sorrow point to the split in families that was occurring as Christianity spread through the empire. Perpetua's statement that he alone of her family would grieve for her may suggest that the rest of her family was Christian, or at least had Christian sympathies. Perpetua and the Christian members of her family surely would have known of Tertullian's tract "On Patience," written only a few years before and circulated in the Carthage Christian community. In this tract, Tertullian specifically says that Christians were not to grieve for the death of a loved one. Instead they should rejoice that the loved one has gone ahead to God.[24] Following Tertullian's exhortation, Perpetua believed the Christian members of her family would rejoice in her martyrdom and the expected salvation that would follow. Her father would grieve alone.[25]

One morning as the prisoners were eating breakfast, they were suddenly taken out for their hearing, which was to be held in the forum on the Byrsa hill. It was usual for the Roman officials to hear cases in this most public space of Carthage. In the martyrdom of Montanus in Carthage in 259, the confessors were brought to the forum in chains, then "led back and forth all over the forum by soldiers who did not know where the procurator wanted to hear [the] case."[26] This anecdote of military confusion shows both the regularity of hearings in the forum, and the lack of a regular trial location within the public area. Since hearings were in the forum, crowds eager for novelty always gathered. This was also the case with Perpetua and her companions. The word spread quickly about the hearing and a "*huge crowd*" gathered at the forum to watch the proceedings. It was there that the small group confronted the rigorously conservative proconsul Hilarianus.

Of the other prisoners, Perpetua simply says they "*admitted their guilt*" when they were questioned.[27] In her case, she described in more detail the questioning that marked the final break with her family and confirmed her call to martyrdom. As her turn came to be questioned, her father appeared with her infant. He dragged Perpetua from the step as she began to climb to the prisoner's dock to undergo questioning. He made a final plea: "*Perform the sacrifice—have pity on your baby.*" Hilarianus, too, tried to call her back to the duties of a Roman daughter and matron. He said, "*Have pity on your father's grey head; have pity on your infant son. Offer the sacrifice for the welfare of the emperors.*" Perpetua refused concisely, "*I will not.*" Hilarianus then asked the one question that was pertinent in the hearing, "*Are you a Christian?*" Perpetua answered, "*Yes, I am a Christian.*"

With this statement, Perpetua repeated the words of the Scillitan martyrs who had died in Carthage twenty years before.[28] Since the reasons for persecuting Christians were vague, the crimes ill-defined, for a magistrate who wanted to pursue the persecution, no further information was needed other than Perpetua's obstinate self-definition. Like martyrs before and after her, by giving up her name and renaming herself as a Christian, Perpetua has taken on a new identity.[29]

The moment Perpetua identified herself as a Christian, she no longer belonged to Rome. Hilarianus would waste no more time in persuasion. As Perpetua's father persisted in his attempt to dissuade his daughter, *"Hilarianus ordered him to be thrown to the ground and beaten with a rod. I felt sorry for father, just as if I myself had been beaten. I felt sorry for his pathetic old age."* Perpetua felt compassion, but her confession had separated her from her father once and for all. Hilarianus passed the sentence, as Perpetua recounted joyfully: *"We were condemned to the beasts, and we returned to prison in high spirits."*[30]

The sentence Hilarianus passed was particularly harsh. The Scillitan martyrs had been beheaded, and for a young Roman citizen to be sentenced to the beasts was highly unusual.[31] This sentence reinforces my opinion that Hilarianus had a contest in the arena in mind when he arrested the group.

Once back in prison, it seems Perpetua thought to resume her role as mother as she continued to her martyrdom. She asked the deacon Pomponius to go to her father, retrieve her infant, and bring him back to the prison. Her father refused. Perpetua's final ties to her family were broken. She would seek salvation alone, leaving her son to find his own path. Perpetua saw signs of divine will in her withdrawal from her son: *"As God willed, the baby had no further desire for the breast, nor did I suffer any inflammation; and so I was relieved of any anxiety for my child and of any discomfort in my breasts."*[32] This seeming evidence of divine approval in the text reinforced the notion that martyrdom was incompatible with maternity.[33] The time of the Maccabean mothers was over; martyrdom was a matter of private conscience, not family ties.

The degree to which Perpetua rejected her maternal role to seek martyrdom was reinforced as the story of her passion was passed on through the Middle Ages. In a trial-transcript form of the Passion written probably in the middle of the fourth century, the author removed the tension Perpetua expressed throughout her own account and simply said the martyr pushed her child aside saying to her parents: "Get away from me you workers of evil, since I no longer know you."[34] In the influential thirteenth-century compilation of saints' lives written by Jacobus de Voragine and known as the *Golden Legend*, the Franciscan drew from the fourth-century version to emphasize again

Perpetua's rejection of family ties. In this account, Perpetua's anxiety for her child disappeared: "Then the father laid her child upon her neck, and he . . . said: 'Be merciful to us, daughter, and live with us!' But she threw the child aside, and repulsed her parents, saying: 'Begone from me, enemies of God, for I know you not!'"[35] Perpetua's family, including her child, were portrayed as "enemies," and in her search for martyrdom, she threw them aside. This account is consistent with Tertullian's warnings about the family's drawing its people from martyrdom, and highlights the strong notion in the early Christian communities that new social bonds were shaped in the confession of Christianity.

DREAMS AND VISIONS

The major part of Perpetua's diary consists of an account of her visionary dreams in prison. Saturus, too, described a dream as the only record he made during his imprisonment. It is not surprising that dreams were accorded such attention, given the prominence early Christians gave prophecy and visions. But the predominant place accorded to these dreams in the text is eloquent testimony to their value both for the dreamers and the subsequent Christians who preserved these dream testimonies with such care. Christian communities not only listened to ecstatic prophecy but recorded such visions for reflection later. In his work "On the Soul" (written after Perpetua's death), Tertullian described almost in passing the importance of recording visions. He told of a woman who during a service "became rapt in ecstasy." He went on to say, "After the services were over and the laity had left, we asked her as is our custom, what visions she had. All her visions are carefully written down for purposes of examination."[36] Perpetua and Saturus carefully recorded their visions, and the Christian community carefully saved them. All these actions were based on their understanding, their memories, of what one did with visions. Further, the visions were preserved by the ritual reading of them during the services.

Before I examine these dreams with the care accorded by Perpetua and her companions, I will first contrast their view of dreams with our own, for Perpetua's contemporaries understood dreams far differently than we do. For the most part, modern dream theorists fall into two basic groups: those who believe dreams reveal only the individual, and those who believe dreams may offer some transcendent insights. Both groups believe that interpretations of dreams may offer insights to help the individual.[37]

Theories that see dreams as revealing only the individual virtually began with Freud, who established for the nineteenth century and beyond the belief that dreams focus backward and inward. In *Interpretation of Dreams*, Freud dismissed the concept of dreams as premonitory: "It would be truer to say instead that they give us knowledge of the past. For dreams are derived from the past in every sense."[38] Although Freudian theory has been changed and refined, most psychoanalytic dream analysis focuses on a dream as a pathway to the individual's unconscious, to his or her past.

Carl Jung established the possibility for modern dream theorists to see dreams as revealing something more transcendent than the individual. By exploring archetypical images in dreams, Jung believed dreams led individuals to a larger consciousness. Jung even allowed for the possibility that some dreams point to the future to anticipate an individual's future development.[39] Jung was not alone in exploring the transcendent in dreams. Kelly Bulkeley argues that even in our modern secular society dreams have a dimension of religious meaning.[40] Even among modern dream analysts who allow for transcendent or even prophetic dreams,[41] none whose works I have read share the ancient belief that dreams may originate from outside the dreaming psyche. Modern dreams originate within the dreamer.

Beyond this concern for the origin of the dream, one of the first things that distinguishes ancient dream wisdom from ours is the ancients' assumption that some dreams were true and some were not. This question does not come up in modern dream analysis because we believe that although some dreams might be more significant or reveal a deeper insight than others, all truly reflect some aspect of the inner life of the dreamer. However, the ancient world believed that dreams did not all come from within the dreamer; some came from other sources and were received into the soul of the dreamer. With the possibility of an outside source for dreams the question of their validity became more important. Virgil in the *Aeneid* offered one explanation for the two kinds of dreams, and his explanation was widely known and quoted in the ancient world: "There are two gates of sleep, one of which is said to be of horn, by which an easy egress is given to true spirits; the other is gleaming, wrought of dazzling ivory but the shades send by it false dreams to the upper world."[42] In this model, dreams offer access to the transcendent world, in this case the world of the dead. From there, spirits send dreams that are either true or false, which raised the important question of how to tell the difference. For this, a skilled dream interpreter was required.

An interpreter was also frequently required for dreams that foretold the future, even if they were acknowledged as "true." In the second century, Artemidorus wrote a summary of dream lore that distilled the status of pagan beliefs on dreams. This work circulated during Perpetua's life and influenced people's understanding of dreams. Artemidorus said there were two general kinds of dreams. The first kind had no particular meaning and derived from the dreamer's present experience. (It would not particularly matter if these dreams were true or false because they were not offering any advice.) The second kind of dream was more important: dreams that predicted the future. This category of premonitory dreams could be subdivided into dreams that predicted directly and those that needed interpretation.[43] These were the dreams for which it was most important to determine whether they came through the gate of horn or the gate of ivory.

Dreams that predict were seen to come from the divine, for the future was known only to the gods. As Artemidorus explained, "For the god presents to the dreamer's soul, which is by its very nature prophetic, dreams in response to future events."[44] Souls were susceptible to the influence of the divine, and there were many ancients who saw in dreams the way individuals were able to come in direct contact with God. For example, the Neoplatonists of the second century thought individuals could reach God through ecstasy, contemplation, and dreams.[45] Initiates into mystery religions frequently had to be invited directly by the deity, usually through a dream.[46] In Apuleius's *Golden Ass*, Isis appears to Lucius in a dream that foretells his salvation.[47] Thus, the pre-Christian world had ample precedent for concern with dreams, their validation and their interpretation. It would have been remarkable if the Christians who shared these ideas would not also have given dreams their close attention, even without the association of dreams with Christian prophecy.

Christians drew their ideas on dreams not only from the classical world but from sacred Scripture. The Old Testament portrayed the dream world as the place where the holy and the secular came together. Jacob's famous dream of a ladder extending to heaven with angels ascending and descending became a prototype for the linking of God and his world.[48] In the Book of Job, Elihu reminds Job that God communicates with men in dreams.[49] In addition, the Old Testament contains numerous examples of famous premonitory dreams, such as the dreams by Pharoah described in Genesis about the seven years of famine that would follow seven years of plenty.[50] The New Testament has fewer examples of divinely inspired dreams, but they are there, particularly in Matthew and Acts.[51] However, simply because there was ample Christian precedent for valuing dreams, that did not mean

Christians were fully comfortable with them. There were always the problems of the origin of the dream (divine or otherwise) and its interpretation (accurate or not).[52]

Christian ambivalence about dreams began in the earliest years and continued throughout the Middle Ages.[53] For the Christian communities in second-century Carthage, Tertullian defined Christian attitudes toward dreams. In his tract "On the Soul," written between 206 and 210, Tertullian included several chapters analyzing dreams, and these became the first Christian study of the subject. Tertullian began by establishing the problem: there has to be a *Christian* "explanation of dreams as accidents of sleep and rather serious disturbances of the soul."[54] After exploring pagan views on dreams, Tertullian established an understanding of his own. Everyone dreams, and dreams derive from three sources: the Devil, God, or the soul itself. The first source can include dreams that are true and false, but they are not to be trusted. The dreams from God are blessings of the Holy Spirit,[55] and it was these dreams that Tertullian valued so much as prophetic utterances. Given this theory, it is not surprising that Tertullian emphasized the importance of knowing the origin of the dream. In this he followed Artemidorus in trusting an interpreter to locate the dream's origin. If it were from the Holy Spirit, it was less important to get a specific interpretation of its meaning. In this he departed from ancients and moderns who emphasize dream interpretation.

For the ancients, for Freud, and for subsequent dream analysts, the dream and the dreamer represented only half the story. Equally important was the dream interpretation. Modern psychoanalytic literature gives at least as much attention to the best way to understand the meaning of a dream as it does to any dream or dreamer. A dream can be understood by a dreamer's free association on the dream, by group projection and discussion, or by direct interpretation by a sensitive counselor.[56] All these methods share the assumption that the dream has something to tell, that it offers insights that will help or heal the dreamer. These techniques also assume that the dreamer wants to know the meaning of a dream. By these last assumptions, modern dream theorists begin to have things in common with ancient dreamers who frequently sought the services of a dream interpreter to help them understand the meanings of their dreams.

Pharoah's dreams required Joseph to interpret them.[57] Artemidorus was a skilled dream master who argued it took an expert to take into account such things as the gender, occupation, legal status, and social position of the dreamer before he could accurately interpret the dream.[58] The ancient pagan and Judaic world shared our modern desires to have the meanings of dreams assessed by experts. As we saw in Tertullian's tract, however, the early Christians did not emphasize the need for dream readers. The fourth-century Neoplatonist Synesius of Cyrene most clearly articulated the attitude that was emerging in the early Christian communities. Jacques LeGoff summarizes Synesius's position: "There was no need to resort to oneiromancers because every man and woman was capable of interpreting his or her own dreams. He saw this, moreover, as one of man's fundamental rights. To each his own dreams and their interpretation."[59]

The origin of the Christian attitude toward personal dream interpretation must be sought somewhere other than in the classic dream literature that virtually always argued for expert analysis. In the second century in Carthage two texts from the biblical apocrypha circulated widely and were valued and read. These were *Second Esdras* and the *Shepherd of Hermas*.[60] In the second century the biblical canon had not yet been established, so Christians treasured such works as highly as those that later would become Scripture. Both of these works deal with dreamers and prophecy and both portray the dreamer as the best interpreter. Such texts changed the nature of dream interpretation for Christians, making it more personal than it had been before.

The apocryphal *Second Book of Esdras* (called the *Fourth Book of Esdras* since the Council of Trent) was written near the end of the first century A.D. The main part of this work is a series of seven revelations that the dreamer is led to understand by the angel Uriel, who also appears in dreams. After Ezra achieved wisdom through these dreams, God spoke through him in prophecy.[61] In this text, the most important question in a Christian context was settled early: the dreams were of divine origin. Presumably, if God cared enough to send a dream to Ezra, He cared enough to make sure that the dreamer understood it. Thus, the interpreter was provided within the dream itself.

This message was even more clear and direct in the *Shepherd of Hermas*, which was written in the middle of the second century and was extraordinarily popular during the early church. Tertullian put it in the category of sacred Scripture, and other early church fathers also valued it.[62] In this text, Hermas was led to wisdom through five dreams or visions. Hermas had dreams within the dreams of spiritual dreamguides who interpreted the dreams for him.[63] Through the interpretations of the dreams, Hermas grew in spiritual understanding until his final vision, when he saw a shepherd. In the dream, he is told that the shepherd has "been sent by the most venerable angel to dwell with you for the rest of your life."[64] The shepherd will remain Hermas's "dream companion," representative of Hermas's newfound wisdom.[65] Like

Ezra, Hermas finished his work with a series of prophecies, or man-
dates for living a Christian life. The dreams, interpreted by people
within the dream itself, form the basis for subsequent prophecy.

Hermas concluded with Ezra that when God selects his vessel, he
empowers that person with the ability to interpret the dream. Many
Christians, perhaps influenced by texts like these, renounced the pagan
practice of consulting dream interpreters who seemed altogether too
much like augurs and diviners. Hermas, in his mandate against false
prophets, says, "For, no spirit granted by God has to be consulted. It
speaks everything with the Godhead's power, because it is from above,
from the power of the divine Spirit."[66] This Christian message led Tertullian and others to worry less about interpreting dreams and more
about whether or not the dreamer was worthy to have a vision from
God. If so, the dreamer could interpret it. Augustine's mother, for example, repeatedly interpreted her dreams to her famous son, and he accepted her interpretation because he was sure that her dreams had been
sent by God.[67]

It was not difficult for Augustine to decide his mother's dreams were
from God because he had already decided she was saintly. As we saw in
the case of prophets in the early Christian communities, it was not
always easy to be certain whether their prophecy was true or, to phrase
it a different way, whether their visions were from God. Christians had
to assess the worthiness of the vessels as well as the strength of the
message.

When it came to confessors, however, the task was simpler. People
who had been selected for martyrdom were seen to have been selected
by the Holy Spirit.[68] Thus, their dreams were accepted as prophetic.[69]
Accounts of martyrs are full of dreams that were premonitory. Eusebius wrote of the dream of Polycarp in which his martyrdom by fire
was predicted in a dream of his pillow bursting into flames.[70] The martyr Renus had a vision that showed him leading his group with lamps,
and he interpreted that dream to mean all would be saved.[71] The list of
martyr visionaries can be extended considerably,[72] but these should suf-
fice to show that the dreams of martyrs-to-be were considered to be always from God. Furthermore, the interpretation of the dreams was not
left to discussion; the confessor interpreted the dream for the faithful.
When Perpetua and Saturus recorded their dreams, it was in this spirit.
They preserved and interpreted their dreams for the community.

In the twentieth century, we can analyze the meaning of the confessors' dreams from many different perspectives. One could take a
Freudian approach to the images, focusing on the phallic dragon and
swords,[73] or one could take a Jungian approach, focusing on the arche-

typical images in Perpetua's dreamworld.[74] Instead, I shall rely on Perpetua's and Saturus's own interpretations of their dreams. This approach concentrates on Perpetua's understanding of her experience and acknowledges the way subsequent readers understood this text. The faithful who for centuries listened to the account of Perpetua's visions accepted her interpretation of her dreams. Of course, Perpetua's interpretations of her dreams were shaped by her understandings of dream interpretation which she brought from her pagan and Christian experiences.

Beyond the direct meaning of these dreams, however, I want to focus specifically on the content of the dreams and the relation between the dream images and the dreamer's waking life, both past and immediate.[75] I will look closely at the images Perpetua saw in her visions, as well as the way she chose to express these images. In our dreams, our minds select impressions that are familiar to us, that are in some way part of our thought world. Cicero noted this tendency of dreams: "It often happens that our thoughts and words affect us during sleep."[76] Although the images may certainly have symbolic meaning that may point to a larger truth, they directly reveal our mental world. I will explore the images that Perpetua's subconscious selected to express the truths she believed she saw. This will reveal how Perpetua's memories were brought to bear on her understanding of her imprisonment and her forthcoming execution. In these mental images, we can see a microcosm of the conflict of cultures that led to the imprisonment of the young mother and her companions. And for me most surprising, we see revealed a remarkable synthesis that led to the confessor going confidently to her death in the arena.

THE CONFESSORS' DREAMS

Once the prisoners had been moved from the darkest prison, Perpetua had her first vision. This dream was solicited. One of Perpetua's fellow prisoners (whom she referred to as "brother"), said to her: *"Dear sister, you are greatly privileged; surely you might ask for a vision to discover whether you are to be condemned or freed."*[77] The Christian community believed an arrest indicated that a person had been selected for martyrdom, thus Perpetua was "privileged." Again, within the context of early Christian understanding, this selection placed her among those who could expect a premonitory dream sent from the Holy Spirit. Perpetua shared her companion's confidence and responded: *"Faithfully I promised that I would, for I knew that I could speak with the Lord, whose great blessings I had come to experience."*[78] We cannot know what "blessings" Perpetua had experienced in the past, but it seems likely she had already had dream-visions, or had participated in other forms of ecstatic experiences in the community. She was too confident in her ability to speak to God for the presence of the Spirit to be new to her. This was perfectly consistent with what she would have learned in the Christian gathering.

Furthermore, Tertullian in his letter to the martyrs reassured them that their imprisonment would not separate them from the experiences they knew in the services. He wrote that prison might confine their bodies, but it was conducive to setting their spirits free. He urged them, "In spirit wander about, in spirit take a walk. . . . The spirit carries about the whole man and brings him wherever he wishes."[79] In the ancient world, people believed dreams sometimes came because the spirit wandered free during sleep. Perpetua could well have taken Tertullian's words to heart and expected fruitful dreams in prison. She tells her brother/companion she will tell him the next day the results of her vision. She continues briefly and confidently: *"Then I made my request and this was the vision I had."*

Perpetua's First Vision

I saw a ladder of tremendous height made of bronze, reaching all the way to the heavens, but it was so narrow that only one person could climb up at a time. To the sides of the ladder were attached all sorts of iron weapons: there were swords, spears, hooks, daggers, and spikes; so that if anyone tried to climb up carelessly or without paying attention, he would be mangled and his flesh would adhere to the weapons.

At the foot of the ladder lay a dragon of enormous size, and it would attack those who tried to climb up and try to terrify them from doing so. And Saturus was the first to go up, he who was later to give himself up of his own accord. He had been the builder of our strength, although he was not present when we were arrested. And he arrived at the top of the staircase and he looked back and said to me: "Perpetua, I am waiting for you. But take care; do not let the dragon bite you. "He will not harm me," I said, "in the name of Christ Jesus." Slowly, as though he were afraid of me, the dragon stuck his head out from underneath the ladder. Then, using it as my first step, I trod on his head and went up.

Then I saw an immense garden, and in it a grey-haired man sat in shepherd's garb; tall he was, and milking sheep. And standing around him were many thousands of people clad in white garments. He raised his head, looked at me, and said: "I am glad you have come, my child." He called me over to him and gave me, as it were, a mouthful of the milk he was drawing; and I took it into my cupped hands and consumed it. And

all those who stood around said: "Amen!" At the sound of this word I
came to, with the taste of something sweet still in my mouth.[80]

When Perpetua requested this dream, she had been preoccupied
with what was to happen to the group. This dream was about salvation,
but it was equally about fear and about the strength of community. The
images she chose drew from various elements of her past experience to
express these ideas. These memories were Roman, Carthaginian, and
Christian.

First, the general association that would have contributed to the
shape of this dream was Perpetua's knowledge that she would have to
face beasts in the arena. The serpent represented a foreshadowing of
that struggle in which she hoped to be victorious "in the name of
Christ Jesus." Perpetua's subconscious could have naturally selected a
snake to oppose her salvation, drawing from images she read or heard
from Genesis. The serpent was given "enmity between you and the
woman" and his head would be bruised by the woman's heel,[81] just as
happened in the dream. Perpetua's dream might also have been influenced by Tertullian's letter "To the Martyrs," wherein he referred to
the devil, saying the martyrs had come to prison "for the very purpose
of trampling upon him." Tertullian further compared the devil that she
was to confront to a snake (or dragon).[82] In dream images, one can expect words recently read from an influential source to mingle with
other recollections, and this is what happens in Perpetua's mind.

Artemidorus also offered insights that might have shaped Perpetua's
dream of the dragon at the foot of the ladder. He argued that ven-
omous animals represented powerful men, and further that the head
signified parents.[83] These interpretations express vividly, albeit symbolically, Perpetua's current situation: she was treading on the authority of her father, a powerful man, in her quest for spiritual progress.[84]
Because she probably knew of Artemidorus's ideas, her mind, strug-
gling with her relationship with her father, might certainly have drawn
on this image to express her concern.

In a dream that demonstrated a longing for a better world, the ladder ascending from this world and the serpent that attempted to im-
pede the ascent were natural and obvious symbols. The ladder recalls
the Genesis account of Jacob's ladder leading to heaven, but Perpetua's
image draws from a much richer background than only scriptural.

Perpetua's mind uses and modifies the images to begin to reveal a
more full expression of her experiences. In the Genesis account, the
ladder is not described in any detail. Yet, Perpetua sees a ladder of
bronze, dangerously framed with weapons. Why would she have seen

the ladder in this way? She may have been reaching for an older, non-Christian example of an ascent to heaven. There was ample precedent in the ancient world for ladders as symbols of crossing beyond to another world,[85] and Perpetua would surely have known of them. Artemidorus believed a ladder in a dream symbolized travel, progress, and danger,[86] all of which work consistently in Perpetua's dream. An ancient Assyrian dream book offered an interpretation that would have applied well to Perpetua's dream: if a man ascends to heaven and the gods bless him, he will die.[87] She may well have been familiar with such dream interpretations that might have shaped the images her mind created. It may also be that the modification to the ladder was a symbolic reflection of her status in prison. The ladder—the path to heaven—was bronze, a weak, soft metal. The weapons affixed to it were iron,[88] much harder than the ladder. Her fear at the strength of the impediments that might get in the way of her salvation may have shaped the image of the ladder itself.

In her narrative, she shows no fear or uncertainty in the path she has chosen, but she knew full well that until a martyr had died constant in the faith, there was no certainty of salvation. She knew this from martyr stories she had heard, for example the stories of the martyrs who died in Lyon in 177, and from the letter from Tertullian that warned repeatedly of the frail flesh that might fail. Her fears may have been expressed symbolically in a ladder much more dangerous than that seen by Jacob.

Furthermore, the ladder as she describes it was shaped by her experience as a Roman/Carthaginian. When she describes the weapons on the ladder, she says quite graphically that someone would be *"mangled and his flesh would adhere to the weapons."* This is what happened in the arena when gladiators and others were killed. It is unlikely that a young Carthaginian of Perpetua's status would not have seen people die in the arena. In her mind, her fear of her upcoming ordeal combined with her previous experience to yield a concrete image that gave vivid shape to her fears. Finally, the images of bronze and weapons were likely shaped by classical authors she had read. Dronke sees echoes of Virgil in the dream as when Pyrrhus breaks into the bronze portals of Priam's palace with weapons like a "snake coming into the light."[89] Perpetua, who grew up reading this literature, drew from it images of struggle and courage.

Perpetua's vision of heaven as a garden also shows a creative mingling in her mind of several Christian sources. The crowd of people dressed in white surely mirror the vision of John in Revelation. For John, these were martyrs whose clothing was washed white in the "blood of the lamb."[90] Perpetua, in expectation of imminent martyr-dom, drew from these consoling images of martyrs in heaven. Yet, John's heaven was not a garden; it was a synagogue or basilica.[91] John's vision was not pastoral, it was resplendent with gold and jewels, the glory of human production.

The Carthaginian community was also familiar with the visionary work written in the mid-second century called the *Apocalypse of St. Peter*. This work offered the first vision of heaven and hell after the Book of Revelation.[92] Peter saw heaven as "a great garden, open, full of fair trees and blessed fruits, and of the odor of perfumes. The fra-grance of it was pleasant and came upon us."[93] As we shall see below, Saturus's vision also saw heaven in the form of a garden, and Saturus even emphasized the fragrance that Peter had recalled. It seems that the image of heaven in the Carthaginian communities owed more to Peter's *Apocalypse* than to that of John, which later became canonical.

The image of the shepherd in Perpetua's dream is easier to explain than her choice of a garden. In the early church, by far the predomi-nant image of Christ was of the Good Shepherd; it appeared on Chris-tian carvings, sarcophagi, and frescoes. Furthermore, a shepherd as welcoming guide to a dreamer had appeared in the *Shepherd of Hermas*. In her vision, Perpetua, like Hermas, gained the company of a com-forting shepherd/guide, although, unlike Hermas, she placed the shep-herd in a garden. She had combined her memories to create a new heavenly vision.

Perpetua's dream offered many elements that revealed the confes-sor's fear of the upcoming ordeal, but it was not predominately about terror. The dream was primarily about community: the Christian com-munity that she joined as she renounced her father, and the community for whom she recorded this vision. In my emphasis on community, I depart from other scholars who have analyzed these dreams, and who have been so impressed by the singularity of these personal visions that they have stressed their individuality. These visions were only partly about Perpetua's personal spiritual growth; they were also about her in-tegration into a new community as she gave up her old one.

The first element that points to her concern for community is the image of the shepherd. In her vision, the shepherd was old with gray hair; he resembled her description of her father.[94] In portraying the shepherd as a older man, Perpetua changes the images that she brought to her dream world. Early Christian art portrayed the Good Shepherd as a young man, and neither did the *Shepherd of Hermas* show the shep-herd as old.[95] In Perpetua's dream, familiar images were changed to replace the father figure she had recently rejected in life. She was welcomed into the heavenly family with paternal caring: *"I am glad you have come, my child."* Her new father was proud of her choice in a way her old father was not.

In addition to the shepherd, another father figure was Saturus, the leader of the small group in prison, and the leader up Perpetua's dream ladder. Perpetua interrupted the narrative of her dream to tell the reader about Saturus. She explained that he was the *"builder of our strength,"* and that he was not arrested at the same time the others were, and later he gave *"himself up of his own accord."* The digression in the middle of the dream narrative is important because it contributes to our understanding of Perpetua's interpretation of her dream. If this dream were in large part about the forging of a new community in heaven, it was important for Perpetua that readers of her vision knew about the leadership of that community. Perpetua may have had to give up a beloved father on earth, but she gained two in heaven.

Another element in her dream that pointed to her concern for a Christian community life was the presence of the *"many thousands of people clad in white garments"* in the garden, recalling the vision in Revelation. Heaven for her was not a lonely place. She could look forward to the same kind of community that had shaped her earthly Christian experience.

This earthly community experience also informed her vision of the heavenly garden. The portion of the dream in which she seems to receive a ritual nourishment of milk from the shepherd while the heavenly community closes her dream with an "Amen" has been much analyzed for its Eucharistic symbols.[96] However, Perpetua had a more specific, local, precedent for this image; Carthaginian Christians ate milk and cheese along with the bread and wine of Holy Communion. Further, at their first Holy Communion the newly baptized were given a cup of milk and honey as a taste of the sweetness of heaven they could later expect.[97] This dream experience collapsed together the ritual community experiences that made Christians part of a new society. When Perpetua awoke with *"the taste of something sweet still in her mouth,"* it was both the taste of honey she had recently received at her baptism and the taste of paradise that she had been promised.

When Perpetua awoke, she "at once" told this dream to her "brother." Because she was able to relate the dream immediately, the "brother" to whom she refers must have been a brother in Christ, a fellow prisoner. Here the words she chose reveal again her bonding with a new community, which was so evident in the dream itself. Her direct interpretation of the dream addressed its prophetic nature, and answered the question that she had posed when she requested the vision: *"[W]e realized that we would have to suffer, and that from now on we would no longer have any hope in this life."*[98] The vision and her certainty of its meaning shows the intricate way Perpetua's memories and previous experiences began to be integrated in a new and comforting synthesis. This dream resolved her hopes for the future and her relationship with her father, and it confirmed the new community to which she belonged. But her maternal role seems not to have been addressed, and perhaps was still unresolved in her mind.

Perpetua's Second and Third Visions

"Some days" after the hearing and after Perpetua had finally separated from her son and broken her maternal ties, the group was at prayer in prison. During this prayer, Perpetua *"suddenly . . . spoke out and uttered the name Dinocrates. I was surprised; for the name had never entered my mind until that moment."*[99] Because it was not uncommon for Christians to utter prophetic words during prayer, Perpetua naturally looked for meaning in her exclamation.

Dinocrates was her younger brother who had *"died horribly of cancer of the face when he was seven years old, and his death was a source of loathing to everyone."* Because Perpetua had not thought of him for a while until his name came to her during prayer, she interpreted the experience in this way: *"At once I realized that I was privileged to pray for him. I began to pray for him and to sigh deeply for him before the Lord."*[100] Perpetua had ample Christian precedent for believing she had the ability to pray effectively for someone. In his letter to the imprisoned martyrs, Tertullian reminded them they had the ability to pray for and help others in the Christian community.[101] As Perpetua exerted this care for others, she was reclaiming a new maternal role after having renounced the old one.

From the earliest martyrdoms, confessors were recognized to have the power to pray for their new Christian family. Eusebius described this care in maternal terms. He claimed confessors had the power to forgive the lapsed, allowing the church to receive "her stillborn children back alive."[102] The martyrs in this case served as mothers giving rebirth to others in the community. After birth, mothers care for their children. Irenaeus described the care confessors showed other Christians in their community also in maternal terms. He said the confessors "bestowed . . . motherly affection on those who lacked. . . . Shedding many tears on their behalf in supplication to the Father."[103] This is what Perpetua was doing for her deceased younger brother. In renouncing her role as a mother of Rome, Perpetua did not really renounce maternal caring; she simply changed the locus. If her first visions were in part about belonging to a community with father figures, these next two visions were about belonging and contributing to that community in a maternal way.

While Perpetua prayed for Dinocrates, she received the following vision as she was sleeping:

> I saw Dinocrates coming out of a dark hole, where there were many others with him, very hot and thirsty, pale and dirty. On his face was the wound he had when he died.... There was a great abyss between us: neither could approach the other. Where Dinocrates stood there was a pool full of water; and its rim was higher than the child's height, so that Dinocrates had to stretch himself up to drink. I was sorry that, though the pool had water in it, Dinocrates could not drink because of the height of the rim. Then I woke up, realizing that my brother was suffering.[104]

Perpetua's previous concern for her son's suffering and his thirst for milk becomes transferred to her thirsty brother. Since her hearing, Perpetua increasingly was focused on the next world, so her maternal care was now for the dead.[105] Perpetua's vision of the afterlife and the suffering of her brother was shaped by pagan and literary views more than by any Christian vision of an early idea of purgatory.[106] She had an image of suffering children from Virgil, whose Aeneas heard the wailing of infants weeping at the threshold of the underworld. In the *Aeneid* underworld, Dido the Carthaginian queen bore the mark of the sword that killed her,[107] as Dinocrates carried the mark of his terminal cancer. Tantalus suffered in the pagan afterlife with an unquenchable thirst, as did many others in the pagan world of death.[108]

Although Perpetua's pagan background shaped this dream, her experience in the Christian community and her knowledge of the intercessory power of martyrs shaped her response to it. She said, *"I was confident that I could help him in his trouble; and I prayed for him every day.... And I prayed for my brother day and night with tears and sighs that this favour might be granted me."*

During this time of prayer for her younger brother, Perpetua and her companions were transferred to the military prison in preparation for the forthcoming games. It is at this point in the text that Perpetua tells us they are to die *"on the occasion of Caesar Geta's birthday."*[109] It may have been coincidental that Perpetua found out the occasion of the games at this time, but it seems equally likely that she chose this point in the narrative to relay this information. Just as she was in the midst of expressing, indeed helping to shape, a new Christian motherly concern for the spiritual health of a family member,[110] the Romans were preparing to celebrate a ritual for the well-being of another child, the emperor's son. This conflict of cultures is revealed in a poignant way as the young mother writes of maternal concern for her dead brother.

After they were moved and while they were in chains in the new prison, Perpetua experienced her third vision:

> *I saw the same spot that I had seen before, but there was Dinocrates all clean, well dressed, and refreshed. I saw a scar where the wound had been; and the pool that I had seen before now had its rim lowered to the level of the child's waist. And Dinocrates kept drinking water from it, and there above the rim was a golden bowl full of water. And Dinocrates drew close and began to drink from it, and yet the bowl remained full. And when he had drunk enough of the water, he began to play as children do. Then I awoke, and I realized that he had been delivered from his suffering.*[111]

Perpetua's maternal care had been effective. Today we frequently judge a child's well-being by his or her appearance, and Perpetua seems to have shared that judgment. Dinocrates was clean, well dressed, and no longer thirsty. The poignancy of her vision is enhanced by the realistic detail of the image of a happy child playing in the water "as children do." Perpetua drew from her memories of family life in her vision of personal and maternal power.[112] Furthermore, these two visions confirmed the first vision in reassuring her that she truly was not cut off from all her social ties as she continued on her spiritual path.

Perpetua's analysis of her dream, that the child had been delivered from suffering, was validated not only by her motherly recognition of a happy child; pagan dream wisdom also confirmed her analysis. Artemidorus said in his dream book that drinking from a bowl symbolized great safety,[113] and a scar "signifies the ending of every care."[114] The efficacy of her Christian prayers was confirmed in her subconscious mind by pagan wisdom. Furthermore, in her dream state, Perpetua preserved her role as a mother, albeit in a changed form. She gave up her son, but cared for her dead brother.

Perpetua's Fourth Vision

The prayers, demeanor, and perhaps visions of the confessors made an impression on the soldier in charge of the prison. Perpetua said that this man named Pudens *"began to show us great honour, realizing that we possessed some great power within us. And he began to allow many visitors to see us for our mutual comfort."* As the day of the contest approached, one of these visitors was Perpetua's father, who made one more appeal to his daughter:

> My father came to see me overwhelmed with sorrow. He started tearing the hairs from his beard and threw them on the ground; he then threw himself on the ground and began to curse his old age and to say such words as would move all creation. I felt sorry for his unhappy old age.[115]

As the previous visions showed, Perpetua was already beyond changing her mind. She had begun to focus on the afterlife and had shifted her community identity to the Christian community of the living and the dead. She had enough compassion left for her father to "feel sorry" for him, yet her response hardly matches the depths of his grief. Her final vision came shortly after this last confrontation and the day before they were to *"fight with the beasts."* She dreamed that

> Pomponius the deacon came to the prison gates and began to knock violently. I went out and opened the gate for him. He was dressed in an unbelted white tunic, wearing elaborate sandals. And he said to me: "Perpetua, come; we are waiting for you." Then he took my hand and we began to walk through rough and broken country. At last we came to the amphitheatre out of breath, and he led me into the centre of the arena. Then he told me: "Do not be afraid. I am here, struggling with you." Then he left.
>
> I looked at the enormous crowd who watched in astonishment. I was surprised that no beasts were let loose on me; for I knew that I was condemned to die by the beasts. Then out came an Egyptian against me, of vicious appearance, together with his seconds, to fight with me. There also came up to me some handsome young men to be my seconds and assistants.
>
> My clothes were stripped off, and suddenly I was a man. My seconds began to rub me down with oil (as they are wont to do before a contest). Then I saw the Egyptian on the other side rolling in the dust. Next there came forth a man of marvelous stature, such that he rose above the top of the amphitheatre. He was clad in a beltless purple tunic with two stripes (one on either side) running down the middle of his chest. He wore sandals that were wondrously made of gold and silver, and he carried a wand like an athletic trainer and a green branch on which there were golden apples. And he asked for silence and said: "If this Egyptian defeats her he will slay her with the sword. But if she defeats him, she will receive this branch." Then he withdrew.
>
> We drew close to one another and began to let our fists fly. My opponent tried to get hold of my feet, but I kept striking him in the face with the heels of my feet. Then I was raised up into the air and I began to pummel him without as it were touching the ground. Then when I noticed there was a lull, I put my two hands together linking the fingers of

*one hand with those of the other and thus I got hold of his head. He fell
flat on his face and I stepped on his head.*

*The crowd began to shout and my assistants started to sing psalms.
Then I walked up to the trainer and took the branch. He kissed me and
said to me: "Peace be with you, my daughter!" I began to walk in triumph towards the Gate of Life. Then I awoke.*[116]

On the night before her ordeal, it is not surprising that Perpetua's
thoughts were dominated by the coming struggle in the arena. This
dream continues her affirmation of the new Christian family into
which she has entered, but it also reveals more about her own changing self-identity (or in Jungian terms, her own individuation).[117]

Her sense of connection to community was reinforced in the dream
by several father figures who replaced the father she had once again rejected just before this vision. The deacon Pomponius who escorted her
to the amphitheatre (wearing in her dream the same white tunic that
the inhabitants of paradise were wearing in Perpetua's first dream) as-
sured her that he was with her through her ordeal. The trainer at the
end kissed her in the Christian ritualized kiss of peace and called her
his daughter. She was accompanied by two young men as seconds in
her ordeal. Although this dream was about her struggle, she was not
alone. The dream (and the dreamer) were framed by male supporters in
a fictive family group.

This dream reasserts the presence of community that had been established in the previous vision. It goes beyond this by offering new insights into Perpetua's sense of her own transformation. Certainly there
is no more vivid image of personal change than Perpetua's dream
image in which she is transformed into a man. Others have struggled to
interpret this complicated and, indeed, somewhat disturbing image.
Does this transformation reflect the reality of a male-dominated world
in which, to achieve power, Perpetua must see herself as male?[118] Is this
a Christian symbol in which the martyr imitates Christ in whom there
was to be no male or female?[119] Is it an image derived from a troubled
mind?[120] Is this a practical accommodation in a dream in which the reality is that women could not fight in this particular form of wrestling
contest (the *pankration*)?[121] Cassius Dio tells us that in A.D. 200 in
Rome a great gymnastic contest took place in which women participated with such vigor that "jokes were made about other very distinguished women as well." Because of the impact of these games, women
were henceforth forbidden to fight in single combat.[122] If Perpetua
had heard of this event, which is likely, the knowledge could have entered her dream in this form.

All these insights shed light on this complicated image. For me, the most compelling part of this image is its signaling of transformation.[123] If one is looking for a metaphor of personal change, one cannot do better than a transformation of one's gender, which is at the heart of one's self-identity. In her dream, Perpetua was changed into a man. Led by the deacon of her new community, she was fully transformed from her old self into a new empowered individual who could stand in the arena and fight for what she believed. Here she was remembering in a dream-form her own baptism—the dramatic change from catechumen to baptized Christian.

Her startling transformation was followed immediately by another surprising image—that of her male seconds rubbing her naked body with oil. There are unmistakably sexual overtones to this image,[124] and not simply to our twentieth-century ears. Perpetua, too, must have noticed. The second-century Greek author Lucian wrote a satire called "Lucius or the Ass" that contains an erotic passage in which the hero and a slave girl named Palaestra (Ms. Wrestler) engage in oil rubdowns in an extended and sexual parody of a wrestling match.[125] Because Perpetua knew Greek, she could have read Lucian's work. She certainly had read Apuleius's *Golden Ass*,[126] which drew from Lucian's satire. Recognizing that Perpetua probably knew of such references, we can understand her parenthetic explanation in her dream narrative, in which she explains that such oil rubdowns are simply part of this kind of wrestling match. This break from the dream narrative gives us a glimpse of the modest Roman matron probably somewhat surprised herself at the nature of her dream.

Just as most of the dream images are rich in meaning and associations from various thought worlds of Perpetua's past, the oil, too, draws various metaphors together. She was certainly correct in joining oil with pagan athletic contests. However, there were also Christian associations. The newly baptized were anointed with oil in ceremonies in which the new members were accepted naked into the congregation. The newly baptized Perpetua surely joined this image to the athletic one.

In addition, in his letter to the martyrs, Tertullian used the same metaphor of the athletic contest to represent the upcoming test as Perpetua did. Tertullian spoke of the Holy Spirit as the martyrs' trainer,[127] and Perpetua's vision of the trainer in purple and so large that he dominated the amphitheater echoes Tertullian's view of the Holy Spirit athletic trainer. Furthermore, Tertullian said that Jesus Christ "who has anointed you with His Spirit" brought the martyrs to the "training ground" of the athletic contest.[128] In Tertullian's metaphor, Perpetua's anointment with oil by the young men was a blessing by Christ. In her dream, then, the modest Roman matron was transformed completely, anointed and ready to battle in a traditional forum against a new kind of enemy.

Although the waking and sleeping Perpetua expected to be confronted by an animal as she would be the next day, she instead was opposed by an Egyptian of loathsome appearance. Perpetua's mind could have selected an Egyptian as the demonlike figure because of Egypt's association with pagan wisdom;[129] she knew of Apuleius's passionate description of the cult of Isis. She also knew of Septimius's identification with the Egyptian god Serapis, so her enemy *was* the "Egyptian" emperor on the occasion of his son's birthday. Her mind's selection of an Egyptian as opponent would have been a natural image to oppose her Christianity. The images of Egyptians as opponents in her experience were even more rich than the associations of paganism with Egyptian deities.

She may also have shared a general Roman prejudice against "barbaric" Egyptians. Juvenal's Fifteenth Satire (written in the mid first century) is entitled "On the Atrocities of Egypt" and demonized Egyptians.[130] In addition, her dream may have drawn on Heliodorus's romance *Ethiopian*, in which the protagonist's last test was to fight in the arena against a gigantic Ethiopian (Ethiopians frequently were equated with Egyptians.) In sum, the gigantic Egyptian embodied many levels of evil for Perpetua, and he was thus a perfect dream opponent.

Perpetua engaged the Egyptian in the traditional Greek-style free-for-all wrestling match, the *pankration*.[131] It is quite likely that Perpetua had seen just such a contest in the arena. Early in the third century, Carthage had received permission to hold Pythian games in honor of Apollo.[132] These games included a wrestling contest similar to that described by Perpetua, and may well have shaped her dream of the contest in the arena.[133] The probability that Perpetua saw such a contest (instead of just having read about it) is increased by the fact that she did not have the accurate terminology for the match. When her narrative was translated into Greek, the Greek redactor corrected the jargon.[134] If she had read about the contest, the terminology would probably have been more precise than if she had simply witnessed it. Thus as her dream mind searched for images of a powerful struggle between good and evil, it probably drew from her experience of watching such a match. It would have been more impressive since it was an unusual festival, and required special permission for its celebration in Carthage.

She fought and defeated the Egyptian with her feet. The striking emphasis on her feet in this dream and indeed throughout the dreams is noteworthy. In her first vision, she began her ascent to heaven by treading on the serpent's head, just as she stepped on the head of the Egyptian in her final vision. Further, in her final vision, she was careful to describe Pomponius's sandals, as well as the gold and silver sandals of the trainer in her dream. Her opponent tried to "get hold of my feet," before she ultimately defeated him by kicking his face and head. It is clear that Perpetua associates feet with power,[135] and these associations so permeated her classical world that they would have been a natural part of her memories. A newborn Roman child was placed at the father's feet in a token of the father's power of life and death over the child. (This image was reversed in Perpetua's narrative when her father threw himself at her feet to plead with her. The power between them had been reversed at that moment.) In the arena, the traditional gesture of the victor was to place one's foot on the head of the opponent.[136]

The power associated with feet extended in people's minds beyond the visible world of children and gladiators. In the pagan world, ritual barefootedness was believed to enhance the power of prayer and petition to the gods. Augustine complained that it was impossible to persuade Christians to abandon the "cultic custom" of barefootedness.[137] Other Christian martyrs used these images of the power of feet in their expressions of their most sacred moment in this life: martyrdom. For example, the martyr Fructuosus marched to the amphitheater. Once there, a lector tearfully begged Fructuosus for the privilege of removing the Bishop's shoes. Fructuosus refused and "strong and rejoicing and certain of God's promise, Fructuosus removed his own shoes." In another case, the most sacred relic of the martyrs Justus and Pastor was one of their shoes.[138] Perpetua had remembered these perceptions of the power of feet, and this notion emerged with strength and clarity in her dream imagery.

Perpetua defeated the Egyptian and received the prize: the branch of golden apples, and the kiss of peace by the trainer/Holy Spirit. Apples were a strong symbol of woman and woman's love in the antique world. The fruit of Aphrodite regularly played a role in marriage and erotic ceremony,[139] and Artemidorus believed apples in dreams symbolized the pleasures of love sacred to Aphrodite.[140] The equation of apples with women surely shaped the Genesis account of the Fall, but for Perpetua the symbol was too joyous and victorious to have been much influenced by biblical account. In searching for an image of victory, Perpetua's mind reached for images from the classical past, and the image was one of a victorious woman. (Just as Aphrodite had won the apple for being the most beautiful of the goddesses, Perpetua, who turned into a man at the beginning of the contest, received the highest prize of womanhood at the end.)

These remarkable visions of Perpetua reveal all the fears and uncertainties one would expect in this circumstance. Images of struggle combined with those of comfort. Images of dislocation merged with those of community acceptance. But what is probably most extraordinary about these visions is the way in which all the competing forces are integrated really very comfortably. I expected to find much more difficulty and anxiety in both Perpetua's narrative and in her dreams. Yet, the experience of this extraordinary young woman shows the way in which people can manage what should be seriously conflicting ideas and emerge with a strong and clear sense of purpose. Perpetua drew from her classical past, both her experiences and her literary background, and she drew from her more recent experiences in her community of Christians.[141] For example, the trainer in her dream, who in Tertullian's words took the place of the Holy Spirit, wore the traditional robes of the African priests of Saturn.[142] These mental images did not clash in her unconscious; instead they blended to form metaphors that Perpetua interpreted clearly and unambiguously into a prophetic vision of her Christian future.

After this extraordinarily complex dream, Perpetua analyzed its meaning with simple clarity: *"I realized that it was not with wild animals that I would fight but with the Devil, but I knew that I would win the victory."*[143]

Saturus's Vision

The leader of the group who had volunteered to join the martyrs also had a vision while imprisoned. Here is his account of his vision that the narrator also claimed was in the martyr's own words:

> *We had died and had put off the flesh, and we began to be carried towards the east by four angels who did not touch us with their hand. But we moved alone not on our backs facing upwards but as though we were climbing up a gentle hill. And when we were free of the world, we first saw an intense light. And I said to Perpetua (for she was at my side): "This is what the Lord promised us. We have received his promise." While we were being carried by these four angels, a great open space appeared, which seemed to be a garden, with rose bushes and all manner of flowers. The trees were as tall as cypresses, and their leaves were constantly falling. In the garden there were four other angels more splendid*

than the others. When they saw us they paid us homage and said to the other angels in admiration: "Why, they are here! They are here!"

Then the four angels that were carrying us grew fearful and set us down. Then we walked across to an open area by way of a broad road, and there we met Jucundus, Saturninus, and Artaxius, who were burnt alive in the same persecution, together with Quintus who had actually died as a martyr in prison. We asked them where they had been. And the other angels said to us: "First come and enter and greet the Lord."

Then we came to a place whose walls seemed to be constructed of light. And in front of the gate stood four angels, who entered in and put on white robes. We also entered and we heard the sound of voices in unison chanting endlessly: "Holy, Holy, Holy!" In the same place we seemed to see an aged man with white hair and a youthful face, though we did not see his feet. On his right and left were four elders, and behind them stood other aged men. Surprised, we entered and stood before a throne: four angels lifted us up and we kissed the aged man and he touched our faces with his hand. And the elders said to us: "Let us rise." And we rose and gave the kiss of peace. Then the elders said to us: "Go and play." To Perpetua I said: "Your wish is granted." She said to me: "Thanks be to God that I am happier here now than I was in the flesh."

Then we went out and before the gates we saw the bishop Optatus on the right and Aspasius the presbyter and teacher on the left, each of them far apart and in sorrow. They threw themselves at our feet and said: "Make peace between us. For you have gone away and left us thus." And we said to them: "Are you not our bishop, and are you not our presbyter? How can you fall at our feet?" We were very moved and embraced them. Perpetua then began to speak with them in Greek, and we drew them apart into the garden under a rose arbour. While we were talking with them, the angel said to them: "Allow them to rest. Settle whatever quarrels you have among yourselves." And they were put to confusion. Then they said to Optatus: "You must scold your flock. They approach you as though they had come from the games, quarrelling about the different teams."

And it seemed as though they wanted to close the gates. And there we began to recognize many of our brethren, martyrs among them. All of us were sustained by a most delicious odour that seemed to satisfy us. And then I woke up happy.[144]

The account of this dream offers a striking contrast to those of Perpetua. It lacks the dreamlike quality of compressed images and surprising associations. It reads more like a polished theological tract designed to present a lesson to a Christian congregation.[145] If it were a dream, either Saturus's dream life is very clear and linear, or he edited it substantially in the recording to be sure that the Christians for whom it was intended would not misunderstand any dream images. Unlike Perpetua, Saturus did not include a statement of the dream's meaning; it seems likely that in his recording of the dream he allowed his interpretation of the meaning to shape his narrative. Whether it was a "real" dream or a record of a pseudodream designed to instruct, it nevertheless expresses the concerns of Saturus on the eve of his execution.

Saturus shows much the same care for the community as Perpetua. However, Saturus's concern is that of a leader of the Christian communities. Echoing the early Christian writers from Paul through Ignatius, he was worried about strife in the congregation. The bishop and presbyter pleaded with Saturus and Perpetua to settle the differences in the quarreling community. In Saturus' narrative, angels reprimanded them and urged them to settle their differences. Saturus was telling the community to avoid fragmenting dissent, and gave divine sanction for this advice. In this exchange, Saturus expressed his view that martyrs, not church officers, were the leaders of the church.[146] With this perspective, it is perhaps understandable that he voluntarily joined the martyrs in prison, rather than continue his position as a leader of the Carthage Christian community.

Saturus saw himself and Perpetua joining the heavenly community that included angels and martyrs who had predeceased them.[147] By directly naming martyrs who had died, Saturus both reestablished his case for the importance of martyrdom, and reassured himself of his salvation after the coming struggle.

In a number of ways, Saturus's vision parallels the first vision of Perpetua. As in Perpetua's vision, the two share the passage to heaven (without any of the others of the group). Heaven for both is a garden with a gray-haired man. (Although Saturus does give the man a "youthful face," which is more consistent with the portrayals of the youthful good shepherd that were available in the art of the Christian community.) Saturus drew in more detail from the Book of Revelation than did Perpetua, keeping the liturgical chant, the gates, and the angels portrayed in some detail. However, like Perpetua, he placed the scene in a heavenly garden, following the *Apocalypse of Peter*. The visions share many of the same images, from the descriptions of the angels to the awareness of feet as symbols of power. Finally, they are similar in concern for community and the shared prophetic vision of their martyrdom. The differences between them—primarily Saturus's concern for hierarchy and organization against Perpetua's very personal visions—may derive from personality, age, gender, or differential power.

All combine to allow us a poignant look into the individual and collective mentalities of the early Christian communities.

FINAL PREPARATIONS

The diary written by Perpetua ended shortly after her account of her final vision. At that point, she was certain of her victory; she had recorded the most important things for the Christians who would be left behind: her dreams that she believed had come from the Holy Spirit. She concluded her diary briefly: *"So much for what I did up until the eve of the contest. About what happened at the contest itself, let him write of it who will."*[148]

Whoever continued the *Passio* next included the vision of Saturus purportedly written with his own hand. After recording his vision, Saturus, too, fell silent in the text. Like Perpetua, he ended his record of his prison ordeal with a visionary guide for the living. The eyewitness then included some information about the other confessors in prison before turning to the events in the amphitheater. The narrator tells us that one of the confessors, Secundulus, died while in prison. The circumstances of his death were not explained, but the cryptic sentence *"Yet his flesh, if not his spirit, knew the sword"*[149] suggests that something happened in prison that caused the soldiers to execute him there by the sword.

The last of the imprisoned confessors to be discussed was the slave Felicity. She was pregnant in the eighth month when she was arrested, and as the narrator described, Felicity's greatest worry was that her condition would keep her from sharing the struggle in the arena with her companions:

> *She became greatly distressed that her martyrdom would be postponed because of her pregnancy, for it is against the law for women with child to be put to death. Thus she might have to shed her holy, innocent blood afterwards along with others who were common criminals.* [150]

Felicity was right about the Roman law; a pregnant woman would not be executed, even if she were a confessed Christian. Accounts of martyrdoms repeatedly showed pregnant women exempt from execution. One example was that of Eutychia, who was arrested with several female companions. The others were executed, and the prefect said of Eutychia: "Since Eutychia is pregnant she shall be kept meanwhile in jail."[151] Although Felicity was a slave, Rome had an interest in her child even if it no longer valued the mother. The child represented property belonging to Felicity's owner, and as such was important.[152] In accor-

dance with the law and with the values of Rome, a pregnant Felicity
would not be executed with her companions.

The narrator said that *"her comrades in martyrdom were also saddened;
for they were afraid that they would have to leave behind so fine a companion
to travel alone on the same road to hope."* The group prayed together and
the Lord answered their prayers by bringing on premature labor pains
two days before the contest in the arena. (It is a bit surprising that Perpetua's diary, which covers the same time period, did not mention this
incident. Were they in separate quarters, because Perpetua was of
higher birth? Perhaps Perpetua's diary was self-consciously intended to
be about herself, so there was no room for Felicity's experience. We
cannot know for sure.)

Felicity bore her child, experiencing the pain of a difficult birth and
the additional ordeal of a taunting guard:

> She suffered a good deal in her labour because of the natural difficulty of
> an eight months' delivery. Hence one of the assistants of the prison guards
> said to her: "You suffer so much now—what will you do when you are
> tossed to the beasts? Little did you think of them when you refused to sac-
> rifice." "What I am suffering now," she replied, "I suffer by myself. But
> then another will be inside me who will suffer for me, just as I shall be
> suffering for him."
>
> And she gave birth to a girl; and one of the sisters brought her up as
> her own daughter.[153]

Just as God relieved Perpetua's maternal responsibilities so she could
focus on her martyrdom, he freed Felicity's burden of motherhood.[154]
Both Perpetua and Felicity had to reject their maternal roles if they
were to proceed to martyrdom, and once again the strong statement in
this account of the need to separate from family to seek God was reaffirmed. At the same time, the message that the Christian community
was a new group that brought solidarity was also reaffirmed. The community that had been arrested together could stay together through the
final ordeal.

Felicity's dialogue with the prison guard expressed the same kind of
secure hope in God's assistance during her martyrdom as had appeared
in the dreams of Perpetua and Saturus. The perceived miraculous de-
liverance of the child was seen as a sign of God's selection of Felicity
as surely as the prophetic dreams that he sent to the other two martyrs.

The time was short from Felicity's delivery to the appearance in the
arena. The very brevity of the statement that Felicity gave up her
daughter points to both the immanence of the martyrdom and the

martyrs' readiness for the ordeal.[155] This ends the portion of the *Passio* that decides the imprisonment of the small group. Perpetua, Saturus, and Felicity had already felt the hand of God and the presence of the Spirit in preparing them for the ordeal that was to come the next day. Secundulus was dead, but the remaining group, the leaders, Saturus and Perpetua, Saturninus, and the slaves Revocatus and Felicity, would face the beasts in the arena the next morning.

five

The Arena

THE AMPHITHEATER

On the fringes of their cities large and small the Romans built amphitheaters. Since Carthage was one of the major cities of the empire, its amphitheater was suitably grand. It was built in the early second century and underwent major reconstruction in the 160s. The external dimensions are estimated at 512 by 420 feet, with an arena area measuring about 212 by 209 feet (slightly shorter but wider than an American football field). It could have held about thirty thousand spectators.[1] This building was second only to the Colosseum in Rome, which had external dimensions of about 603 by 512 feet.[2]

All that is left of Carthage's great amphitheater today are the subterranean corridors through which prisoners and animals were brought into the arena. The rest is ruins; the stones years ago had been pillaged for other uses. Although we can no longer see the amphitheater as it dominated the edge of Roman Carthage, the narrative of a twelfth-century traveler can recall for us the impressive sight:

> There is a theatre which has no parallel in the entire world. The form of the building is circular and it consists of fifty surviving vaults. Above each vault there are five rows of arches, one rising above the other, all of the same form and size, made out of blocks of stone of the type called *Kaddzan*, of incomparable beauty. Above each row of arches, there is a circuit of panels, on which there are various reliefs and strange figures of persons, animals and ships, made with incredible skill.[3]

Like other arenas, it was in the shape of an oval that had four gates leading to the axes. All the gates led into a vaulted service corridor underneath the seating. The subterranean gallery (which remains today) extended the full length of the arena on both axes, crossing in the center. Along with this gallery, there were subterranean rooms. The prisoners (and the animals) were led into the subterranean chambers, from where they could emerge directly into the center of the amphitheater. This would offer easy access to the arena, and provide dramatic interest for the spectators.[4]

The two major gates, the Gate of Life (Porta Sanavivaria) and the Gate of Death (Porta Libitinensis), were located on the narrow axis of the arena. During contests, the victors left the arena through the Gate of Life, and the slain or dying were removed through the opposite gate. The Porta Libitinensis led to a chamber that usually served as the final execution chamber of the dying before they were removed for burial.[5] The Gate of Life had appeared in Perpetua's vision as a symbol of her victory over the devil/Egyptian.

This impressive arena was located on the northwest edge of the ancient city, on the edge of the city grid built by the Romans. It was probably built in part of Kedel limestone, a very hard, rose-tinted stone[6] that would have looked striking as it dominated the skyline of that area of the town. The amphitheater was oriented on the Roman grid—the long axis aligned with the decumani roads and the short with the cardine. It was located at the junction of Decumanus 1 south and Cardo 29 west. Decumanus 2 south was a major thoroughfare, and probably most people walked along it to get to the amphitheater. It is about a ten-minute walk from the Byrsa hill in the center of Carthage, and on days of games the road must have been packed with people going to the arena.[7]

As one might guess from the scale and expense of both the arena and the events produced there, the amphitheaters of Rome and Carthage served a more important function than simple entertainment. They formed a central part of Roman religious sensibility, which was so concerned with ritual ordering and controlling the world.[8] A proverbial saying from the ancient world expressed the strong identification of Roman well-being with the games in the Colosseum:

> As long as the Colosseum stands, Rome shall stand;
> When the Colosseum falls, Rome will fall;
> When Rome falls, the world will fall.[9]

By such statements, it is easy to see that the Romans took the games very seriously and surrounded them with ritual significance. It is more difficult for the twentieth-century observer to understand exactly what function the games served. Thomas Wiedemann offers the clearest explanation of the importance of the activities in the amphitheaters of the empire:

> [The arena] was the limit of Roman civilisation in a number of senses. The arena was the place where civilisation confronted nature, in the shape of the beasts which represented a danger to humanity, and where social justice confronted wrongdoing, in the shape of the criminals who were executed there, and where the Roman empire confronted its enemies, in the persons of the captured prisoners of war who were killed or forced to kill one another in the arena.[10]

On the days of the games, Romans (even if they were far from Rome) assembled in the arena to reassure themselves that indeed they could control nature, as they watched thousands of animals killed; that they could destroy their enemies as they watched criminals sentenced to the beasts and the flames; that they could even conquer death (or at least the fear of it) as they watched gladiators bravely bare their throats for the death blow.[11]

In addition to controlling and ritualizing the natural and social ordering of the world, the arena served a political function. Here citizens could enhance their reputation by spending private fortunes to sponsor games. In Carthage, this was particularly true for the animal "hunts." As we saw in chapter 2, Carthaginians used mosaics (some of questionable taste) to decorate their homes. In some of these, they commemorated animal hunts that they sponsored. Like the boxers illustrated in chapter 2, these seem a little strange and brutal for modern decorating tastes. For example, see figure 5.1 showing a lion killing a horse (or wild ass) in all its bloody detail. These mosaics most likely commemorated the generosity of the patron who funded the show.[12]

In the best Roman tradition, private honor and public good intersected in the arena, where private generosity served a ritual function for the community. The most munificent individual was the emperor himself.[13] Throughout the empire, gladiatorial games were given by priests of the imperial cult, so the emperor himself was the focus of the ritual ordering of the Roman world that took place in the arena.

When Perpetua and her companions were sentenced to die in the games celebrated on the occasion of Septimius Severus's son's birthday, it called forth a complex series of images and religious metaphors. Criminals (or traitors to the state) would be sacrificed so that the state would be strengthened. This strengthening was more important on a

Fig. 5.1 Animal contest (mosaic). Bardo Museum, Tunis. Photograph by Bob Balsley.

symbolic level than on any practical level that might try to argue that Perpetua was an actual threat to the state. In his study on violence and the sacred, René Girard clearly and perceptively observed that the "purpose of the sacrifice is to restore harmony to the community, to reinforce the social fabric. Everything else derives from that."[14] This describes exactly the nature of the sacrifice of Perpetua and her companions: the violence perpetuated against them was to ensure ritually the continuity and peace of the state. This sacrifice was appropriately celebrated on the birthday of the Caesar Geta.

The sacrifice of Perpetua and her companions had a particularly Carthaginian twist. If a celebration/sacrifice for the emperor's son were to take place in Rome, it would involve gladiator contests. These were much more prestigious than the execution of criminals—not much of a gift in Roman eyes. But in Carthage, with its history of human sacrifice, the execution of Christians seemed an appropriate birthday present.

A space reserved to make such significant statements about power, life, and death could hardly help but be sacred, particularly because Roman religion was so space conscious. Yet, the space of the arena was not considered sacred simply because it was there. In fact, there were specific ritual activities that made the space of the arena sacred to pagans. As Tertullian expressed this idea when he forbade Christians to attend the arena: "It is not the places in themselves that defile us, but

the things done in them, by which the places themselves . . . are de-
filed."[15] So, for Tertullian, it was not that the space was used for killing
that caused it to be sacred to pagans and thus to defile Christians. He
objected more broadly to the "things done" in this space. By exploring
these "things done" we can identify the rituals that made places holy for
the Romans.

Tertullian warned Christians not to attend the games in the arena
because these games constituted idolatry in that they were all dedicated to pagan gods. However, as one reads through Tertullian's warnings, particularly described in his tract "Spectacles," one can note that
it was not simply the existence of the games but specifically the rituals
surrounding the games that claimed the space of the arena for the
pagan gods. He wrote,

> How many sacred rites are observed, how many sacrifices offered
> at the beginning, in the course, and at the end of the procession,
> how many religious corporations, furthermore, how many . . .
> priesthoods, how many bodies of magistrates are called upon to
> march in [the sacred procession].[16]

There is a series of activities that ritualize an action in the Roman
mind. These activities are (1) purification, which prepared the individual for the sacred, and which frequently included a ritual meal; (2) in-
vocation, calling on the god; (3) vision, or the acknowledgment of the
presence of the holy; (4) procession, by which the sacred was made
public, and the space marked out as sacred; and (5) fulfillment of the
sacred ritual, which in the most significant Roman rituals marked a
victory over death. This is the same sequence that marked the celebration of the Mystery of Isis as described by Apuleius. Apuleius was virtually a contemporary with Perpetua, and the crowd assembling in the
arena on that day in March would have been perfectly familiar with this
ritualizing sequence of events. And they would have recognized its appearance in the arena.

The most popular activity of the arena and the one most surrounded by ritual was the gladiator contest. Gladiators began their
arena ritual with a solemn meal. On the night before a match, they
took part in a sacred banquet called the *cena libera*.[17] This meal and the
ritual surrounding it offered purification for the men who would participate in the religious ritual on the following day. It introduced the
sacred.

The next feature that both proclaimed the sacred and made the
space of the arena sacred to the games was a procession, called the
pompa. This procession was what Tertullian described in his prohibition

above. It consisted of a number of elements that marked it as creating sacred events. First was costuming. When gladiators entered the arena in the ceremonial *pompa*, they wore purple- and gold-embroidered fine fabrics.[18] The procession was accompanied by music, as Tertullian noted with disdain: "that whole wretched business [of the procession was conducted] . . . to the tune of flutes and trumpets."[19]

The visionary element for the gladiators was the sight of the emperor if he were in attendance, for these games were always dedicated to him. Finally, at the end of the contest, gladiators celebrated victory over death, whether by defeating their adversaries or by defeating their own fear of death. In either case, the crowd participated in the central mystery of the gladiator games, a celebration of immortality, or at least the wish for it.

Thus, when the spectators and confessors went into the arena, they were entering a space of religious significance. This space on the edges of the civilized town was central to the society that felt it depended on spectacles of violence to ensure social peace and order. However, before the rituals began, people from Carthage and the surrounding regions came eagerly to see the spectacle and, as is always the case with a crowd, they came bringing many expectations with them.

THE SPECTATORS

As people crowded into the arena, they came in excited anticipation of witnessing a spectacle. Further, it was not only a spectacle to amuse and divert the crowd but a religious ritual designed to affect and transform the witnesses. Even though the initial cause of arena shows might have been religious, it does not necessarily follow that the effects on the viewers were either uniformly religious or even uniform at all. It was expected that the process of watching people die in the arena would have an impact on the viewer. That much is clear. What becomes harder to understand from this temporal distance is what exactly would happen to the witnesses to such events. We may gather to watch sports events and be temporarily transformed by the crowd enthusiasm. We may be bonded closer together by the collective support we give to a football team. We may be horrified when a valued player is hurt when the accepted violence of our sports goes a bit awry. But we do not go to such displays to watch people die. The emperor Claudius was said to have had all defeated *retiarii* killed instead of sparing them because these gladiators fought without helmets. Thus the emperor and the crowd could watch them die with their faces exposed and follow the course of their death agony.[20] This was the central event in the amphitheater: watching people die.

There seems to have been an even greater significance in watching death in the arena in North Africa. With their long tradition of human sacrifice, North Africans adapted the Roman traditions and understood them in their own context of sacrifice.[21] When Christians died happily in the arena, it echoed the Carthaginian tradition of laughing children dying at the hand of the sacrificial priest.[22]

One of the surprising things about the structure of the ancient amphitheaters is that, large as they were, they offered a quite intimate experience for all the participants (whether in the arena or in the stands). Because the seating in the arena at Carthage is in ruins, one cannot tell exactly what the participants would have experienced while there. However, the amphitheater at El Djem, in Tunisia, dates from the third century and is still virtually intact. It was modeled on the one in Carthage but is slightly smaller. The seats rise rapidly, with little space between the seating and the arena floor. The acoustics are excellent; even viewers at the top would have heard what was going on in the center. The wealthier citizens seated in the first two tiers would have had a clear and immediate view of the subtleties and nuances of the action in the arena. The experience of watching someone die would have been vivid and involving.

Given the intimacy of the arena, it is not surprising to note that the crowd did not sit as simple voyeurs to the death throes of the condemned. They felt themselves participants, not only in the decision of granting life or death to gladiators but in the sacred ritual of achieving victory over death by conquering one's fear of it. If a gladiator appeared cowardly during the fight, as Seneca wrote, the crowd turned "from spectators . . . to adversaries."[23] A gladiator who tried to escape death while fighting would surely be condemned to it by his adversary, the crowd. Once defeated, a gladiator should embrace death bravely. If he betrayed his fear or reluctance to bare his throat to the sword, the crowd felt disgraced. They had participated in this ritual, and the gladiator was to mirror their bravery. Similarly, the crowd had expectations about the death of criminals. Criminals could (and should) die a cowards' death, and when the crowds' expectation of this was violated (as was frequently the case with the death of the martyrs), the crowd was often infuriated.[24] The Carthaginian martyrs violated these expectations by dying as bravely as the most highly trained gladiator.

Spectators might also participate in the collective violence of the arena more directly. Emperors at times arbitrarily ordered a spectator into the arena, or violence sometimes broke out in the stands. The audience came to interact with, not just to react to, the spectacles. Further, the Romans enjoyed the permeability of the boundary between spectator and participant.[25]

Knowing that people came to the arena to participate in a death ritual, to celebrate life by confronting death, does not really tell us the impact of the experience on the participants. Because we have no rituals offering this kind of confrontation, we have to rely completely on the descriptions in the texts for our understandings. The texts seem to offer three possible reactions or impacts on the audience: spectators may be affected positively or negatively, or they may be just bored.

In part, a positive effect on the audience was generated by the ritual and religious structure of the day's events. All the elements of the arena from the ceremonial meal to the parade focused people's attention on the sacral nature of the proceedings. This alone was to have a salubrious effect on the participants bonded together in a ritual designed to please the gods.

Beyond that general good, Romans believed that there was a positive character-building quality of the arena experience that would improve the individuals who participated. Watching people die was to stimulate bravery within the spectators themselves. Pliny the Younger said of the spectacles that they "inspired the audience to noble wounds and to despise death."[26] Livy said that there was "no better schooling against pain and death" than watching criminals in a death struggle in the arena.[27] Other authors attributed the greatness of Roman armies to the schooling they received while watching gladiators fight in the arena. People learned that they should "not be afraid of armed enemies in war or be frightened by wounds and blood."[28]

It may be that watching people who have overcome their fear of death offers a way for people to overcome their own fear. It may also be that as people watch violence and blood, they are desensitized to the experience. This is the argument that shapes the concern expressed about modern society that enjoys violent movies and television. Similar observations may be made at bullfights today: newcomers turn away at the sight of the bull's blood; experienced watchers cheer the skill of the matador. During Roman times, an inability to look at executions was considered childish, to be outgrown with experience. A Roman historian recalled that even Septimius Severus's son Caracalla, as a child, recoiled from arena violence: "If ever he saw condemned criminals pitted against wild beasts, he wept or turned away his eyes."[29] In an adult, it was considered moral weakness to turn away from the sight of

a criminal's blood.[30] Like many a young Roman, Caracalla would out-
grow his aversion to violence.

Even if one were desensitized to death as a spectacle, one still
watched for extraordinary deaths. Again, drawing from examples of
bullfights, once one can watch the death of the bull, one notices different ways to kill. This awareness of the spectrum of how people could
face death led to appreciation of, indeed, frequently awe of, how martyrs faced death in the arena. Criminals were not gladiators, trained to
hold their necks out unflinchingly to the blade. Yet, martyrs frequently
met death as bravely, and these brave deaths had a great impact on the
audience. Justin Martyr was converted to Christianity by watching
Christian martyrs die. He wrote, "I watched them stand fearless in the
face of death and of every other thing that was considered dreadful." [31]

For all the writers who saw positive effects in people who steeled
their nerves, watched blood flow in the arena, and learned how to die,
there were as many who saw negative results in. As might be expected,
many Christians thought it inappropriate and indeed harmful to attend
the shows in the amphitheater. The good effect witnessed by Justin did
not apply universally. Tertullian was particularly strong and articulate
in his belief that Christians should avoid the arena altogether. He begins his long tract "On Spectacles" by stressing that the shows in the
amphitheater were religious, mirroring the rituals that people experienced elsewhere in pagan culture. Therefore, according to Tertullian,
by simply being at the arena, Christians were participating in pagan
worship. Tertullian's example of a Christian woman who attended the
theater shows his view:

> For we have the case of that woman . . . who went to the theatre
> and returned home having a demon. So, when in the course of ex-
> orcism the unclean spirit was hard pressed with the accusation that
> he had dared to seize a woman who believed, he answered boldly:
> "I was fully justified in doing so, for I found her in my own do-
> main."[32]

For Tertullian, all the spectacles from theater to circus to amphitheater
were pagan rituals, and thus inhabited by the pagan gods, whom he
considered demons. This was the most obvious Christian objection to
the shows.

Tertullian expressed another objection to Christians' going to spectacles, and this one lies at the heart of early Christianity almost as
much as avoiding paganism. One of the central features of the Christian communities of the second century was that they perceived them-

selves as communities—people linked together by ties that were so strong that they replaced other ties of family and of state. The survival of these communities depended upon their recognition of themselves as a group to the exclusion of other groups. The experience of spectators in an arena, however, bonded the crowd together in a different community, a community of spectators. Tertullian showed his awareness of crowd behavior, of the way individual will subsided when the excitement of the crowd could sweep one away. He warned Christians not to attend the arena, even to witness Christian martyrdom, for they would not be able to avoid the exuberance of the cheering crowd: "What will you do when you are caught in that surging tide of wicked applause? . . . Will you therefore not shun the seats of Christ's enemies . . . and the very air that hangs over it and is polluted with sinful cries?"[33] When Christians in the stands participated in the activity of the audience, for Tertullian they participated in the collective sin that created martyrs in the arena.

The shows, and particularly those performed to honor the cult of the emperor, were designed to form a sense of community and loyalty to that community. This was the case on the day Perpetua was to die to celebrate the emperor's son's birthday.

This goal of bonding a community could obviously cut two ways: it was good if you wanted to be part of that community; bad if you did not. Tertullian understood this clearly, and wanted to avoid becoming a member of a pagan community. Some pagans, too, objected to the overwhelming sense of community (or crowd) that took place in the arena. The Stoic Seneca criticized the games along these lines: "To consort with the crowd is harmful. . . . But nothing is so damaging to good character as the habit of lounging at the games. . . . I come home more greedy, more ambitious, more voluptuous, even more cruel and more inhuman, because I have been among human beings."[34] For him, the collective emotions of the crowd diminished his striving for a higher good. Tertullian, too, continued his attack on the collective crowd mentality that dominated in the arena. His description of the crowd entering the circus might be familiar to anyone who attends sporting events: "Look at the populace, frenzied even as it comes to the show, already in violent commotion, blind, wildly excited over its wagers."[35]

Observers of the bad effects of the spectacles did not end their critique with observation of crowd behavior. Tertullian also noted the effect of the passionate involvement on individuals. He said, "No one ever approaches a pleasure such as this without passion; no one experiences this passion without its damaging effects. These very effects are incitements to passion."[36] Some pagans and Christians alike objected to the spectacles for this reason: instead of receiving an uplifting moral lesson of stoic indifference to pain and death, sometimes individuals were swept away by emotion. Many pagans (particularly the educated) and Christians believed that a moral life was achieved best by overcoming one's passions and relying on one's reason. Yet, at the spectacles, it seems to have frequently been one's passions that dominated. Tertullian articulated this principle succinctly when he wrote "There is no spectacle without violent agitation of the soul."[37] This view was shared by many pagan observers whose most frequent objection to gladiatorial games and other such spectacles was that they "engaged the emotions so much that it clouded . . . reason."[38] Such passions impeded the longing for the divine that characterized many pagan philosophies.

This abstract criticism of the emotions that became engaged in the arena is reaffirmed by the anecdotal evidence described in the sources. Prudentius (a Christian writer, so admittedly not supportive of the games) criticized the Vestal Virgins' reaction to the brutality in the arena. Their religious privilege ensured them excellent seats to witness the ritualized battles, but their reactions as described by Prudentius reflect more the personal, emotional impact of the spectacle than any religious ritualization:

> She to the amphitheater goes to view
> The bloody fights and human deaths, and looks
> With holy eyes on wounds received for bread.
> She sits there, fillet crowned, enjoying the shows.
> O soft and tender heart! At blows she stands,
> And when a victor stabs his rival's throat,
> She calls him her delight; the gentle maid
> Bids him by thumb turned up to strike his foe,
> So that no breath of life may in him stay,
> While from the thrust he gasps in agony.[39]

The virgin in Prudentius's account was stirred by the sight of blood to sexual lust, and this association permeated other writings. Tertullian censured women who "surrendered their bodies" to the arena gladiators,[40] but it was not only the Christians who accused witnesses to killing of having inappropriate passions stirred. Juvenal, the acerbic first-century satirist, accused Roman matrons of lusting for gladiators in the arena as they watched them spill blood. "The sword is what they dote on, these women," wrote Juvenal. Further, he warned men that the longed-for sons in their cradles resembled a favorite gladiator more than themselves.[41] Juvenal was simply one of many Roman writers who accused women of being stirred to lust by the passions in the arena.

Seneca, who shared the desire to have people learn a stoic disregard for death, nevertheless shared a dislike for those who were so carried away by their passion to see blood spilled in the arena that they had lost a rational balance. He particularly criticized those who stayed in the arena during the lunch break to watch the criminals killed. Seneca argued that there was no skill to be observed in killing criminals, so there was no moral lesson available there.[42] In fact, for Seneca, not only was there no moral lesson, there was actual harm to the individual in watching the killing of defenseless criminals: "Granted that, as a murderer, he deserved this punishment, what crime have you committed, poor fellow, that you should deserve to sit and see this show? . . . Do you not understand even this truth, that a bad example reacts on the agent?"[43] In the view of the Stoic, the audience was harmed by witnessing executions that did not display examples of noble deaths.

Romans recognized that there was a fine line between the benefits gained from learning to face (or watch) death in the arena and becoming too involved in the passions generated there. The young son of Septimius Severus who cried as a child at the executions grew to love the spectacles immoderately. According to one of his biographers, the emperor moved away from Rome to try to take his two sons away from the city and particularly the games:

> [The emperor] . . . saw that their enthusiasm for the shows was more disreputable than was proper for emperors. Their keenness and rivalry over the shows was always a source of contention and antagonism, distracting the senses of both brothers by adding fuel to their quarrels and making them into personal enemies.[44]

Septimius's removal of his sons from the games seems to have done nothing to improve their characters. They grew up cruel, quarrelsome, and violent. We can see, however, that the biographer and the emperor shared the perception that it was possible to be affected badly by the environment of the arena.

The most famous example of an individual who was swept into the passions of the arena is that of Augustine's friend Alypius. Alypius had followed a life of the mind, untempted by lust (unlike his friend Augustine), and had gone to Rome to study the law. In Rome, "he had been quite swept away, incredibly and with a most incredible passion, by the gladiatorial shows." At first, as a Stoic, he was opposed to the games which seemed to appeal to base emotion. One day, his friends forced him to join them. He said, "You can drag my body there, but don't imagine that you can make me turn my eyes or give my mind to the show. Though there, I shall not be there." So, foolishly, Alypius believed he could go to the show and avoid the emotional involvement. However, once there, the sound of the crowd's roar penetrated his ears.

> [H]e was overcome by curiosity and opened his eyes, feeling perfectly prepared to treat whatever he might see with scorn and to rise above it. But he then received in his soul a worse wound than that man, whom he had wanted to see, had received in his body. . . . He saw the blood and he gulped down savagery. Far from turning away, he fixed his eyes on it. Without knowing what was happening, he drank in madness, he was delighted with the guilty contest, drunk with the lust of blood. He was no longer the man who had come there but was one of the crowd to which he had come. . . .
> There is no more to be said. He looked, he shouted, he raved with excitement; he took away with him a madness which would goad him to come back again.[45]

Alypius's experience represented the worst that both pagans and Christians feared for the audience in the arena. He was taken from the life of the mind; he was swept into the collective bloodlust of the crowd, and he was addicted by the strong emotions he felt.

As powerful as the emotional reaction to the spectacle was, there nevertheless were people who in time became desensitized to the killing and reacted to the spectacles with boredom. This is perhaps not surprising, for part of the motivation behind the games was to desensitize people so they would no longer shirk from the sight of blood. As children learned to face the cruelty without flinching, some of their elders grew bored. Marcus Aurelius said, "The shows in the amphitheater and similar places grate upon you as an everlasting impression of the same sight and the constant repetition makes the spectacle uninteresting."[46] This reaction of boredom on the part of some of the audience led the patrons of the shows to ever-larger and more creative spectacles.

The morning hunting spectacles demonstrate this problem vividly. There were only a few ways to introduce novelty into the killing of animals. Exotic animals could be shown and paired. Seneca mentions a bear being chained to a bull, and Tertullian describes lions fighting tigers.[47] More often, emperors attempted to impress the audience with sheer numbers of animals. Cassius Dio says six hundred animals were killed during one of Augustus's presentations. At the inauguration of the Colosseum in Rome under Titus, nine thousand animals were killed. The largest number of animals in one *venatio* seems to have been the eleven thousand killed in honor of Trajan's triumph after his second Dacian war.[48] Of course, the irony here is that it is difficult to imagine anything more tedious than watching men with light arms killing eleven thousand animals.

The same boredom principle applied to the killing of humans in the arena. Gladiator shows increased the numbers of pairs of gladiators fighting, and tried to pair the weaponry in interesting ways. More specifically relevant to understanding the martyrdom of Perpetua, organizers of even criminal executions attempted to bring some novelty to the executions. Criminals sentenced to die in the arena were sent either "to the beasts" or "to the flames," so there was not a great deal of flexibility for novelty. When prisoners were sentenced to the beasts, the organizers could vary the animals to offer variety to the audience. Another way to vary executions was to combine them with theatrical presentations: the condemned were made to reenact mythological stories as they died.[49] In his history of the church written in the early fourth century, Eusebius described a persecution in which a governor made "a theatrical show of the blessed ones and displaying them to the crowds."[50] The goal was not simply execution or purely torture but entertainment as well.

Dressing the condemned in costumes of gods and goddesses sometimes enhanced the ritual significance of the execution, turning it into a sacrifice to benefit the community. Costuming, however, could serve more than one purpose. It also could offer variety in the presentation of the executions. Tertullian described such theatrical executions, which he probably observed in Carthage before he renounced attending spectacles.

> We once saw Attis, that god from Pessinus, castrated, and a man who was being burned alive played the role of Hercules. Then, too, at the gladiators' midday performance, in the midst of the cruelties of the entertainment, we laughed at Mercury testing the dead with his red-hot iron. We watched Jupiter's brother [Pluto], too, hammer in hand, dragging away the corpses of the gladiators.[51]

In this description, we can see that in addition to the re-creation of mythic themes (the self-castration of Attis), even the mundane acts of the arena, testing the presumed-dead gladiators and removing the bodies, were sometimes made theatrical by the addition of costuming. Tertullian articulately criticized the strange paradox of combining theater with death when he described the amphitheater as the place where "over human blood and the filth resulting from the tortures inflicted, your gods do their dancing and provide plots and stories for the guilty."[52]

The Roman author Martial described a paradoxical re-creation of the myth of Orpheus. The arena was decorated to resemble a sacred grove filled with animals where Orpheus was to play his lute and enchant the wild beasts. However, the conclusion was that the condemned dressed as Orpheus was torn apart by a bear.[53] This execution would have satisfied the need for novelty both in the presentation and in the surprise reversal of the myth by making Orpheus die.

These few examples can serve to indicate the degree of effort taken by the organizers of both the games and executions to keep the interest of the crowd engaged. They would not have gone to such lengths if boredom were not an issue. It must have been a fine line between the desired effect of desensitization to pain and death, and the thorough contempt of it reflected in a bored audience. It seems that the creative use of costume, setting, and the unexpected sometimes could re-create the surprise and power of watching executions. Plutarch captured this re-creation when he described an unusual execution of criminals sentenced to die by the flames:

> But there are some people, no different from little children, who see criminals in the arena dressed often in tunics of golden fabric with purple mantles, wearing crowns . . . and, struck with awe and astonishment, the spectators suppose that they [the criminals] are supremely happy, until the moment when, before their eyes, the criminals are stabbed and flogged, and that gaudy and sumptuous garb bursts into flames.[54]

In this case, the juxtaposition of the beautiful costuming that should mark a happy celebration with the sudden, brutal death jarred some viewers out of their apathy into seeing the spectacle as if they were once again "little children." Boredom was banished by surprise.

The audience who came to the arena on the edge of Carthage on that day in March must have included people who reflected all these views. Most probably came enjoying the community feeling as the crowd gathered to celebrate the birthday of the emperor's son. Some certainly recognized the important sacred aspect of the event where humans would be sacrificed in the traditional Carthaginian manner to bring benefit to the community at large. Some came to experience the Stoic disregard for pain, and others surely came drawn like Augustine's friend Alypius by the lure of blood. Without a doubt, some came hoping for something unexpected to occur, a novelty that would set these executions apart from the average.

It may have been the custom in Rome for educated Romans to skip the criminal executions that took place at the noon break, but in

Carthage such executions were in the tradition of human sacrifice, and as such were extremely popular. In fact, in the provinces the executions sometimes occupied the whole day, forming the main spectacle instead of an interlude.[55] This was likely the case in Carthage. There was no danger of people leaving the arena instead of watching Perpetua and her companions die.

In addition to these pagans with diverse motives, there were probably many Jews, for Carthage had a large Jewish community. If Eusebius's description of the martyrdom of Polycarp could apply to the Jewish community in Carthage, the "Jews as usual [joined]. . . in with more enthusiasm than anyone."[56] Finally, there were undoubtedly some Christians in attendance to watch the martyrdom of five members of their community. We know there was at least one who wrote the eyewitness account of the execution that followed Perpetua's personal account of her imprisonment, and this narrator wrote of other Christians in attendance. Many accounts of martyrdoms include descriptions of Christians who came to watch. The letter recounting the martyrdom of Montanus and Lucius about fifty years after the death of Perpetua described the composition of the crowd: "From everywhere there came a crowd of pagans with the Christians in a body, just as they had accompanied many other of God's witnesses."[57] In spite of Tertullian's exhortation to avoid the whole spectacle, it seems clear that by the middle of the third century, it was customary for Christians to come to the executions. Furthermore, the account of Montanus suggests that such attendance had been the practice for some time.

In the same way that pagans came to the games to learn bravery in the face of death, Christians came to learn how to die for the faith. The letter of Montanus emphasizes this goal of Christian attendance. The martyrs were an example to the Christians in the crowd by both their deeds and their words. The crowd could see "the martyrs of Christ witnessing to their glorious joy by the cheerfulness of their faces so that even without a word they would have drawn the rest to imitate their courage." However, the martyrs did not just let their actions speak. They addressed the crowd repeatedly in long speeches urging them to stay strong in their faith. Montanus summarized: "Hold your ground courageously, my brothers, and fight perseveringly. You have good models; let not the treachery of apostates lead you to ruin, but rather let our own endurance strengthen you for the crown."[58] Just as the small group of martyrs that went into the arena on that day in 203 may have been strengthened by watching previous martyrs die, there were surely many Christians there to watch God's power expressed in the witness in the arena of Perpetua and her companions.

THE MARTYRS

As the spectators came to the arena with a series of expectations, the martyrs, too, had a sense of what to expect when they were tested. They likely had watched people die in the arena before, so they knew the range of possibilities in how to face death. Their resolve had surely been strengthened by accounts of others who had faced death bravely. In his letter to the prisoners, Tertullian had reminded them of people who died bravely, although the strong tradition of Carthaginian sacrifice probably meant they hardly needed to be reminded. Tertullian argued that if all these pagans showed so little fear of death, why should Christians flinch from it?[59]

They also had before them stories of the bravery of earlier Christian martyrs. The twelve Scillitan martyrs had died bravely in Carthage only twenty years before, and members of the Christian community in Carthage must surely have read the Acts of these martyrs that have been preserved until now. Perpetua and her companions may well have reminded themselves of the last words of one of these martyrs: "Today we are martyrs in heaven. Thanks be to God!"[60]

Even Saturus's vision in prison linked the experience of these martyrs to those who had gone before. In his heavenly vision, he met "Jucundus, Saturninus, and Artaxius, who were burnt alive in the same persecution, together with Quintus who had actually died as a martyr in prison."[61] The confessors in prison awaiting their testing did not see themselves as alone. Saturus's vision makes perfectly plain that they were strengthened by the recollection of their predecessors. This community of the dead with the soon to be so continues to be a theme throughout the records of the martyrdoms. The person who recorded the Acts of the martyrs Marian and James, who died in North Africa in about A.D. 259, explicitly said he recorded the account so "the ordinary men who constituted God's people might be given strength in the test of their faith by the sufferings of those who had gone before."[62]

All these examples of Christian courage did not mean that fortitude was a foregone conclusion. There were many examples of Christians who lacked the strength to carry out their convictions. Eusebius, in his careful chronicle of the events of the early church, gave accounts of Christians who were not strong. In an early recorded account of martyrdoms, those in Lyons in A.D. 177, Eusebius tells of ten Christians who renounced Christ at almost the last moment, "causing us great distress and inexpressible grief, and damping the enthusiasm of those not yet arrested."[63] Just as the constancy of some martyrs spurred others on to bravery, the weakness of others spawned timidity. Even arriving in the arena was no guarantee that the will would not fail. The narrative of the martyrdom of Polycarp (which took place in about 155) told of a man named Quintas "whose courage failed him at the sight of the beasts."[64] Eusebius found this failure of Quintas so impressive that he elaborated on the simple statement in the original narrative: "[O]n seeing the beasts and the threatened torments to follow [Quintas] broke down completely and ended by throwing away his salvation."[65] It is no wonder that Tertullian wrote to the prisoners, trying to steel their resolve. The possibility of failure was always present.

Yet, the small group was consoled by more than recollection of previous martyrs. As shown in Felicity's dialogue during her childbirth, the confessors fully expected God to be immediately with them in the arena helping them through their ordeal. This divine presence and aid marks virtually all the martyr stories, and we can be sure this group hoped for such aid. They would have echoed Justin Martyr's famous phrase that challenged the Roman persecutors and revealed much about the Christian attitudes: "You indeed may be able to kill us, but you cannot harm us."[66]

The martyrs in prison had also been reassured by the visions of Perpetua and Saturus that had promised victory in the arena and eternal life to follow. Perpetua ended her diary with her final vision. This vision served as the culmination of her personal, spiritual quest, representing as it did an invitational dream marking her as belonging to God. Seemingly, she had nothing more to say in her own words. Yet, although her personal, interior quest seemed finished, she still had to fulfill the public culmination of her path to salvation. That would happen on the next day in the arena. At this point, Perpetua entrusted her diary to someone in the Christian community of Carthage and charged him with the task of recording the public elements of the passion of the martyrs. The eyewitness picks up the narrative on the day before the games: *"[W]e shall carry out the command or, indeed, the commission of the most saintly Perpetua, however unworthy I might be to add anything to this glorious story."*[67]

Tensions had mounted as the time for the martyrdom grew closer. The highly superstitious Carthaginians were uncertain how much magic these Christians possessed, and the military tribune in charge of the prison restricted their amenities severely for fear they might escape. As the scornful eyewitness wrote of the jailer's superstitions: *"[B]ecause on the information of certain very foolish people he became afraid that they would be spirited out of the prison by magical spells."* Perpetua dealt forthrightly with the tribune, saying:

Why can you not even allow us to refresh ourselves properly? For we are the most distinguished of the condemned prisoners, seeing that we belong to the emperor; we are to fight on his very birthday. Would it not be to your credit if we were brought forth on the day in a healthier condition?

The officer became disturbed and grew red. So it was that he gave the order that they were to be more humanely treated; and he allowed her brothers and other persons to visit, so that the prisoners could dine in their company.[68]

Perpetua cleverly and ironically appealed to his patriotism and loyalty to the emperor to gain some comforts on their last night. It is likely that among the visitors who came to dine with them was the one to whom she entrusted her diary along with the task to record their passion.

Just as gladiators had a ritual meal before their appearance in the arena, so did the condemned Christians. As the eyewitness to the execution wrote, *"The day before the games, they were eating their last dinner, which is usually called the 'free banquet,' though they didn't call it that but made it instead a love feast [agape]."*[69] Here we can directly see the process of ritual conversion by which an action sacred to the Romans, the ritual meal before the arena, was transformed into a Christian ritual, the last communion meal. The pagan sacrifice of traitors to the state for the emperor's birthday was being converted into a Christian sacrifice.

Not only family and supporters came to see the confessors on their last night; many others who were simply curious to see the condemned walked the short distance from Carthage to the prison near the amphitheater. The confessors used this gathering as an opportunity to spread the word of Christ. *"They spoke to the mob . . . [and] warned them of God's judgement, stressing the joy they would have in their suffering, and ridiculing the curiosity of those that came to see them."*[70] Saturus, the most reckless of the group, challenged and mocked the crowd of onlookers: *"Will not tomorrow be enough for you? Why are you so eager to see something that you dislike? Our friends today will be our enemies on the morrow. But take careful note of what we look like so that you will recognize us on the day."*[71] It must have been remarkable for the Carthaginians to see condemned criminals (including young women) behaving as bravely as the staunchest gladiator on the night of the ritual dinner. *"Everyone would depart from the prison in amazement, and many of them began to believe."*[72] In a world hungry for spiritual certainty, the strength of the young confessors was impressive.

As one might expect, the group talked about what might await them the next day. Saturninus seemed to see a contest in his martyrdom. He *"insisted that he wanted to be exposed to all the different beasts, that his crown might be all the more glorious."* Saturus revealed his fears: *"[H]e dreaded nothing more than a bear, and he counted on being killed by one bite of a leopard."*[73] Saturus's preferences were based on sound knowledge. The big cats stunned their victims with a single blow or effectively killed with one bite. Other animals dragged and ripped at their victims less efficiently.[74] The great early martyr Ignatius too hoped for a speedy kill by a lion: "All I pray is that I may find them swift."[75] If the women spoke of their preferences, it was not recorded.

The morning of the execution, the martyrs were led to the arena.[76] In Rome, condemned prisoners were transported to the arena in carts at the first hour of the morning.[77] In Carthage, the holding area seems to have been close enough to the arena that the prisoners were led on foot. Whether with carts or on foot, the parade from the prison to the arena had all the elements of the Roman *pompa*, and the description by the eyewitness strongly suggests that the Christians were consciously claiming this ritual as a Christian one marking this time and space as sacred to Christianity. The observer wrote that the martyrs *"marched from the prison to the amphitheater joyfully as if they were going to heaven."*[78] Already the reader is signaled to transform the arena from a pagan pit of horror into the doorway to heaven.

Perpetua marched with confidence. Showing the pride of a Roman matron rather than any shame of a criminal, the young woman faced the crowd bravely, *"putting down everyone's stare by her own intense gaze."*[79] In describing Felicity, the narrator recalled again the theme of the necessity to renounce maternity in order to achieve martyrdom, interpreting her state of mind in these terms: *"Felicity, glad that she had safely given birth so that now she could fight the beasts, going from one blood bath to another, from the midwife to the gladiator, ready to wash after childbirth in a second baptism."*[80]

Many accounts of martyrdoms emphasize the ritual procession of the martyrs as signaling a sacred event. For example, the description of the celebratory procession of the martyr Flavian, who also died in Carthage some years after Perpetua, reinforced the importance of the sacred march: "Even now the entire atmosphere of the march proclaimed a martyr about to reign with God."[81] So it is likely that in the course of the procession, the witnesses, both pagan and Christian, knew they were watching an act of ritual importance.

Costuming formed part of the ritualizing process. The account of the Passion of Perpetua focuses on costuming as a way of marking the distinction between whether the occasion of the execution was to be sacred to Rome or to Christ. As the party reached the gates of the amphitheater, the Romans wanted to force the men and women to dress in costumes of the priests of Saturn and the priestesses of Ceres. The choice of Saturn and Ceres, the favored deities of Carthage, was not accidental. Here, again, the North African tradition of human sacrifice played out in modified form in the arena.[82]

Perpetua, acting again as spokesperson for the group, refused to dress in such costumes. She said, *"We came to this of our own free will, that our freedom should not be violated. We agreed to pledge our lives provided that we would do no such thing. You agreed with us to do this."* This speech is particularly interesting, for it has Perpetua acknowledging her complicity in the sacrifice. The martyrs came to this point of their "own free will." In this, she emphasizes the Carthaginian belief that a sacrifice had to be voluntary to be effective. There seemed to be a bargain struck here: the emperor would have his willing sacrificial victims, and the Christians would have their martyrs. However, the costuming would have shifted the bargain too heavily toward pagan ritual. Clearly, for her the ritualizing acts were to claim this time and this space for Christianity, and she did not want any ambiguity on that score. She won her point: *"Even injustice recognized justice. The military tribune agreed. They were to be brought into the arena just as they were."*[83]

Perpetua's victory over the tribune seemed to confirm this procession as sacred to Christianity. As was appropriate to sacred processions, this one was accompanied by music, albeit Christian music: As she marched, *"Perpetua then began to sing a psalm: she was already treading on the head of the Egyptian."*[84] Her prophetic vision of victory in the arena was coming true.

As they marched, Perpetua was content to show her scorn for the crowd by meeting their stares directly. The men in the small group were more confrontational: *"Revocatus, Saturninus, and Saturus began to warn the onlooking mob. Then when they came within sight of Hilarianus, they suggested by their motions and gestures: 'You have condemned us, but God will condemn you' was what they were saying."* As the spectators were used to being involved in the events in the arena, they took collective affront at the arrogance of the martyrs: *"At this the crowds became enraged and demanded that they be scourged before a line of gladiators."* The martyrs were pleased that by this additional torture they could emulate the sufferings of Christ.[85]

Many of the stories of the martyrs show that the crowd was an active participant in the events. Eusebius was perhaps most vivid describing the crowd's behavior in Lyons: "[The martyrs] heroically endured whatever the surging crowd heaped on them, noisy abuse, blows, dragging along the ground, plundering, stoning, imprisonment,

and everything that an infuriated mob normally does to hated enemies."[86] Spectators who came to the arena to take an active role in the
proceedings were seldom disappointed. It is no wonder that Tertullian
warned Christians against becoming part of the crowd.

The first of the martyrs to face the beasts were the men. Saturus, Saturninus, and Revocatus were brought into the arena to be exposed to
the wild animals. Condemning criminals *ad bestias* is more complicated
than it might appear. Animals, no matter how vicious, are not predictable, so elaborate efforts had to be made to try to ensure that the animals would indeed attack the condemned. Animals were starved before
the spectacle, or sometimes some animals had been specially trained to
devour people.[87] One way to try to ensure that the animals focused on
the intended victim was to tie the criminal and the animal together. In
attempts to further control the killing, victims were frequently tied to
fixed platforms or moveable ones. Figure 5.2 shows a North African
mosaic depicting a condemned man being wheeled toward the big cat.
All these efforts required the presence of animal trainers (or con-
trollers) in the arena. These men used whips to drive the condemned to

Fig. 5.2 **Men condemned to the beasts** (mosaic). Villa di Dar Buc
Amméra Mosaic, Zliten, Libya. Photograph courtesy of the German
Archaeological Institute, Rome. Drawing by Alicia Nowicki.

the beasts or to steer the beasts to the appropriate victim. Tertullian not surprisingly spoke with scorn of a trainer who "pushe[d] another to the lion"[88] and subsequently claimed he was not a murderer.

All these preparations were never sufficient to ensure predictable behavior of the wild beasts. Accounts repeatedly relate incidents of animals that refused to attack their victims. The prototype was the tale of Androcles and the lion, but Christian stories are also full of such accounts. Saint Thecla was thrown to the lions but the cat lay down at her feet in awe of her virgin body instead of attacking her.[89] Saint Euphemia was thrown into a pit with wildcats that also refused to harm her.[90] Blandina was hung on a cross to serve as food for the wild beasts, but they all refused to touch her, so she was returned to the jail.[91] Although the Christians watching and recounting such incidents attributed the animals' behavior to divine intervention, in fact, having people killed by wild animals was always an uncertain business.

Saturninus got his wish by confronting two different animals. At the beginning, he and Revocatus were "matched with a leopard." The martyrs were not killed in this confrontation, but then they were to face other beasts. Saturninus was bound to a platform and attacked by a bear. Saturus was tied to a wild boar, but the boar ignored the martyr and dragged him along as it gored the gladiator who had tied the two together. (The gladiator died a few days later from his wound.) Saturus then joined the bound Saturninus awaiting attack by a bear. It seemed as though Saturus's worst fear of being mangled by a bear might come true. However, the animal refused to come out of the cage, so Saturus was brought back to a gate unhurt to wait while the women were brought into the arena for their ordeal.[92]

To please the crowd, the organizers of the games had planned something special for the women. The narrator wrote: *"For the young women, however, the Devil had prepared a mad heifer. This was an unusual animal, but it was chosen that their sex might be matched with that of the beast."*[93] It seems that executing women was somewhat unusual in Carthage, and they wanted to highlight this novelty by having them confronted by a female animal. Professor Brent Shaw has offered further interpretation of the symbolic reasons for the use of a heifer against the women. The release of a bull signaled sexual dishonor, usually revealing the woman as a known adulterer.[94] The choice of the beast and the change in the animal's expected gender would have added further dimensions to the symbol of sexual degradation. Shaw offers the suggestions that perhaps the cow suggested that the women were not sufficiently sexual to be guilty of adultery, or even implied a "different sort of sexuality" for the women.[95] With the brevity of the eyewitness's explanation, we will likely never be sure exactly what the organizers of the execution had in mind, or how the spectators viewed the symbolic character of the heifer.

Prisoners in the arena frequently were confined in some way to make them more accessible to the animals. When criminals were to be killed by a bull, they were first enmeshed in a net.[96] This was the case with Blandina, one of the martyrs at Lyons, who was enmeshed in a net and repeatedly tossed by a bull.[97] Consequently, Perpetua and Felicity were brought into the arena stripped naked except for the enmeshing nets. However, the crowd acted in an unexpected way when confronted with the young women: *"Even the crowd was horrified when they saw that one was a delicate young girl and the other was a woman fresh from childbirth with the milk still dripping from her breasts. And so they were brought back again and dressed in unbelted tunics."*[98]

This incident shows the power of the crowd to be actively involved in and influence the events even as they transpired in the arena. Why was the crowd so horrified to see the naked young women? It was probably not simply their nudity. A terracotta found in Africa portrays a naked woman exposed to the beasts,[99] so nudity was not unprecedented. Perhaps the crowd was offended by the echo of the procession to Isis in which priests dripped milk through a golden breast. Most likely, the crowd shared the belief expressed by both Perpetua and Felicity that motherhood was incompatible with martyrdom.

Perpetua's text shows the degree to which Christians were expected to break the social obligations of motherhood if they were to achieve martyrdom.[100] As significant as the social links that bound mothers, however, motherhood represented a physiological state that seems to have also been inconsistent with martyrdom. Mothers made milk, martyrs blood.

Classical understandings of physiology linked blood with milk. Fetuses were nourished in the womb on menstrual blood, and after childbirth, the mother's body transformed the blood into milk to nourish the infant.[101] Not only were the substances of blood and milk linked, but "menstruation, pregnancy, and lactation represented different stages of one process and . . . a woman could or should not occupy more than one stage at a time."[102] Thus, women who were lactating should not bleed and vice versa. These deep-seated beliefs certainly must have affected people's attitudes toward mothers' becoming martyrs. The crowd sent the women back to be clothed so they would not have to face the incongruity of lactating mothers shedding their blood in the arena.

Once the women were clothed in a way agreeable to the crowd, the wild heifer was released. Wild cows can be just as fierce and lethal as bulls. Sometimes modern matadors are paired with wild cows to add diversity and danger to the event. Cows charge differently and are said to charge with their eyes open (unlike bulls). The release of a wild heifer instead of a bull in no way would have lessened the threat to the two women. The narrator tells the details of the martyrs' confrontation with the animal and their survival of the attack:

> First the heifer tossed Perpetua and she fell on her back. Then sitting up she pulled the tunic that was ripped along the side so that it covered her thighs, thinking more of her modesty than of her pain. Next she asked for a pin to fasten her untidy hair: for it was not right that a martyr should die with her hair in disorder, lest she might seem to be mourning in her hour of triumph.
>
> Then she got up. And seeing that Felicity had been crushed to the ground, she went over to her, gave her her hand, and lifted her up. Then the two stood side by side.[103]

The careful details and the eyewitness's interpretation of them probably reveal more about the narrator's mind than about Perpetua's. It is hard to imagine that Perpetua would have been thinking of modesty or of the appropriate hairstyle for triumphal death while being tossed by a wild beast. However, these details show that the narrator wanted to make a point about Perpetua's perfection (in his eyes, modesty marked this) and about the joyful quality of a martyr's death. The women were probably dazed, waiting to see what would happen next.

The first charge of the heifer seemed to be enough for the crowd. *"The cruelty of the mob was by now appeased, and so they were called back through the Gate of Life."*[104] Their being summoned to this gate seemed to be an affirmation of the truth of Perpetua's vision in which she went to this gate after her victory over the Egyptian. It signaled that they had suffered enough from the beasts, and had emerged alive from this ordeal. However, unlike in Perpetua's vision, the reprieve at this gate did not mean they would be ultimately victorious in the contest. Instead, it marked only a delay in the execution, not a commutation of the sentence. At the gate, the martyrs were joined and comforted by their Christian supporters. Perpetua leaned on a catechumen named Rusticus, and at that point she awoke from an ecstatic trance: *"She awoke from a kind of sleep (so absorbed had she been in ecstasy in the Spirit) and she began to look about her."*[105]

The strength the martyrs showed during their ordeal was seen to be the result of divine presence in the arena. When Perpetua was tossed by the wild heifer that attacked her, she apparently did not feel any pain. When she recovered from her trance, she said: *"When are we going to be thrown to that heifer or whatever it is?"* When she was told that she had already faced the beast, *"she refused to believe it until she noticed the marks of her rough experience on her person and her dress."*[106] It is quite possible that Perpetua went into shock at the force of the contact. Victims of a car accident often do not recall the impact. Blandina, too, seemingly did not feel the impact of the bull tossing her about the arena: "Time after time the animal tossed her, but she was indifferent now to all that happened to her."[107] Whatever physiological explanation there might be to account for the martyrs' state, within the context of late Roman culture, the state of ecstasy indicated the presence of the Holy Spirit. Felicity had told the jailer that God would help them during the ordeal in the arena, and all believed that to have been so. The presence of the Spirit in the arena confirmed that the arena had been made sacred to Christianity during these proceedings.

While Perpetua stayed at the Gate of Life waiting for her final martyrdom, she took the opportunity to address the Christians, including her brother, who had gathered around her. She urged them to remain strong in their beliefs: *"You must all stand fast in the faith and love one another, and do not be weakened by what we have gone through."*[108] She need not have worried. All the evidence indicates that the examples of martyrdom served to strengthen witnesses rather than the reverse. This was especially true because the prevailing belief was that the Holy Spirit was present and helped the confessors endure their ordeal.[109]

As Perpetua and Felicity were comforted at the Gate of Life, the attention of the crowd turned again to Saturus, who had been waiting at another gate. He addressed a soldier, named Pudens: *"It is exactly as I foretold and predicted. So far not one animal has touched me. So now you may believe me with all your heart: I am going in there and I shall be finished off with one bite of the leopard."*[110] As we have repeatedly seen, prophecy in addition to ecstasy was a sign of the presence of the Holy Spirit, and Saturus saw in the events of the arena a fulfilling of his request that he die quickly by a leopard. As the contest was ending, a leopard was released and *"after one bite Saturus was so drenched with blood that as he came away the mob roared in witness to his second baptism: 'Well washed! Well washed!'"*[111]

It is hard to know exactly what the crowd had in mind when they shouted this phrase. *Saluum lotum* (well washed) was a greeting of good omen as people departed the Roman baths.[112] In this case the crowd may have been using the phrase ironically to mock the confessor who had so arrogantly mocked them as he approached the arena. Another possible explanation for the phrase is a strictly North African one. The phrase may have been a "ritual exclamation during a sacrifice to Saturn."[113] If this is so, then the crowd drew from Carthaginian tradition to see the events as a traditional human sacrifice to the old gods. (This is further suggested by the initial desire to costume the martyrs in clothing of Saturn and Ceres.) Whatever the call meant to the crowd, the eyewitness turned this mocking phrase into praise by identifying the blood of martyrdom with the washing in baptismal waters: *"For well washed indeed was one who had been bathed in this manner."*[114]

Figure 5.3 shows a graphic and horrible mosaic commemorating just such an event as Saturus's ordeal. Remarkably, Saturus did not die immediately from the attack by the leopard. He had further interaction with the guard, Pudens, asking him for a ring from the guard's finger. Then the martyr dipped the ring into his wound and returned it to the guard *"as a pledge and as a record of his bloodshed."*[115] Shortly afterward, Saturus fainted from loss of blood.

As we can see from this narrative, being sentenced to the beasts did not necessarily mean that the animals would kill the martyrs. It seems that almost inevitably with such sentences, the wounded were taken to the Gate of Death to be killed by gladiators. Saturus was *"thrown unconscious with the rest in the usual spot to have his throat cut."* However, the crowd once more got involved in the proceedings. They were not yet satiated with the sight of the martyrs. The eyewitness described the crowd's request, while condemning the crowd for its participation in the martyrdom of the faithful: *"The mob asked that their bodies be brought out into the open that their eyes might be the guilty witnesses of the sword that pierced their flesh."*

A platform was available for the executions so that the crowd would have a clear, unimpeded view of the deaths. They perhaps wanted to see if the martyrs would face their last moment as bravely as they had faced the ordeal of the beasts. They were not disappointed. The martyrs walked bravely to the platform without hesitation. They bid each other farewell in a ritual way, recalling Christian religious services: *"[K]issing one another they sealed their martyrdom with the ritual kiss of peace."* Just as, in the services, the kiss sealed the prayers, here the ritual kiss ended the ordeal that they believed bound the small group together in salvation.

Then they proceeded to the scaffold, led once again by the indomitable Saturus, who had recovered from his faint enough to be the first up the stairway to the platform. Just as in his dream, he led the way up the stairs to be followed by Perpetua. All the martyrs before Perpetua *"took the sword in silence."* The martyrs demonstrated their victory

Fig. 5.3 Leopard attacking man (mosaic).
Sollertiana Domus (Thrysdrus), Room xxiv. Photograph by Anna
Gonosová, courtesy of Corpus des Mosaïques de Tunisie, III, 1, and Dr.
Margaret Alexander. Drawing by Alicia Nowicki.

over death in the Roman way, unflinchingly greeting their death.
Seneca, the Stoic, expressed the Roman sentiment: "I have been freed
from fear; henceforth I shall not hesitate to bare my neck on the scaffold."[116] The martyrs did not hesitate to bare their necks. In their confidence of an expected afterlife, they conquered their fear of death.

The last martyr to die was Perpetua. She, too, bravely exposed her
neck, but her death was not so quick. As the witness explained, she *"had
yet to taste more pain."* The gladiator who was charged with executing

the martyrs was inexperienced. When he turned his blade to Perpetua, he misstruck and hit her bone (most likely the collarbone) and the martyr screamed in pain. Yet, this did not give her a fear of death or of the blade. Perpetua *"took the trembling hand of the young gladiator and guided it to her throat."* In the respected tradition of Carthaginian women from Dido on who took their own lives in a cause greater than their own, Perpetua killed herself in the arena. The eyewitness, a Carthaginian himself, praised the act of sacrificial suicide: *"It was as though so great a woman, feared as she was by the unclean spirit, could not be dispatched unless she herself were willing."*[117]

Here in the arena on the outskirts of Carthage a number of great forces and powerful ideas came together and were expressed by the death of the small group of believers and witnessed by the crowds. The power of Rome in the person of the emperor was demonstrating the identity of a state larger than the many peoples that inhabited it. The confessors who refused to sacrifice to this symbolic principle became the martyrs who were sacrificed to ensure the health and continuity of imperial power. The long history of Carthage praised the ideal of suicide and sacrifice of individuals to ensure the well-being of the city. The crowd who watched the blood spilled in the arena drew from this tradition. They no longer publicly sacrificed children to Saturn, yet the deaths of the young people in the arena satisfied the need to keep chaos away by the sacrifice of some of the living.

Yet, within these old worlds of Carthage and Rome, new spiritual aspirations and new social connections had appeared. The martyrs died for their own longings for a different world. In this they shared the spiritual longings of many of the spectators, who hoped for a closer connection between the human and divine worlds. The sacrifice of the martyrs was not simply personal, however. Their deaths were to help bind the nascent new communities that would ultimately form a new structure in the ruins of Rome. Many of the acts of the martyrs, from Perpetua's recording her dreams and talking to the people gathered at the Gate of Life to Saturus's giving a bloodied ring to the guard, were designed to create memories that would strengthen the new community and give it life to continue. Their sacrifice was not for the health of the emperor's son; it was for the health of the Christian communities. The blood of these martyrs would be the seed to grow new converts, and the subsequent history of Christianity in Carthage proved this to be true. The eyewitness concluded his narrative with a plea for these communities to remember and learn from the sacrifice of the martyrs:

[A]ny man who exalts, honors, and worships his glory should read for the consolation of the Church these new deeds of heroism which are no less significant than the tales of old. For these new manifestations of virtue will bear witness to one and the same Spirit who still operates, and to God the Father almighty, to his Son Jesus Christ our Lord, to whom is splendor and immeasurable power for all the ages. Amen.[118]

six

Aftermath

It is the nature of accounts of martyrs that they close with finality. The stories inevitably end with the death into eternal life of the martyrs. For the recorder of these events, nothing more needed to be said, indeed could be said. Of course, in this world things do not end so definitively. Life does go on, but it proceeds shaped in some way by the events that have taken place. Although it is impossible (even undesirable) in this short space to give a full history of the development of the Christian communities in Roman North Africa, I nevertheless want to point to some of the developments that occurred and perhaps were shaped by the martyrdom of the small group in Carthage. In this way, I will avoid the easier path of closing with the death of the martyr in favor of the more realistic one of trying to show how life does go on.

In the course of this discussion, I shall show how many of the ideas that had shaped Perpetua's experience were changed or ended. The future lay with a newly constituted Christian community that embodied the whole empire. Perpetua's experience was a microcosm of the kind of intellectual and emotional synthesis that would occur as the empire itself became Christian. Furthermore, current experiences quickly become memories to be integrated into and accommodated to new circumstances. Therefore, I will also trace the fortunes of the *memory* of Perpetua, which far outlasted the moment of her martyrdom.

ROME AND CARTHAGE

Perpetua and her companions were sacrificed on the occasion of Septimius Severus's son Geta's birthday. Such sacrifices were to guarantee the health and prosperity of the man and the dynasty. In this case, it was not to be efficacious. The childhood of Septimius's two sons, Caracalla and Geta, had been marked by a rivalry that was beyond the norm. Roman historians who described the reign of Septimius all remarked on the animosity between the brothers. Herodian sums up the childhood: "As brothers they were also mutually antagonistic; this dated back to their rivalry as children when they quarrelled over quail fights or meetings in the cock-pit or wrestling bouts with each other. . . . [A]nything one liked, the other hated."[1] Septimius knew that their animosity was excessive and dangerous. He repeatedly reminded them of historical examples in which the enmity between royal brothers ended in disaster. He showed them the wealth they would inherit, and warned them that all would be lost in a fratricidal civil war. Herodian, the emperor's biographer, described all these efforts and summarized the futility of Septimius's efforts: "They simply would not listen and grew worse as they threw off all restraint."[2]

In 208 the aging emperor (already more than sixty and suffering badly from gout) decided to go to war in Britain.[3] Herodian tells us that part of the emperor's motivation for engaging in this campaign was to attempt to reconcile his sons,[4] although these efforts did not involve having the sons work together. Septimius left his younger son, Geta, in southern Britain to handle administrative tasks, and took Caracalla with him to the battlefield.[5] Dio Cassius tells us that the emperor particularly did not trust his violent elder son, who was plotting to kill his younger brother, and even to try to kill his father if possible. Caracalla seems to have intended to kill his father in front of the army by approaching him from the rear with drawn sword. He was prevented by the warning shouts of the witnesses.[6]

Septimius continued his efforts to reconcile his sons to joint rule. In 209, while on campaign, he promoted Geta to the rank of Augustus, equal to his brother. Septimius must have known that he had not much longer to live and was doing all he could to persuade his sons to share the empire.[7] Septimius died of his illnesses in York, England, in 211. On his deathbed, he gave his sons final advice: "Be harmonious [with each other], enrich the soldiers, and scorn all other men."[8] It was good advice, but seemingly no one doubted that the young emperors's mutual animosity would prevent them from sharing rule.

The young men ended their British campaign and returned to Rome (carefully avoiding each other), each attempting to conspire to kill the other. Caracalla finally achieved his purpose by a ruse that was described by Dio Cassius. Unable to reach his brother, who was well guarded, Caracalla persuaded his mother to summon both sons to her apartment unattended so they could reconcile. As Geta saw centurions enter, who had been summoned by Caracalla, he ran to his mother and clung to her, pleading that she save him. "And so she, tricked in this way, saw her son perishing in most impious fashion in her arms, and received him at his death into the very womb, as it were, whence he had been born; for she was all covered with his blood."[9] She was not even able to mourn her younger son for fear of the wrath of the elder.[10] Caracalla embarked on a systematic attempt to eradicate even the memory of his younger brother. Geta's name was erased from all inscriptions, and portraits were defaced to remove the boy from the family groupings. Figure 6.1 shows Septimius Severus with his wife and two sons. The face of Geta (who was said to have resembled his father) is erased.

Dreams and omens, which were so central in Perpetua's and Septimius's experiences, continued to give meaning to historians of the next generation. The Romans who recorded this fratricide recalled omens that foretold Geta's death. One remembered that at the birth of Geta, someone announced that a purple egg had been laid by a palace hen.

Fig. 6.1 Julia Domna; Septimius Severus; *below right,* **Caracalla;** *below left,* **the erased figure of Geta** (painted wood panel). Courtesy Antikensammlung, Staaliche Museen zu Berlin, Preussischer Kulturbesitz. Photograph by Ingrid Geske-Heiden.

The toddler Caracalla seized the egg and broke it, whereupon Julia said jokingly, "Accursed fratricide, you have killed your brother." In another instance, someone recalled that at the sacrificial celebration of the birthday of the infant Geta, the sacrificial victim was killed by a boy named Antoninus (another name for Caracalla).[11]

It was always the habit of superstitious Romans to look backward for omens, for patterns that gave order to events. In the Roman fashion, we could recall the children taken from the breasts of Perpetua and Felicity before their martyrdom in blood on the birthday of Geta and see an ironic parallel in the young emperor slain on his mother's breast. However, that small, provincial event in North Africa did not make it to the attention of the Roman historians recounting the great events of Severan rule, so they could not see in it a portent of things to come. However, whatever else the martyrdom of the small group achieved for Rome, the health and well-being of Caesar Geta was not one of the benefits.

As we look closely at events like a martyrdom, in the Christian tradition we prefer to look for justice for the villains of the actions. Such perhaps might be the case with the death of Caesar Geta and the decline of the fortunes of the Severii. But, of course, such justice is not necessarily forthcoming. Perhaps the most visible "villain" of the events in Carthage was the procurator, Hilarianus, who presided so vigorously over the trial of the group. After the martyrdom, his career progressed most satisfactorily for a Roman. He rose to senatorial rank and his son, Publius Aelius Apollonios, had a successful military career and produced a son duly named after his grandfather, Publius Aelius Hiliarianus.[12] The procurator's role in presiding over the execution seems to have produced no observable ill effect.

After the murder of his brother, Caracalla ruled for only five years. He spent most of that time with the army, following that portion of his father's advice. In his religious inclinations, he seems to have followed his father's interests in the North African cults. According to one of his biographers, "He brought the cult of Isis to Rome and built magnificent temples to this goddess everywhere, celebrating her rites with even greater reverence than they had ever been celebrated before."[13] Caracalla did not introduce the cult of Isis to Rome, but he could well have increased its importance, and the elaborate rituals Apuleius described as taking place in Carthage would have been repeated in Rome.

Caracalla seemingly ignored Christians but nevertheless did make one important ruling that was to have a strong, albeit unforeseen, consequence on Christian persecutions. As Dio Cassius says almost in passing for such a consequential act, "he made all the people in his empire Roman citizens."[14] Scholars have pointed out that the actual ramifications of such a decree were really rather slight. In his detailed work on religion and authority in Roman Carthage, Professor J. B. Rives, however, has convincingly shown that this decree had serious implications for the religious identity of Rome and for the young Christian communities.

As we have seen, the spatial nature of Roman religion was ill suited to an empire with loyalties that were divided into localities and local deities. Caracalla's declaration of universal citizenship created one people of the diversity of the empire, and imperial policy changed to try to impose a universal religion to reflect that universality.[15] The worship of the emperor had always been the logical cult to serve as a focus of the collective empire, and Caracalla's new policy gave added impetus to the cult.

The most immediate result of this policy for the Christian communities of Carthage and elsewhere in the empire was that the nature of the persecutions dramatically changed. Before Caracalla's edict, we have seen that persecutions were sporadic and dependent upon the inclinations of local magistrates to pursue them. Individuals were charged mostly with stubbornly coming to the attention of the authorities. Perpetua and her companions died under this policy. From the mid third century until the end of the persecutions in the beginning of the fourth century, things changed. The emperor Decius in 250 issued an edict requiring all citizens to offer sacrifice to the gods. As Rives observed, "His motive seems to have been a desire to join together, by force if necessary, all the inhabitants of the empire in one religious act."[16] After such a sacrifice, the individual would receive a document that contained a declaration of essentially religious conformity: "I have always and without interruption sacrificed to the gods, and now in your presence in accordance with the edict's decree I have poured a libation, and sacrificed and partaken of the sacred victims."[17] This testimony bound the individual to obedience to the Roman cult and joined him or her to the citizenship that Caracalla had decreed but had not enforced.

These decrees of uniform cult practice fell hard on the Christian communities. Just as on a small scale Perpetua and her few companions could not perform the sacrifice, so large groups of martyrs were created under the persecutions of Decius (circa 250) and Diocletian (303–304). This was the last attempt by the emperors to force religious uniformity by trying to impose an imperial cult. Religious uniformity came to the Roman empire only in the middle of the fourth century, when Christianity became the official religion of Rome. However, before that time many more martyrs were created.

Of course it is certain that Caracalla had no intention of creating either a universal religion or new armies of Christian martyrs when he decreed universal citizenship. As his historian had noted, he was looking only for more sources of revenues to try to ensure his army's loyalty. But there was nothing that would preserve the rule of this cruel young man. He was murdered in 217.

Carthage continued to prosper under the emperors of the Severan dynasty; they continued to exploit the economic importance of their homeland. A Roman historian writing a generation after the death of Perpetua described the leisurely pursuits of the young men of Carthage: "They had been brought up in absolutely peaceful conditions, forever whiling away their time in festivals and easy living, completely divorced from weapons and instruments of war."[18] These peaceful conditions left the Carthaginians unprepared for changed political circumstances that they would confront at the end of the Severan dynasty with the death of Septimius's grand-nephew, Alexander, in A.D. 235.

Under the next emperor, Maximinus, the North Africans did not fare so well. We have seen how much discretion the procurators of the provinces had in determining provincial policy, and according to Herodian, Maximinus's procurator wanted to come to the emperor's attention by vigorously exacting confiscations and taxation in Carthage and the vicinity. A rebellion broke out in North Africa and a North African, the eighty-year-old Gordian, was proclaimed emperor. Gordian was not from Carthage but from Thysdrus, near the eastern port city of Hadrumentum. A few years before the rebellion, a giant amphitheater was begun in Thysdrus (in modern El Djem), and it is possible that as a leading citizen of that region, Gordian was responsible for financing its construction.[19] Gordian's rebellion was short-lived. The newly proclaimed emperor went to Carthage to make that the center of his power, but as Herodian had told us, the inhabitants of third-century Carthage were ill equipped to wage war. Within a year, emperor Gordian's son (Gordian II) was dead, and Gordian himself had committed suicide in despair. His death added one more suicide to the Carthaginians' memory of sacrificial suicides that had marked the turning points of their history. The leading citizens of Carthage were killed and the countryside was plundered.[20]

As if political difficulties were not enough, plague raged through North Africa between 252 and 254. In this time of disasters, Orosius tells us that the North Africans turned to their traditional remedy, human sacrifice: "They sacrificed men as victims, and they brought to their altars adolescents who had not reached puberty as a way of seeking the enemy's mercy."[21]

Human sacrifice notwithstanding, the plague took its toll. In addition, the unsuccessful attempt to replace the powerful Severan dynasty with another that might lead North Africa to further power and prosperity cost the province dearly. The production in parts of the country was so damaged that they could no longer meet the increasing tax burdens. Public building erected by private donors that had so marked the prosperous second century came to a virtual halt in the mid third. It is possible that even the great amphitheater at El Djem was never completed or used.[22] Perhaps that more than any other indicator marks the decline of the fortunes and spirit of Roman North Africa. The superstitious Romans had always linked their destiny with their ability to exert their power in the arenas. After the disaster of the usurper emperor Gordian, the region of Thysdrus had neither the actual nor symbolic power to flaunt in the public arena.

Carthage continued to be a wealthy, important city of the empire until its fall to the Vandals in A.D. 439. Its amphitheater continued to be a focus for the community's activities,[23] although the games were not as lavish as during its high point. However, the real influence of Carthage from the third century on was not to be political. Instead, from that time, the people of Carthage who are remembered and who made a significant impact on the course of Western culture were members of the Christian community of that city. The political fortunes of the city hardly outlasted the victorious exertion of that power with the execution of Perpetua and her companions in the public arena. The strength of the Christian community that was seen so clearly in the small group of martyrs came to the forefront in the next generation.

THE CHRISTIAN COMMUNITY

When Saturus had his vision on the eve of his martyrdom, one of his central concerns was for peace and harmony within the Christian community. It turns out that he was quite right to be concerned. As presented in accounts of passions of martyrs, the practice of Christianity was clear and pure. When Perpetua said, "I am a Christian," and was prepared to die for that statement, it offered a vision of Christianity that was unencumbered by the many choices that faced Christians daily. As people tried to live Christian lives in more peaceful times, what frequently emerged was the human inclination to disagree.

Under Caracalla's rule, his cruelty was not directed against Christians. The Christian communities of Carthage and elsewhere were left to retreat from the intensity of times of persecution, which called for heroic individual effort. The communities grew rapidly by new converts. Many of these new converts no doubt were inspired by the examples of the martyrs, but peaceful times always favor membership by people more moderate than those exemplified by the martyrs.[24] Yet, the very success of these growing communities with their increasingly diverse congregations led to disagreement within them.

Some Christians, like the eloquent and influential Tertullian, longed for the passion of the age of the martyrs that seemed to subside only a few years after the persecutions had ceased. Not only did there seem to be fewer people willing to die for the faith, the Holy Spirit that people believed gave the gift of strength to the martyrs seemed to be more distant from the congregations. No longer did the spirit of prophecy dominate the church services. Studies of glossolalia show that speaking in tongues subsides in a few years, and it is certain that the Spirit seemed no longer so visibly present during worship services. In fact, Origen, in the early third century, complained that services were being conducted in an atmosphere of "gossip and triviality."[25]

Many orthodox Christians did not mind this change. In fact, some church leaders welcomed authority over inspiration as a way to keep peace and unanimity in the congregations. Others longed for the intensity of the early years. An inevitable issue arises as a religious sect becomes successful: how to maintain the vigor that attracted converts and at the same time attract "less heroic" members.[26] In most religions, movements periodically arise that reinvigorate the spirit of the sect, and this was true in the early Christian centuries.

In the middle of the second century, even before the death of Perpetua, a movement known as the New Prophecy arose in a village in Phrygia (modern Turkey) that tried to revitalize the Christian congregations.[27] This movement (known after the fourth century as Montanism) was founded by Montanus, a recent convert to Christianity who had ecstatic experiences and spoke prophesies. He attracted two women, Priscilla and Maximilla, who left their husbands and experienced gifts of ecstasy and prophecy. The writings that recorded their prophecies spread and were valued among their followers.

The New Prophecy emphasized a belief in the continuing presence of the Holy Spirit visible in the prophetic words of Christians. It also advocated the rigor of a besieged church, urging fasts and preparation for martyrdom. The ideas spread to North Africa, and after 207 Tertullian's works show a strong resemblance to the movement, but probably less because he was converted than because he shared the sensibilities of the three prophets.[28] Tertullian quoted their prophecies[29] as he continued to urge communities not to depart from the rigor and passion of the early ages. If he increasingly moved to extremes in advocating no compromise with the pagan world,[30] it was likely as much from his frustration with the activities of the Christian community of Carthage as from his contact with the prophecies of Montanism.

One of the works from Tertullian's Montanist period, "The Chaplet," can illustrate his dilemma and the mood of Carthaginian Christians. In 211, at the death of Septimius Severus, his two sons followed the tradition of giving each soldier in the army a gift of money. When the gift was distributed, it was traditional for each soldier to wear a crown of laurel. One North African soldier refused to wear the crown, arguing that it was inconsistent with his Christian beliefs. He was arrested and prepared himself for martyrdom.[31] Tertullian used the incident to argue not so much against the pagans as against Christians who were willing to compromise with the pagan world in such apparently small things as apparel. He accused them of talking "like pagans" as they said of the soldier: "Why does he have to make so much trouble for the rest of us Christians over the trifling matter of dress? Why must he be so inconsiderate and rash and act as if he were anxious to die? Is he the only brave man, the only Christian among all his fellow soldiers?"[32]

Indeed, Tertullian wanted no Christian to serve in the army,[33] unrealistically forbidding even that compromise with Rome. He further poignantly complained about Christians who reject the hallmarks of his Christianity, martyrdom and prophecy (which by 211 he identified as the New Prophecy of the Montanists). He said, "Yes, I should not be surprised if such people were not figuring out how they could abolish martyrdom in the same way as they rejected the prophecies of the Holy Spirit."[34]

There can be no doubt that Tertullian was right that some, probably most, Christians would have happily seen the end of the persecutions. Christian thinkers like Clement of Alexandria argued that Christians need not die for their faith; instead their faith should lead them daily to live a Christian life.[35] Tertullian, however, longed for the time when he and others could see the working of the Paraclete, "the source of all endurance,"[36] in the testing of Christians in the arena. This dichotomy did not end with the death of Tertullian or with the condemnation of the Montanists but instead continued to be a struggle in North Africa between what we might call the rigorists and the realists.

The account of the Passion of Perpetua did not escape the controversy between orthodox and Montanists. There were many elements in the account that resembled Montanist beliefs. The text was about martyrdom, and the power the Spirit gave the confessors. In Saturus's dream, bishops appealed to the martyrs for guidance,[37] thus symbolically placing martyrs above the established church hierarchy. In Perpetua's dreams, she had the power to pray for her dead brother's welfare. Furthermore, the text praised prophecy and visionary dreams as gifts from the Spirit. The eyewitness to the passion framed his account with biblical citations that echoed sentiments of the New Prophecy: "In the last days, . . . I will pour my Spirit and the young men shall see visions and the old men shall dream dreams."[38]

Do these similarities mean that Perpetua or the eyewitness were Montanists? The church in Carthage had not yet split into such clear distinctions.[39] The Christian communities shared the strong belief in prophecy, and surely Christians approaching martyrdom would imagine that the last days of the world had arrived.[40] However, even if the text and the martyrs were not produced by a group of followers of the New Prophecy, nevertheless their visions seem to have influenced subsequent Montanists. For example, a fourth-century observer, Epiphanius, described a Montanist ritual in which participants were given bread and cheese in a ritual meal.[41] Douglas Powell perceptively suggests that because there were no references to Montanist use of cheese in rituals before 203, they may have been influenced by the dream of Perpetua in which she is given milk in the garden.[42] Perpetua's dreams may have become memories to shape the rituals of the unorthodox.

That both the orthodox and the heterodox could value the same text is testimony to the fact that the religious sensibilities of the two groups were very similar in 203. They diverged more strongly during the years when peace allowed the church to flourish and Christians to relax their vigilance a bit. One can almost feel compassion for Tertullian, that principled and rigid man who was in his element when he was urging confessors to stand firm and prepare for the ultimate test. As the world changed, instead of changing with it, Tertullian became more extreme and more angry as he tried to browbeat the Carthaginian Christians into returning to a purer form of faith that he believed was the only vehicle for the workings of the Holy Spirit. Tertullian lived to be about eighty-five years old and died circa 240. His search for a pure Christian community never abated, and toward the end of his life, he may have founded his own sect, the Tertullianists, to be more rigorous than the Montanists.[43] He certainly died without ever having compromised his rigorous stand on the incompatibility of the church with the world.

In the third century, most of the Christian communities moved away from Tertullian's position, and authority moved to leaders with a different view.[44] But the divisions remained. Saturus's vision warning against animosity within the church proved prophetic, and in North

Africa the principal and most disruptive division was essentially between those who wanted a pure church of martyrs and those who had
more patience with Christians whose faith was stronger than their
courage.

The tension between these two groups would not surface until the
church again faced persecution. In the meantime, during the peace
from 203 to 250, the church experienced remarkable expansion. The
general lack of optimism in North Africa after the political fortunes of
the region fell in the unsuccessful revolt by Gordian must have contributed to people's turning to a group that offered hope. One such
convert was Cyprian, a wealthy, highly educated member of Carthage's
elite who could have looked forward to continuing as a leader of the
community. Instead, after reading the passion in Tertullian's works, and
wrestling with his own despair, Cyprian converted to Christianity. He
showed a continuation of the strong longing for the divine that so
shaped the experience of Perpetua and her contemporaries. Writing
after his baptism, Cyprian described the emptiness of pagan life in
everything from the spectacles in the arena and theater to public life in
the forum to private family life.[45] Despairing of finding satisfaction in
these things, Cyprian discovered peace and solace in Christian teachings: "[T]here is one peaceful and trustworthy tranquility, one solid and
firm security. . . . There can be no want, when once the celestial food
has filled the breast."[46] Christianity was the only institution in the troubled third century that could offer this kind of certainty and peace.
Many people converted; most did not have the kind of fortitude that
Cyprian would eventually show.

Many of the new converts were, like Cyprian, wealthy. The church
became rich, and although building for secular purposes waned in the
third century, church building expanded. (See the Christian buildings
on the outskirts of the old Roman grid shown in figure 2.2.) The basilica in Carthage that is said to have been Cyprian's lies on the outskirts
of the old city on a beautiful bluff overlooking the sea. This was prime
real estate, worthy of a church growing in membership and power. We
may be sure that the beauty of the location would not have been lost on
Cyprian, who wrote so movingly about the benefits of visual aesthetics:
"We delight our eyes by the pleasing view, and likewise instruct the
soul by what we hear and nourish it by what we see."[47] Upper-class
Carthaginians used to beauty and pleasure brought such values into
Christian worship.

With more converts and greater wealth, the church grew in hierarchy. By 245, North Africa had ninety bishops,[48] and beneath each was
a well-developed hierarchy of priests, deacons, and lectors. These

church leaders were no longer elders leading a flock of the faithful but professionals who received stipends.[49]

When Cyprian was elected bishop in 248 (only two years after his conversion), he brought to the job a clear sense of hierarchy and organization based on his experience as an upper-class Roman. He described the role of bishop in terms reminiscent of a provincial governor, and could command a large staff very much like that of the governor.[50] This new church organization was made up of many converts searching for meaning and peace, a group that would be severely tested when new persecutions broke out.

In 250, the emperor Decius began another persecution, and many in the Carthaginian community who had ignored Tertullian's warnings were not prepared for new "last days." It was not like the previous ones, which were highly arbitrary in their impact. This persecution was designed to bring all the citizens of the empire into conformity with a single rite; all citizens were supposed to perform a ritual sacrifice and prove it by obtaining a certificate testifying to the act. There were examples of heroic resistance among some Christians who would not perform the ritual sacrifice even though they were arrested and tortured.[51] But these were by far in the minority.

On the day set for the ritual sacrifice, Christians were summoned to the forum. Some—like the martyr Pionius with his companions—were brought in chains into the forum near the top of the Byrsa hill, watched by crowds of "Greeks, Jews, and women" on the upper stories of the surrounding buildings. [52] Non-Christians gathered to see the martyrdom, but as Pionius spoke eloquently, they were silenced.[53] Finally, he was martyred by burning.[54]

However, some Christians did not even wait to be arrested. The temple verger questioning Pionius reminded the confessor that many Christians came to sacrifice of their own accord, with no pressure.[55] This was not mere rhetoric; so many rushed to the marketplace in the forum on top of the Byrsa hill that all could not be accommodated in one day. By evening, the magistrates had to delay the sacrifices and cause the Christians to come back.[56] Other Christians avoided performing the ritual by bribing others to sacrifice and thus obtain the required certificate in their name.[57] Many wealthy Christians were motivated not by fear of imprisonment but by fear of confiscation of property.[58] This large-scale defection of Christians posed a much greater threat to the church than the persecutions that had taken a few lives.

Cyprian had left Carthage during the persecution to avoid the necessity of sacrificing (an act for which he was criticized by many).

When he returned, he found the Christian community in disarray. It is to his enduring credit that he was able to bring it together again. The principal problem was what to do with the people who had lapsed in this time of trial. Had Cyprian been of the rigid cast of a Tertullian, the church might not have recovered.

Cyprian tempered his rigor with compassion, saying that the lapsed could be readmitted to the Christian communities after a period of penance.[59] Furthermore, Cyprian placed the control of the readmittance of lapsed Christians in the hands of the bishops and priests, who would be guided by decisions made in church council. By this step, Cyprian undercut the spiritual power of the confessors, who were forgiving their fallen friends on the basis of the power they had acquired by their courage in the face of persecution.[60] The confessors were acting completely consistently with precedent and the power that had previously been accorded martyrs. It was this power that had allowed Perpetua to dream she could heal her dead brother and Saturus to envision curing dissenting congregations. The fifty years that had passed, however, had changed the circumstances. If the church was to be saved, it would be saved by the hierarchy, not by charismatic confessors.

In this crisis of the faith, Cyprian saw clearly that the salvation of the Christian communities lay in their unity. In this he followed the early Christian congregations who valued their peace and harmony, and dreaded any disagreements that would break apart the fragile societies. In his famous tract "The Unity of the Catholic Church," Cyprian warned that the dissent within Christian communities was more threatening than persecution from without.[61] His vision of the Christian community was that it was where "those of one mind dwell; they persevere in concord and simplicity." Christians would be ". . . harmonious in affection, clinging to one another faithfully in the bonds of unanimity."[62] This unanimity would be achieved under the guidance of a bishop and with the pastoral care for Christians who might not measure up to the strength of the early martyrs.

When the next wave of persecutions came in 259, more Christians withstood the pressure, and bishops knew what to do with the lapsed. That year, Cyprian himself was martyred. This time most martyrs were not taken to the arena for the crowds to cheer at their deaths; there were too many Christians in the community. Now Christians were executed at various locations. Cyprian was beheaded at the Villa of Sextus where the proconsul was relaxing.[63]

Cyprian's call for harmony and unanimity was heard by many. The martyrs Montanus and Julian, who were executed in 259, had Cyprian's bond of community in harmony in mind during their last hours. The two martyrs had quarreled, when Montanus had a vision urging reconciliation. He then said, echoing Cyprian, "Wherefore, dearest brothers, let us all cling to harmony, peace and unanimity in every virtue."[64] For all the work and exhortation of great theologians like Cyprian, and for all the dreams of martyrs from Saturus to Montanus, harmony in the Christian communities of Carthage and North Africa was not to be long-standing.

The kind of unanimity envisioned by Cyprian probably could exist only in small homogeneous congregations, not in a universal church. Already in Cyprian's time the divisions between the lax and the rigorous were apparent. During the next forty years the church expanded tremendously. In North Africa alone, the number of bishops probably doubled between 260 and 303, and most of the gains were in the countryside,[65] where sensibilities were quite different from those of the great cities like Carthage. In 303, when Diocletian signed an edict that began what would be the final persecution, the diverse congregations were no more ready to stand together than they had been in 250.

Diocletian's persecution was intended to continue the policy begun by Decius. Imperial unity was to be established by cultic conformity. Christian churches were to be destroyed and sacred books handed over to be burnt. This second requirement created the new controversies in North Africa. If a Christian handed over the sacred Scriptures to the authorities and yet did not perform a sacrifice, had he or she violated Christian law? This happened frequently, even among the bishops. Even the bishop of Carthage handed over Christian writings (asserting they were only those of heretics) to the authorities.[66] Christian purists would find even such compromises with authority to be unacceptable, especially when compared with the few like Felix, bishop of Thibiuca, who was martyred rather than accept any compromise.[67] Once again the stage was set for a conflict between those who believed that true Christians were those who rigorously refused to compromise, and those who believed it acceptable to sway a bit in these changing winds so that the church as a whole could survive until a calmer period.

This problem was even more complicated than the similar situation that Cyprian had confronted fifty years before because of an added social problem. The people in a position to have Scriptures to turn over to authorities were the bishops and priests; those more likely to be martyred were the common people. When the persecutions ended a few years later, could the same bishops who had destroyed Scriptures continue to lead their congregations? This dilemma recalled Saturus's dream that placed martyrs over priests—the purists would have agreed with Saturus.

The controversy came to a head in Carthage in 311, when Caecilian was ordained bishop. The purists believed he had been ordained by a bishop who had handed over sacred Scriptures. Therefore, some bishops who believed his ordination was invalid appointed another bishop in his place, Donatus. The patronymic "Donatism" was given to the split in the North African church that was to last for centuries.[68] The Donatists had separate church buildings, separate hierarchy, and separate Christian communities. They saw themselves in the tradition of the early martyrs like Perpetua and adhered to the uncompromising rigor of men like Tertullian. They believed they were a church of the chosen who could hope for imminent martyrdom by a world that was corrupt. The world of Rome may have been corrupt, but after the last persecutions of Diocletian, it no longer created Christian martyrs. The followers of Donatus, however, continued to be martyred.

The age of the orthodox martyrs and the besieged Christian communities ended in 313 with the acceptance of Christianity by Constantine. After this time, the church increasingly gained the support (material and spiritual) of the Roman power structure. The challenge of fourth-century theologians was not to preserve communities in the face of persecution but how Christians would live in an increasingly Christian empire. It was a North African who largely articulated and shaped the ideas of this new kind of Christian community for western Europe: Augustine, the bishop and prolific writer who spent ten years fighting the separatism of the Donatists.

Augustine had been born in 354 in Thagaste (in modern Algeria), about 150 miles from Carthage. He was reared by a Christian mother and pagan father, and like many promising young Romans from the provinces, studied hard to rise through the administrative ranks of the late empire. When he was seventeen, he went to Carthage to continue his education, and like most youths who go to the big city from small towns, was captured by the passions of the place. In his *Confessions*, Augustine wrote, "I went to Carthage, where I found myself in the midst of a hissing cauldron of lust," and he tells how he enjoyed the theater and the passions it generated.[69]

Augustine recalled that throughout his sinful years his famous mother, Monica, never doubted that he was destined for conversion to Christianity. Just as Septimius believed his dreams foretold his imperial destiny, and Perpetua's dreams promised her salvation, Monica's dreams promised salvation for her son.[70] In 387, Monica's predictions came true; Augustine was baptized. He became Bishop of Hippo Regius, on the coast north of his birthplace. Until his death in 430, Augustine exerted a monumental influence that would be more enduring than that of the North African emperor Septimius Severus. Among his many contributions was his view of the relationship of the Christian community with the world. In this, he rejected the rigor of the Donatists and made the ideal of the Christian communities not martyrdom but a peaceful life. He transformed the vision that had driven Tertullian, Perpetua, and many others during the passionate early centuries of a besieged Christianity.

From 401 onward, the orthodox church repeatedly condemned the position of the Donatists. Augustine joined church councils at Carthage at which the church articulated its position, and in his writings he presented the view of the church that was to prevail. Christians, both pure and not, belonged to the universal church, and this church (and all its members) was part of society, that is, obedient and loyal members of the Roman empire. Constantine, by supporting Christianity, accomplished what Decius and Diocletian by persecution could not. He set the stage for an empire that was unified through a common religious identity.[71] Even salvation came not from the visible presence of the Holy Spirit in the Christian congregations and in the martyrdoms in the arena but through obedience to ecclesiastical hierarchy.[72] Augustine was prepared to welcome the Donatists back into the universal church in spite of their "errors," but he was as frustrated by their intransigence as the proconsuls who tried the early Christians were by theirs. He complained that "they stir up rebellion and enmity against the unity of Christ by persisting in their error."[73]

This vision is strikingly different from that of the Christian communities that had appealed to Perpetua and her companions and had drawn the uncompromising passion of Tertullian. The Donatists were guided by an older vision and became increasingly fanatic as they fought for the lost cause of keeping Christian communities separate from the corrupting world.[74] As their vision of the proper relationship between a pure church and an impure world faded, they clung to the ideal of martyrdom as the main thing that separated them from the impure church. Augustine describes their suicidal quest with an uncharacteristic lack of compassion, writing that instead of coming to pagan festivals to destroy idols, Donatists came "solely to be killed." Further, some joined armed bands for the purpose of forcing the authorities to kill them, thus achieving martyrdom. Finally, Augustine says, "it was also their daily sport to kill themselves by jumping off steep crags, or by fire or water."[75]

Augustine contrasted this suicidal search for martyrdom with a picture of the new Christian communities living in harmony with the world:

> If you were to see the effects of the peace of Christ: the joyful throngs, their eagerness to hear and sing hymns and to receive the word of God, the well-attended, happy meetings . . . you would say that it [was] . . . not to be compared by any standard of judgment to that unnumbered throng, [who believe they] should destroy themselves in flames kindled by themselves.[76]

This was the choice that was offered to North African Christians as they selected which church to follow. The persuasion of Augustine was supplemented by the coercion of the state; for example, after 412, there was a large tax levied against anyone who did not join the Catholic church.[77]

One would think that such efforts would have quickly ended people's allegiance to the Donatist movement, but this was North Africa, the land that held the ideal of human sacrifice longer than anywhere else in the ancient Mediterranean. The suicidal intensity of the new martyrs when the age of martyrdom had passed, combined with cultural and political anger,[78] prevented reconciliation until new invasions of Goths and eventually Moslems rendered the dispute moot.

By the late fourth century, some of the intellectual streams that had shaped Perpetua's experience had dried up. The Roman struggle to ground a divinity in a particular space was solved by the Roman adaptation of the transcendent Christian God. The longing for the presence of the divinity was satisfied by the belief in the incarnate Christ and the continuing presence of the Holy Spirit. The necessity to renounce one's family to join the Christian community was also gone.

Some intellectual currents just went underground for a while. Although church leaders like Augustine wrote against suicide, the Carthaginian ideal of sacrificial suicide came back repeatedly as Vandals and Arabs invaded the region. Great turning points of Carthaginian history continued to be marked by women's suicides. The community discord that Christians from Paul to Saturus had warned against subsided under episcopal authority but burst out again with a vengeance with the Donatist controversy.

The ideal of martyrdom, however, which had been a relatively new idea for Perpetua, became a central cultural memory. But this ideal had to change to serve the new Christian communities that were part of the world, not separate from it. The age of the martyrs may have been over, but the brave witnesses of the faithful left a great impact on the church and its theology. Still, as with any historical event, the way it was remembered was more important than what happened, and to understand the impact of the martyrs, we have to look at the way their memory was preserved. In this context, we can return to the poignant diary of Perpetua that has served as a focus of her memory.

MEMORY AND THE TEXT

As the analysis of Perpetua's and Saturus's dream records has shown, their sacrifices were not only for their own salvation but for the benefit of the faithful left on earth. This is why they recorded their visions and experiences. The account of the martyr Pionius, who died in Carthage in 259, during the persecution that took Cyprian, addresses this directly: "[We are] . . . to share in the remembrances of the saints, fully aware that to call to mind those who have passed their lives in the faith wisely with all their hearts gives strength to those who are striving to imitate the better things."[79]

Probably, the martyrs who were urging the recollection of their deeds imagined that the example they were setting was to encourage their companions to be strong in the face of expected persecution. These examples strengthened martyrs from Justin to Perpetua to Cyprian and to many others. In Tertullian's famous phrase, the "blood of martyrs is seed"[80] from which would grow more converts and more martyrs. However, once the persecutions were over, the memory of the martyrdoms had to serve a different purpose.

After the fourth century, the memory of martyrdoms was a way of recalling the power that the martyrs had acquired by their confession and of using this power to benefit the living community of the faithful. As Peter Brown has shown us in his classic work on the cult of saints in antiquity, martyrs became the powerful "invisible companions" who served many of the same functions as powerful patrons had during the ancient world.[81] The power of heaven was linked to the frailty on earth through the intercession of the martyr in the same way that the confessors had used their power to forgive the lapsed in their congregations.

For the memory of martyrs (and other saints) most effectively to benefit the community, two things were needed: some physical remains and a text. It was possible to preserve memory with one or the other of these, but the preservation of both offered the most efficacious result.

The preservation and veneration of the physical remains of martyrs—bones and other relics—strikes many modern readers as strange and even unsavory. This was a Christian innovation that seemed disgusting even to the Roman pagan world. To the Romans, dead bodies were polluting. Traditionally, they cremated bodies and buried them outside the city walls to avoid the perceived contamination of the dead.

Celsus in the second century stated the strongly felt pagan position: "For what sort of human soul is it that has any use for a rotted corpse of a body? . . . [C]orpses should be disposed of like dung, for dung they are."[82] A third-century Christian text proudly articulates a different approach to corpses: "We Christians do not abominate a dead man because we know he will live again. Assembling in cemeteries, we offer up on the graves themselves the Eucharist, which is . . . not only Christ's body but also the likeness of our bodies in heaven."[83]

Although this text links respect for the dead body with a belief in resurrection, this is not a necessary association. Ancient Jews could believe in resurrection while still recoiling from the pollution of corpses. Carolyn Walker Bynum has shown that the third century marked a significant turning point in the belief of resurrection, not only of the soul but of the body itself.[84] Tertullian was instrumental in seeing resurrection as "reassemblage of bits," and Bynum emphasizes Tertullian's sense of justice in his articulation of a theology of resurrection. The stern theologian believed that the whole person had to be rewarded or punished. The body, too, must share in the benefits or punishments for its behavior on earth.[85] The fourth-century "Acts of Phileas the Martyr" clearly continue this idea, when Phileas insists that both soul and body will receive the "recompense for the good deeds done for God."[86]

Yet, there is more to this valuing of the bodies of the dead than the belief that these physical remains would share in the resurrection. The experience of martyrdom and its recollection convinced people that it was not simply the strong faith or firm will of the confessor that gave him or her the strength to withstand the ordeal.[87] The body itself had received an infusion of power that permitted it to be strong during torture. In the Passion of Perpetua, the martyr was in a state of ecstasy when she was in the arena, so her body did not suffer from the impact of the heifer. This notion of spiritual power helping the body is repeated in most of the accounts of martyrdom. Marian, who was tortured in Carthage in the third century, received grace, and the text says that "he was so tortured that the very pain gave him joy. . . . Marian, with his faith in God, grew great in body as well as soul."[88] Before his ordeal, the martyr Montanus received a vision of the dead Cyprian, who reassured him, "The body does not feel this at all when the mind is entirely absorbed in God."[89]

Although the soul of the martyr went quickly to its reward, the faithful believed a spiritual power remained physically in the body after death. According to the texts, this power was immediately visible to the faithful. The account of Pionius's martyrdom describes the awe observers felt when they saw that his body was undestroyed after Pionius had been burnt to death: "[It was like] . . . that of an athlete in full array at the height of his powers. His ears were not distorted; his hair lay in order on the surface of his head; and his beard was full as though with the first blossom of hair. His face shone once again—wondrous grace!"[90] Whether or not we believe that the fire left his body untouched, indeed improved, the metaphoric meaning of this text is that the body itself had received spiritual power.

Martyrs's bodies themselves had been transformed into vessels of holiness. After Marian's mother had watched her son be decapitated for his faith, she was happy at the strength of his flesh, and "again and again with religious devotion she pressed her lips to the wounds of his neck."[91] The spiritual strength left in the bodies was perceived to benefit those it touched. When Saturus gave the guard his ring dipped in his own blood, he was giving a gift that would have been seen as very powerful. This belief led both to a strengthening of the theology of the resurrection of the body, and to the growth of the cult of the dead that manifested itself most visibly in the veneration of relics.

The living venerated the holy dead, and the veneration of their memory meant a reverence for the parts of the dead that were left behind. In the late fourth century, Victricius wrote: "I touch remnants but I affirm that in these relics perfect grace and virtue are contained. . . . He who cures lives. He who lives is present in his relics."[92] The full theology of relics is present in Victricius's words. The grace that the martyr had while living persisted in his remains. Further, the miraculous cures that took place in the presence of the relics testified to the martyr's immortality, and if he were still alive, then he was alive in the bones that remained on this earth.

This set of beliefs caused a dramatic change in the world of late antiquity. Romans, who had avoided corpses as polluting, now treasured body parts. For example, a wealthy Carthaginian woman, Lucilla, had purchased a bone of a martyr. She took it to church with her and kissed it before she took the Eucharist.[93] Here is a public, indeed ostentatious, display of wealth and piety focused on a relic.

Peter Brown has noted that this change in mindset also changed the very topography of the ancient cities. Cemeteries outside the walls that had been ignored by pious Romans became centers of the ecclesiastical life of pious Christians.[94] Martyrs's bodies were buried with great ceremony to become centers of worship.[95] People vied to have the holy dead buried near their own burial chambers.[96] The living did pilgrimages to these burial places and focused people's spiritual longings on the spirit-filled bones the martyrs had left behind.

Another pious Carthaginian noblewoman, Megetia, exemplified the passion people brought to these shrines. The shrine of Saint Stephen (near Carthage) consisted of an iron grill protecting a cubicle that contained the relics, so people could see but not touch the precious bones. When Megetia came, she was carried away with the "longings of her heart . . . [and] her whole body." She beat herself against the grill until it collapsed and she "pushed her head inside and laid it on the holy relics resting there, drenching them with her tears."[97] For Christians like Megetia, the relics served to bring divinity present, to earth, thus satisfying the longing that so marked the earlier pagan Roman texts.

The shrines became the sites not only of private devotion but of public worship. During the persecutions, Roman authorities recognized how important these burial sites were to the Christians and tried to prevent their use as centers of worship. After some executions, the Romans tried to destroy the bodies, both to cast doubt on the resurrection of the flesh and to prevent Christians from venerating the relics. After the martyrdoms in Lyon in 170, the authorities swept the ashes of the martyrs into the river.[98] After the martyrdom of Saint Vincent, the proconsul tried to feed his remains to wild animals and, when that failed, attempted to sink them in the sea.[99] Under the persecution of Valerian, Christians were forbidden to enter the burial areas of Christians.[100] Of course, when the persecutions were over, the veneration of martyrs centered at the location of their remains flourished.

The physical remains of martyrs helped keep their memory strong and brought their spiritual power to the service of the community, but the bones were not sufficient in themselves. Remains offered somewhat fragile memories, and they were vulnerable to loss. Braulio of Saragossa in the seventh century poignantly described the confused state of relics. In response to a request for relics to be sent to another church, Braulio wrote that he had many precious relics, but "not a single martyr's relics [are] so preserved that I can know whose they are." His predecessors had removed all the labels to make them less vulnerable to theft.[101] Although such action certainly would have made precious relics less interesting to thieves, it also made them less useful as triggers to memory.

The relics were strengthened in their veneration if they were accompanied by a text that preserved the memory of the deeds that had rendered the remains so powerful. The narrator of Perpetua's text knew the power of the written word, for he wrote of the importance of the "recollection of the past through the written word." He was not alone in this recognition. Worshippers of Saint Patroclus of Troyes had trouble preserving his cult, as Gregory of Tours described: "The

men of that place had paid little reverence to this martyr, because the
story of his sufferings was not available. It is the custom of the man in
the street to give more attentive veneration to those saints of God
whose combats are read aloud."[102] The reading of the passion of the
martyr brought the saint immediately to memory. People felt the martyr's power and presence and the sick were cured and the spiritually
hungry were filled.[103]

Saint Augustine knew the power of the recorded word in preserving
the memory of the power of saints. He said that there were as many
miracles happening around the holy dead in North Africa in the fourth
century as there had been in biblical times in Palestine. The only difference was that these miracles did "not enjoy the blaze of publicity
which would spread their fame."[104] The memory of the martyrdom of
Perpetua was preserved vividly at her shrine where the martyrs's bones
were buried because her powerful text brought her experience alive
each time it was read.

By the second century, it was customary to commemorate the anniversary of martyrs deaths at a celebration at their shrines.[105] The
precedent was already set before Perpetua died. After her death, she
and her companions would have immediately been accorded the veneration they had earned. By the reign of Constantine in 313, when
Christianity was free to flourish, the anniversary of Perpetua's martyrdom had already appeared in the official calendar of the church of
Rome.[106] The martyrs were buried in the Basilica Maiorum on a high
plateau to the south of the city[107] visible to the faithful (see figure 2.2).
The place was marked by a burial inscription,[108] so it fulfilled one of
the requirements of a memorial to sanctity: the presence of physical
remains. This was the site of great annual festivals on the "birthday" of
the martyrs, that is, the day of their martyrdom, when they were
"born" into eternal life.

By the time of Augustine, then, the martyrdom of Perpetua was an
established part of the annual cycle of celebrations in Carthage. People heard the account of her passion and venerated the text almost as if
it were Scripture.[109] However, the besieged Christian communities of
the third century for whom Perpetua preserved her dreams were different from the communities of the fourth century who were guided to
salvation by their bishop. Perpetua's text was explained and modified by
churchmen who wanted to shape the vision offered by the powerful and
personal account of the martyr.

Subsequent commentators on the *Passio* continued to emphasize the
strong morals of faith, salvation, and the presence of the Holy Spirit.
However, two principal things seemed to have troubled the commen-

tators from the fourth century. One was the troubling hierarchy that placed martyrs and confessors equal or superior to priests and bishops. This problem was most simply addressed by churchmen taking control of the text itself. As we shall see, bishops surrounded the reading of the popular text with homilitic commentary. Thus, instead of letting the text speak directly to the community of the faithful, they guided the understanding of the words, subtly changing the message of the independent young martyr and, perhaps more important, controlling its dissemination. Just as Cyprian co-opted the power of confessors by making them into priests, Augustine co-opted the power of Perpetua's text by turning it into a subject of sermons.

The second and more troubling problem implicit in the *Passio* was a gender problem. Perpetua had overturned the social order of the Roman Empire by standing on her own, and indeed by assuming leadership of the small group (or at least sharing it with Saturus). The stone on the burial shrine of the martyrs commemorated all the martyrs, beginning with the men, Saturus, Saturninus, Revocatus, and Secundulus, and ending with the two women, Felicity and Perpetua. Yet, it was the women who captured popular imagination, and by the fourth century the festival day was in their honor. The women had continued the reversal of the social order by taking leadership in the cult of the martyrs. The fourth-century church was one that did not stand outside the social order but was part of it. How would this socially conservative church of Augustine reconcile itself to the strong young women who were so venerated in Carthage?

The most obvious way to shape the message offered by the martyr was to rewrite the text, making it less direct and personal while preserving the memory of the martyrdom. Many of the acts of the martyrs were rewritten to make them more consistent with prevailing church doctrine, or to put it another way, to bring them up-to-date and make them relevant to the experiences of Christians at any given time.[110] When a fourth-century redactor rewrote (and shortened) the account of the martyrdom of Perpetua, it is clear that gender was very much on his mind.[111] In his account of the trial, he separated the men from the women, so that during the questioning of the two women he could focus on their social roles. He asked Felicity about her husband and created a husband for Perpetua, claiming he joined her family at her trial. In this way, the redactor emphasized the women's place in the family, and when Perpetua rejected her family, the writer removed all tension from the young martyr's decision, thus reducing the sympathy that the audience would bring. Perpetua was described as pushing away her infant and family, calling them evil.[112] The women remained martyrs, but the account made them less appealing as role models, and thus less threatening to the social order.

Rewritten versions of the accounts of some martyrs' passions were popular and prevailed as the text to be read on the saint's day. However, by the fourth century, Perpetua's original text was already too popular for people to accept a replacement. Therefore, Augustine offered sermons to point to appropriate morals in the text and to explain the troublesome portions of the diary. By trying to shape people's understanding of the text, the bishop was taking control of the worship of the martyr. We have several of Augustine's sermons written for the festival day of Saints Perpetua and Felicity,[113] and we have one sermon written a bit later in Carthage, possibly by Quodvultdeo, bishop of Carthage in the middle of the fifth century.[114]

There were a number of lessons in the account of Perpetua's passion that the bishops accepted and highlighted. Augustine accepted the validity of Perpetua's visions foretelling the martyrs' victory.[115] He emphasized the martyrs' overcoming of a fear of death and pain, and the gift of ecstasy that was given Perpetua so that she "felt not the battle against the maddened cow." He spoke certainly of their salvation, and of the martyrs' ability to pray for other members of the community.[116] These lessons were the core of the cult of saints that said that the bodies of the martyrs received power that was then available to the community of the faithful. It is extremely likely that the *Passio* of Perpetua was so popular in large part because these central lessons were so readily visible in the text.

As we have seen, however, the fourth century was different from the early third. Augustine not only emphasized points in the text that were there from the beginning but used the *Passio* to draw new morals relevant to the fourth-century church. The age of the martyrs had brought about a theological interest in the resurrection of the flesh, and this promise was emphasized by Augustine. He said the martyrs' souls would receive "the same bodies wherein they suffered unworthy torments." Furthermore, this lesson applied to others as well. "[E]very body shall be restored and the whole man shall receive that which he deserveth."[117] Although there was nothing directly in Perpetua's text that spoke to the resurrection of the flesh, the experience of martyrdom itself seemed to allow for this kind of moral lesson.

Augustine had to stretch further when he tried to apply the circumstances of Perpetua's martyrdom to the overall condition of the fourth-century church. Perpetua's text was written by and to a church besieged, not a church victorious. Augustine explained carefully that the age of martyrs was not only over but overturned. He said that the children of the people in the arena who "raged against the martyrs' flesh" now praised the martyrs' glory. Descendants of those who gathered in the arena now gathered in church. As he summarized, "[T]hat was unholy then, and now is nothing." This church is not a threatened one. For Augustine, this meant that there was space for compassion where once there was not. Instead of challenging the tormentors and threatening them with retribution, as Saturus did in the arena, Augustine "pities" the tormentors' blindness.[118] Ignorance, not evil, killed the martyrs, and this was a radical change that was necessary in an age that was more plagued by splits within the church than by threats from without. These examples show that a powerful text can be and was made relevant to contemporary issues.

Lessons of resurrection and compassion were not necessarily explicit in the original text, nor were they contradicted. Augustine and Quodvultdeo spent most of their time explaining and interpreting gender issues that emerged from the text. This suggests that this tricky issue of gender roles gave the bishops the most trouble in the fourth century.

One troubling aspect of the portrayal of the women in the account of the martyrdom was their relationship to their families. One of the central features of the Christian communities in the second century was their perception that Christians had to follow the biblical injunction to renounce one's family to follow Christ. So on the one hand, fourth-century commentators had to support this action that had so much historical and scriptural precedent. Augustine praised Felicity's ability to give up her husband in favor of Christ, and commended both women for giving up their children in exchange for the love of Christ.[119]

On the other hand, the church in the fourth century was part of society, with all the necessary support for family ties that entailed. As part of his pastoral duties, Augustine was called upon to sort out the tension between people's (particularly women's) calls to spirituality and their family obligations. For example, he reprimanded Ecdicia, a fourth-century matron who followed a call to celibacy and refused to obey her husband, saying that her spiritual aspirations did not free her from her social duties to her family.[120] Perpetua's narrative, with its lesson of complete renunciation of family ties, seems to have presented a problem to the bishop walking a fine line between spiritual independence and family obligations.

In his second sermon on her text, Augustine dealt with this issue by trying to shape the audience's understanding of the events. First, he addressed the question that has plagued commentators ever since the text was written: Where was the virtuous matron's husband? Augustine saw the absence of the husband as part of the unfolding of a divine plan that all martyrdoms in retrospect seemed to represent. Perpetua's trial was portrayed as a temptation by the devil, and in Augustine's interpretation, the devil knew that Perpetua was strong enough to withstand the temptation of "fleshly love" that her husband represented. Therefore, the devil did not even try to tempt her with the husband's presence. Instead, according to the bishop, the devil knew the strength of the daughter-father tie, so sent Perpetua's father to tempt the young woman to renounce Christ.[121] By casting the events into a metaphysical level, Augustine reduced Perpetua to a virtuous, passive participant in a drama that was staged to offer moral lessons for future generations of believers.

Augustine further emphasized Perpetua's role as dutiful daughter even within a setting that called for her to withstand the "assault of filial love." Although Perpetua stood firm during her test, Augustine stressed that she did not "transgress the commandment which biddeth honour be paid to parents." The bishop explained to the audience that the daughter had to disobey her father but had compassion for him, and she never rejected his "nature" nor "her own birth."[122] None of these lessons were in the forefront of the text, but Augustine's sermon stressed them, and this emphasis served to keep Perpetua portrayed as a dutiful daughter. Christianity for Augustine was not inconsistent with family ties, indeed *should* not be so. Therefore, the lessons drawn from the account of a martyrdom also should not contradict social obligations. In reshaping Perpetua's memory, the bishop had to forget her renunciation of family and the formation of her new fictive family. Her memory was recast so it would be consistent with the fourth-century church.

Even more problematic for Augustine was the portrayal of the two women, and particularly Perpetua, as the central characters in the text. This was inconsistent with Augustine's strong belief in an appropriate hierarchy in which men led and women obeyed.[123] Anyone reading the text itself had to be struck by the strength of Perpetua and even her leadership in the events.[124] It was she who obtained better conditions for the prisoners and ensured that they would not have to dress in pagan costume for their martyrdom. The greatest evidence for the respect accorded the women in the story is that the celebration day was named for the martyrs Perpetua and Felicity even though there were four men in their company. In his sermons, Augustine reshaped the memory of this extraordinary woman to have her fit his perception of a more suitable matron.

One way that Augustine tamed the independence of the martyr was by repeatedly framing her accomplishments within a context of Eve's fall. According to the bishop, the serpent Perpetua stepped on in her vision was the same one who caused the first woman to fall. The devil tempted the two martyrs in the same way he had successfully tempted Eve, and Felicity did not simply endure the pains of childbirth, she "suffered the pain of Eve."[125] These constant juxtapositions of Perpetua with Eve (which were absent in the text itself) served to remind the audience that these virtuous women were anomalies in a world that fell due to the actions of a woman, the "sex [that] was more frail."[126]

Feminine frailty served as the link for Augustine to discuss Perpetua's vision of being transformed into a man. In the *City of God*, Augustine made clear that resurrected bodies of women would retain the appearance of women, including their genitalia. Women would not be resurrected as male.[127] So, Perpetua's vision was not a preview of the world to come. Instead, Augustine saw the transformation of Perpetua as a divine demonstration showing that women *were* weak and thus only someone "manly" could withstand the kind of testing that had confronted the martyrs. As he said, "even in them that are women in body the manliness of their soul hideth the sex of their flesh." And again, God "made these women to die in a manly and faithful fashion."[128]

Augustine returned to the transformation of Perpetua in his tract on the nature and origin of the soul. He stressed that Perpetua's transformation into a man was reflective of the complete transformation of the womanly interior into a male one. He said that her mind had been as changed as her body. There had to be no trace of the woman left in her, for in her dream her body did not "keep the shape of its vagina. For in that female flesh no male genitalia were to be found."[129] In this life, male and female were dramatically different, and they remained so in Augustine's explanations. In the bishop's hands the accomplishment of the women and the dream of Perpetua served to illustrate a lesson of feminine frailty and imperfection that was wholly absent from the original text.

Finally, Augustine returned repeatedly to the question of why the day was named after the two women: Why were they, not Saturus, Saturninus, Revocatus, or Secundus, preserved most vividly in the memory of the martyrdom? It seems that the obvious answer was that it was Perpetua who wrote the most dramatic portions of the text. But such an explanation would give a great deal of credit and power to the woman, and Augustine did not do so. Instead, he saw the naming of the day as part of God's plan to give a lesson to subsequent generations. Throughout the sermons, Augustine repeatedly made a pun on the names of the two women.[130] He said that all martyrs withstand the trials so "that they may rejoice in perpetual felicity. . . . And therefore although there was in that contest a goodly company, with the names of these two the eternity of all is signified." The day was named after the two women so that all would remember that martyrdom brought with it perpetual felicity and, further, that all Christians could receive that same reward.[131] Once again, Augustine removed much of the women's credit for their achievement, making their fame a function of the moral lesson given by their names. He said directly that the day was named for them "not because women were preferred before men" but to show that people can earn "perpetual felicity" through manly behavior.[132] This repeated emphasis on the pun was out of character for the eloquent orator, but it shows the lengths to which he went to make the day of these women martyrs consistent with a view of church and society that was inconsistent with the early third century in which they died.

Quodvultdeo, the bishop of Carthage in the mid fifth century, continued the same themes that Augustine had established to explain the gender discrepancy. Quodvultdeo, too, could not understand why the names of the women were placed above those of the male martyrs; for him, the "weaker" women could not have exceeded the men in bravery. He solved the dilemma by explaining that the frail women were helped by divine grace (given them in the "milk" Perpetua received from the shepherd in her vision) to overcome their womanly nature. Like Augustine, he was amazed that the weak women, heirs to Eve, could have overcome the "fevers of the flesh," the rigors of childbirth, and the demands of maternity to accept martyrdom.[133] For him, the text was not about the strength of these women but, by contrast, highlighted what he saw as feminine frailty, and this is what he stressed to his congregations as he explained the text they had just heard.

For centuries the faithful of Carthage remembered the martyrdom of Perpetua. The recollection was strengthened by the presence of her remains in the basilica that formed the sacred space of the memory. Her deeds were annually recalled by the public reading of her diary, and constantly made relevant (whether we like the interpretation or not) by churchmen commenting on the text. In the turmoil of the late empire, however, the spacial center of the cult was lost. The Vandals took over the basilica for their own worship,[134] and after the Arab conquest in the seventh century, the relics were lost. Her memory was not lost, however. The cover illustration shows a mosaic of Perpetua that was made in Ravenna at the end of the fifth century as a recollection of her martyrdom.

In the nineteenth century, the French excavations in Carthage restored the physical space of the memory of the martyrs. The stone that

Fig. 6.2. Carthage amphitheater ruins with the chapel dedicated to Perpetua and Felicity. Photograph by Bob Balsley.

marked the graves of the martyrs was found and (heavily) restored. More visible was the work done in the amphitheater by the White Fathers, who wanted to recapture the remains of Christian North Africa. The great structure of the Carthage amphitheater had fallen to rubble in the intervening centuries, and all that remained was the ground floor and the subterranean passages through which the martyrs had come into the amphitheater. The churchmen built a small chapel dedicated to Perpetua in the passage to mark the place of the passion and to give physical space again to the memory of the small group. (Figure 6.2 shows a photograph of the ruins of the arena with the roof of the chapel visible, protruding a bit above the subterranean passage.) The White Fathers were right; the ruins of the amphitheater offer a powerful physical reminder of the martyrdom that occurred here. If Augustine was right that memory required physical remains as well as a text, then perhaps that was what the White Fathers were intending to restore.

The physical memorial to Perpetua's passion may have disappeared for a while, but the diary in which she recorded her experiences, feelings, and dreams as she prepared for martyrdom did not lie forgotten. Virtually from the moment of its writing it became public property, not only to be read but to be interpreted and explained, first by the eyewitness to her passion, then by churchmen giving sermons surrounding the text, and by writers (including me) through the ages analyzing the clear, direct words of the martyr. Sometimes Perpetua's words were refracted through a lens of gender that caused male writers like Augustine to add to the text meanings that had nothing to do with the intelligent, passionate young Roman matron. As Brent Shaw sensitively notes, "From the very start [the text] was buried under an avalanche of male interpretations, rereadings, and distortions."[135]

The text was also refracted through a temporal lens. Obviously, the world, the church, and people's sensibilities have changed since the third century. Augustine felt he had to explain and reinterpret the text to make it relevant to the fourth-century audience. These reinterpretations did not end in the fourth century. Modern Freudian scholars have seen psychoanalytic meaning in the text.[136] Some modern theologians see in the text evidence of women's serving as priests during the early church. As Margaret Miles notes, "*The Martyrdom of Saints Perpetua and Felicitas* is an unusually vivid example of the appropriation of a woman's writing as support for theological and ecclesiastical concerns that her text does not acknowledge as her own."[137]

This constant reinterpretation of the text is not necessarily a bad thing. In this opinion, I depart from most who have commented on the history of Perpetua's memory. We talk of great literature as being "timeless," and by this we do not really mean that it stands outside time. Instead, we mean that it can speak to human experience through many times. This is what the direct and powerful text of Perpetua does. It is so human that it lends itself to human experience in many times and for both genders. That is not to say that we should so transform her text that it no longer speaks with the voice of the young martyr. That would be creativity, not memory.

In Perpetua's diary, we can see the way she brought the memories of her Carthaginian and Roman past to serve the immediate experience of her martyrdom, to be relevant to her present. What we do when we read the text is much the same. We use the memory of her actions and her words to enhance the meaning of our own experience. Throughout history that has been the definition of great people and great literature, and for this they are remembered.

Notes

INTRODUCTION

1. Eusebius, *The History of the Church*, trans. G. A. Williamson, (Harmondsworth, 1984), 341–42.
2. Ibid., 342.

ONE: ROME

1. T. Barnes, *Tertullian. A Historical and Literary Study* (Oxford, 1971), 70, argues for senatorial rank for the family. More convincing is B. Shaw's argument for decurial rank in "The Passion of Perpetua," *Past and Present* 139 (1993): 11.
2. See E. Cantarella, *Pandora's Daughters: The Role and Status of Women in Greek and Roman Antiquity* (Baltimore, 1987), 11.
3. See J. Hallett, *Fathers and Daughters in Roman Society* (Princeton, 1984), for an excellent discussion of the centrality of this tie.
4. Pliny the Younger, in *Women's Lives in Greece and Rome*, ed. M. R. Lefkowitz, et al., (Baltimore, 1982), 144.
5. See, for example, Jerome, "To Eustochium" in *Jerome: Letters and Select Works*, trans. W. H. Fremantle (Peabody, Mass., 1995), 22.
6. See B. Rawson, ed., *The Family in Ancient Rome: New Perspectives* (Ithaca, 1986), 8.
7. See ibid., 40, and S. B. Pomeroy, *Goddesses, Whores, Wives and Slaves: Women in Classical Antiquity* (New York, 1975), 170; both emphasize the importance of education to Roman daughters.
8. Quintilian, "Institutes of Oratory," in Lefkowitz et al., *Women's Lives*, 235.
9. Ibid.
10. Rawson, 22, and Pomeroy, 164. However, see B. Shaw, "The Age of Roman Girls at Marriage: Some Reconsiderations," *Journal of Roman Studies* 77 (1987): 30–46, who argues that the late teens were probably a more customary age for young women to marry.
11. Rawson, 22.

12. "Passion of Perpetua," in *The Acts of the Christian Martyrs*, comp. and trans. H. Musurillo (Oxford, 1972), 109. Shaw, "Passion of Perpetua," 11–12, figures her marriage age at about eighteen or nineteen. I think this calculation is off by a year or two, although with the scarcity of information it is impossible to tell for sure.

13. Peter Dronke, *Women Writers of the Middle Ages* (Cambridge, 1984), 282–83, summarizes the arguments proposed for the absence of Perpetua's husband from the text.

14. Shaw, "Passion of Perpetua," 25.

15. M. A. Tilley, "One Woman's Body: Repression and Expression in the *Passio Perpetuae*," in *Ethnicity, Nationality and Religious Experience*, ed. P. C. Phan (New York, 1991), 62.

16. Ibid., 58.

17. S. Dixon, *The Roman Mother* (Norman, Ok., 1988), 24, 233. See also Cantarella, 134.

18. W. H. C. Frend, *Martyrdom and Persecution in the Early Church: A Study of Conflict from the Maccabees to Donatus* (Oxford, 1965), 104–5.

19. Cicero, *De Natura Deorum*, trans. H. Rackham (Cambridge, 1967), 131.

20. Augustine, *City of God*, trans H. Bettenson (Harmondsworth, 1972), 155.

21. Ibid., 144.

22. Celsus, *Celsus: On the True Doctrine*, trans. R. J. Hoffmann (Oxford, 1987), 87.

23. Ibid., 118.

24. Apuleius, "Florida," in *The Apologia and Florida of Apuleius of Madaura*, trans. H. E. Butler (Westport, Conn., 1970), 193.

25. F. Dupont, *Daily Life in Ancient Rome*, trans. C. Woodall (Oxford, 1993), 75.

26. Symmachus, "Third Relation," in *Ancient Roman Religion*, ed. F. C. Grant (New York, 1957), 249.

27. Livy, "History of Rome," in Grant, 49.

28. Augustine, 145.

29. Celsus, 118.

30. M. Lyttleton and W. Forman, *The Romans: Their Gods and Their Beliefs* (London, 1984), 37.

31. Livy, *Livy*, vol. 5. trans. B. O. Foster (Cambridge, 1963), 235.

32. Symmachus, "Third Relation," in Grant, 249.

33. Pomeroy, 206.

34. Ibid., 207–8.

35. Ibid., 207, and R. S. Kraemer, *Her Share of the Blessings* (Oxford, 1992), 62.

36. Tertullian, "On Monogamy," in *Disciplinary, Moral and Ascetical Works*, trans. R. Arbesmann et al. (New York, 1959), 17.

37. See Kraemer, 62–70, for the importance of this aunt tie in Roman society.

38. D. W. Amundsen and C. J. Diers, "The Age of Menarche in Classical Greece and Rome," *Human Biology* 41 (1969): 125–32.

39. Pomeroy, 206.

40. Kraemer, 54.

41. Livy, "History of Rome," in Grant, 51–53. See also S. Perowne, *Caesars and Saints: The Rise of the Christian State, A.D. 180–313* (New York, 1962), 54.

42. N. Lewis et al., *Roman Civilization Sourcebook*, vol. 2, *The Empire* (New York, 1966), 64.

43. Virgil, *Aeneid*, trans. A. Mandelbaum (New York, 1981), 158.

44. F. Millar, *The Emperor in the Roman World* (Ithaca, 1977), 542–43. See ibid., 517–49, for a discussion of this form of petition.

45. J. H. W. G. Liebeschuetz, *Continuity and Change in Roman Religion* (Oxford, 1979), 198.

46. Lyttleton and Forman, 77.

47. A. Momigliano, "Roman Religion of the Imperial Period," in *Religions of Antiquity*, ed. R. Seltzer (New York, 1989), 220.

48. P. Veyne, *Bread and Circuses* (London, 1990), 308–9.

49. See J. B. Rives, *Religion and Authority in Roman Carthage from Augustus to Constantine* (Oxford, 1995), 98, for a clear explanation of how the figure of the emperor was the only thing that tied the empire together.

50. "Acts of the Scillitan Martyrs," in Musurillo, 87.

51. Rives, 51. Rives offers an excellent analysis of the imperial cult in Carthage that yields theoretical insights having much wider application.

52. Ibid., 59–60.

53. There are a number of good studies of Septimius Severus. The best general biographies remain A. Birley, *Septimius Severus: The African Emperor* (London, 1971) and M. Platnauer, *The Life and Reign of the Emperor Lucius Septimius Severus* (Westport, Conn., 1970). His life is extensively chronicled by the Roman historians as well, particularly Herodian, Dio Cassius, and in the collection known as *Historia Augusta*.

54. Scriptores Historiae Augustae, "Sep Sev," in *Historia Augusta*, trans. D. Magie (Cambridge, 1967), 1:407, 419.

55. Ibid., 419.

56. Perowne, 52, argues that this "resurgence of the east" in temporal power also represented a resurgence in "spiritual power" that actually facilitated the ultimate victory of Christianity, an eastern religion.

57. Birley, 117–18.

58. Scriptores Historiae Augustae, "Sep Sev," 37.

59. See Platnauer, 48–53, for a discussion on the controversy surrounding the possible date of Caracalla's birth.

60. Birley, 272.

61. Herodian, *History*, trans. C. R. Whittaker (Cambridge, 1969), III, 8, 313. Dio Cassius also commented on the elaborate and expensive games, in *Dio's Roman History*, trans. E. Cary (Cambridge, 1961), 239–41.

62. Lewis, *Ecstatic Religion* (New York, 1989), 559.

63. Dio Cassius, 157.

64. Scriptores Historiae Augustae, "Sep Sev," 373.

65. Dio Cassius, 167–71.

66. Scriptores Historiae Augustae, "Sep Sev," 411.

67. See J. G. Davies, "Was the Devotion of Septimius Severus to Serapis the Cause of the Persecution of 202–3?" *Journal of Theological Studies*, n.s. 6, 1954, 73–76, for a description of the changing style of Septimius's depiction.

68. Frend, 327.

69. R. E. Witt, *Isis in the Graeco-Roman World* (Ithaca, 1971),53.
70. Plutarch, "Isis and Osiris," in *Moralia*, trans. F. C. Babbitt (Cambridge, 1962), 5: 69.
71. Scriptores Historiae Augustae, "Sep Sev," 409.
72. So argues Davies, 73–76.
73. So suggests Frend, 320.
74. Eusebius, *The History of the Church*, trans. G. A. Williamson (Harmondsworth, 1984), 239.
75. Lyttleton and Forman, 78.
76. E. R. Dodds, *Pagan and Christian in an Age of Anxiety* (Cambridge, 1985).
77. Platnauer, 156.
78. R. MacMullen, *Paganism in the Roman Empire* (New Haven, 1981), 115.
79. Dodds, 7.
80. Lucian of Samasota, *Lucian*, trans. M. D. Macleod (Cambridge, 1967), 3: 165.
81. Ibid., 155.
82. Plutarch, 9.
83. Liebeschuetz, 200.
84. Lyttleton and Forman, 91, and Liebeschuetz, 198–200.
85. Scriptores Historiae Augustae, "Sep Sev," 37.
86. Lewis, 570.
87. Liebeschuetz, 217, expresses this idea: "His philosophy was concerned with deity as a source of power, and with establishing a relationship between it and the individual by many means, including magical ones."
88. Apuleius, "Florida," 193–94.
89. Ibid., 186.
90. Augustine, 318–30.
91. Apuleius, "Apology," 105.
92. Ibid., 62.
93. Ibid., 77, 87.
94. Ibid., 76.
95. Dio Cassius, 233. Pomeroy, 174, sees Julia's activity as indicative of women's intellectual pursuits during this period; this is much more plausible than Dio's more simplistic political explanation.
96. R. M. Seltzer, ed., *Religions of Antiquity* (New York, 1989), 255.
97. Apuleius, "Apology," 41.
98. Celsus, 98.
99. Liebeschuetz, 198–200.
100. Seneca, "Epistle XLI," in Grant, 273.
101. Apuleius, "Apology" 87.
102. Augustine, 318.
103. Celsus, 92–93.
104. Ibid., 54.
105. Plotinus "The Six Enneads," in *Great Books of the Western World*, ed. M. J. Adler (Chicago, 1991), 11:519.
106. Ibid., 298.
107. Apuleius, "Apology," 96–97.
108. Dio Cassius, 225.

109. Herodian, 313.
110. Seltzer, 274.
111. Apuleius, *Golden Ass*, trans. Jack Lindsay (Bloomington, 1960), 239.
112. L. H. Martin, *Hellenistic Religions* (Oxford, 1987), 62.
113. See Kraemer, 74, 78, for the wide appeal of mystery religions and the cult of Isis to women.
114. Pomeroy, 218.
115. Apuleius, *Golden Ass*, 237.
116. Martin, 77.
117. Ibid.
118. Ibid., 78.
119. Pomeroy, 222.
120. Apuleius, *Golden Ass*, 239–42.
121. R. Stark, *The Rise of Christianity* (Princeton, 1996), 199.
122. Apuleius, "Apology," 77.
123. Ibid., 79.
124. Plotinus, 298.
125. Martin, 97.
126. Augustine, 249.
127. Witt, 94.
128. J. Ferguson, *Greek and Roman Religion* (London, 1980), 252.
129. Apuleius, *Golden Ass*, 236, 246.
130. Scriptores Historiae Augustae, "Sep Sev," 335. For Septimius's emphasis on dreams, see ibid., 373, and Dio Cassius, 167, 253.
131. Apuleius, "Apology," 79.
132. Lucian, "Alexander the False Prophet," in *Lucian*, trans. M. D. MacLeod (Cambridge, 1967), vol. 4. See also A. D. Nock, "Alexander of Abonutei-chos," *Classical Quarterly* 22 (1928): 160–62.
133. Lucian, 225.

TWO: CARTHAGE

1. B. H. Warmington, *Carthage: A History* (New York, 1993), 25.
2. Appian, *Appian's Roman History*, trans. H. White (Cambridge, 1964), 565–67. See also David Soren et al., *Carthage* (New York, 1990), 148.
3. Soren, 150. For an excellent description of the excavations of the houses and streets of second-century-B.C. Carthage, see S. Lancel et al., "Town Planning and Domestic Architecture of the Early Second Century B.C. on the Byrsa, Carthage," in *New Light on Ancient Carthage*, ed. J. G. Pedley (Ann Arbor, 1980), 13–23.
4. Warmington, 133–34.
5. Ibid., 152–53; Warmington writes succinctly: "They were always strange to their neighbors."
6. Herodotus, *The History*, trans. D. Grene (Chicago, 1987), 352–53.
7. Polybius, "Histories," in *Ancient Roman Religion*, ed. F. C. Grant (New York, 1957), 157–58.
8. Livy, *Livy*, trans. B. O. Foster (Cambridge, 1963), 5: 221.

9. Plutarch, *Moralia*, trans. F. C. Babbitt (Cambridge, 1962), 10: 165.

10. Plutarch, "Marcus Cato," in *Lives of the Noble Grecians and Romans*, trans. J. Dryden (New York, n. d.), 431.

11. Ibid., 431.

12. Soren, 148.

13. Appian, 633–35, records this as the number of people who requested and received safe conduct from the fortress before its fall.

14. Ibid.

15. Ibid., 637.

16. Livy, 385–87.

17. Villeius Paterculus, in O. Kiefer, *Sexual Life in Ancient Rome* (New York, 1993), 42.

18. J. H. W. G. Liebeschuetz, *Continuity and Change in Roman Religion* (Oxford, 1979), 169.

19. Appian, 643.

20. I would like to thank the archaeologist Susan Stevens for pointing this out to me.

21. See Soren, 166, for a description of the governance organization of the province.

22. Appian, 645.

23. Soren, 171.

24. My thanks for conversations with archaeologists Susan Stevens, Joann Freed, and Colin Wells, who have worked in Carthage for years and who know the stones of this city.

25. J. B. Rives, *Religion and Authority in Roman Carthage from Augustus to Constantine* (Oxford, 1995), 23.

26. My thanks to Professor Gregory Aldrete at the University of Wisconsin-Green Bay for this information.

27. Apuleius, "Florida," in *The Apologia and Florida of Apuleius of Madaura*, trans. H. E. Butler (Westport, Conn. 1970), 200–201.

28. Rives, 27.

29. Ibid.

30. See ibid., 161.

31. Ibid., 162.

32. Ibid., 65–66, 162.

33. Tertullian, *Pall. 1. 2*, in Rives, 155.

34. Soren, 174.

35. J. K. Evans, "Wheat Production and Its Social Consequences in the Roman World," *Classical Quarterly* 31 (1981): 434.

36. See S. Raven, *Rome in Africa* (New York, 1993), 79–96, for a discussion of the North African agricultural patterns and the late-first-century diversification.

37. Pliny, *Natural History*, trans. H. Rackham (Cambridge, 1960), 4:301.

38. Raven, 101.

39. K. M. D. Dunbabin, *The Mosaics of Roman North Africa* (Oxford, 1978), 10, 21, 24.

40. Ibid., 47.
41. Soren, 189.
42. Ibid., 191–92.
43. B. Shaw, "The Passion of Perpetua," *Past and Present* 139 (1993): 10.
44. Some authors have accepted the town identification as probable: Shaw, 10. Others have rejected it: T. Barnes, *Tertullian. A Historical and Literary Study* (Oxford, 1971), 72.
45. Raven, 55.
46. Apuleius, "Apologia," in *The Apologia and Florida of Apuleius of Madaura*, trans. H. E. Butler (Westport, Conn., 1970), 201–2.
47. Augustine, *Confessions*, trans. R. S. Pine-Coffin (New York, 1980), 45.
48. Rives, 27, describes how the magnificent buildings "were matched by a vivid intellectual and cultural life."
49. Apuleius, "Florida," in *The Apologia and Florida of Apuleius of Madaura*, trans. H. E. Butler (Westport, Conn., 1970), 199.
50. Ibid., 210.
51. Ibid., 200. See also Soren, 221–22.
52. Augustine, *Confessions*, 55.
53. Apuleius, "Florida," 202.
54. Heliodorus, *Ethiopian Story*, trans. W. Lamb (London, 1961), x.
55. S. A. Stephens and J. J. Winkler, eds., *Ancient Greek Novels: The Fragments* (Princeton, 1995), 19.
56. P. Dronke, *Women Writers of the Middle Ages: A Critical Study of Texts from Perpetua to Marguerite Porete* (Cambridge, 1984), 285.
57. Stephens and Winkler, 80.
58. Ibid., 39.
59. Ibid., 78.
60. Heliodorus, 5–24.
61. Stephens and Winkler, 25.
62. Ibid., 75.
63. Heliodorus, 272.
64. Ibid., 277.
65. Apuleius, *Golden Ass*, trans. Jack Lindsay (Bloomington, 1960), 105–42.
66. P. G. Walsh, *The Roman Novel* (Cambridge, 1970), 218–19.
67. Perhaps the best short description of the horror of ancient cities and its impact on the rise of Christianity may be found in R. Stark, *The Rise of Christianity* (Princeton, 1996), 147–62.
68. A. Rouselle, *Porneia: On Desire and the Body in Antiquity*, trans. F. Pheasant (New York, 1988), 128.
69. 2 Kings 3:26–27.
70. Deut. 12:31.
71. Exod. 22:28b.
72. J. D. Levenson, *The Death and Resurrection of the Beloved Son* (New Haven, 1993), makes an excellent case for the presence and transformation of the ideal of sacrifice in Judaism and Christianity.
73. 1 Kings 16:31–33.

74. Levenson, 20.
75. Ibid., 4, 36.
76. Jer. 19:5–6
77. Warmington, 148, notes there is no surviving evidence for human sacrifice among the Phoenicians of Tyre.
78. L. E. Stager and S. R. Wolff, "Child Sacrifice at Carthage—Religious Rite or Population Control?" *Biblical Archeology Review* 10, no. 1 (January-February 1984), 44.
79. Levenson, 20.
80. Stager and Wolff, 44.
81. Ibid., 39.
82. Levenson, 22.
83. Ibid., 26.
84. Augustine, *City of God*, trans. H. Bettenson (Harmondsworth, 1972), 277.
85. Diodorus, *Diodorus of Sicily*, trans. R. M. Geer (Cambridge, 1962), 179–81.
86. Plutarch, *Moralia*, 2: 493.
87. Tertullian, "Apology," in *Apologetical Works and Minucius Felix*, trans. R. Arbesmann et al. (New York, 1950), 29, 31. See Rouselle, 120–21, for a fine discussion on the importance of laughter during sacrifice.
88. Minucius Felix, "Octavius," in *Apologetical Works and Minucius Felix*, trans. R. Arbesmann et al. (New York, 1950), 388.
89. Plutarch, *Moralia*, 2: 493.
90. These ideas are summarized in Augustine, *City of God*, 32–33. For an excellent summary of the topic, see A. J. Droge and J. D. Tabor, *A Noble Death: Suicide and Martyrdom among Christians and Jews in Antiquity* (San Francisco, 1992).
91. Virgil, *Aeneid*, trans. A. Mandelbaum (New York, 1981), 103–4.
92. Augustine, *City of God*, 32.
93. Augustine, *Confessions*, 34.
94. Herodotus, 528.
95. Appian, 635–37.
96. S. Brown, *Late Carthaginian Child Sacrifice* (Sheffield, 1991), 156.
97. Minucius Felix, "Octavius," 388.
98. Tertullian, "Apology," 30.
99. Rouselle, 109.
100. Ibid., 115.
101. Tertullian, "Spectacles," in *Disciplinary, Moral and Ascetical Works*, trans. R. Arbesmann et al. (New York, 1959), 79.
102. Wiedemann, *Emperors and Gladiators* (New York, 1992), 107.
103. Raven, 64.
104. Ibid., 225.
105. Stephens and Winkler, 187.
106. Apuleius, *Golden Ass*, 173.
107. Tertullian, "To the Martyrs," in *Disciplinary, Moral and Ascetical Works*, trans. R. Arbesmann et al. (New York, 1959), 25–28.
108. Tertullian, "Spectacles," 104.

THREE: CHRISTIAN COMMUNITY

1. J. B. Rives, *Religion and Authority in Roman Carthage from Augustus to Constantine* (Oxford, 1995), 225, makes this compelling argument.

2. W. T. Faversham, "The Origins of Christianity in Africa," *Studia Patristica* 4 (1961): 512–17.

3. Rives, 217.

4. Ibid., 215.

5. Ibid., 221.

6. W. H. C. Frend, "The Seniores Laici and the Origins of the Church in North Africa," *Journal of Theological Studies*, n.s., 12 (1961): 280–85, and Frend, *Martyrdom and Persecution in the Early Church: A Study of Conflict from the Maccabees to Donatus* (Oxford, 1965), 361–62, argue for a strong Jewish origin of the Christian communities in Carthage. T. Barnes, *Tertullian. A Historical and Literary Study* (Oxford, 1971), 273–76, on the other hand, devalues the evidence for this development. In absence of evidence to the contrary, logic argues for the former position.

7. W. H. C. Frend, *The Rise of Christianity* (Philadelphia, 1984), 257.

8. See, for example, "Pionius," in H. Musurillo, comp. and trans. *The Acts of the Christian Martyrs* (Oxford, 1972), 139.

9. A. F. Segal, *Rebecca's Children: Judaism and Christianity in the Roman World* (Cambridge, 1986), 142. See E. Pagels, *The Origin of Satan* (New York, 1995), for an intelligent and sensitive account of the way we as Christians have demonized those who are closest to us.

10. Especially convincing and original is R. Stark, *The Rise of Christianity: A Sociologist Reconsiders History* (Princeton, 1996), 49–71. Also good, especially for the discussion of the historiography of the controversy, is J. T. Burtchaell, *From Synagogue to Church: Public Services and Offices* (Cambridge, 1992).

11. J. G. Gager, *Kingdom and Community: The Social World of Early Christianity* (Englewood Cliffs, N.J., 1975), 129.

12. Stark, 18.

13. Ibid., 19, 37.

14. Segal, 43.

15. Ibid., 180.

16. Frend, *Rise of Christianity*, 100.

17. Ibid., 39. See 2 Tim. 3:15.

18. Stark, 7.

19. Tertullian, "To Scapula," in *Apologetical Works and Minucius Felix*, trans. R. Arbesmann et al. (New York, 1950), 160.

20. I want to emphasize that these numbers in no way reveal absolute data but, instead, are only general estimates to give a sense of the situation in Carthage.

21. Stark, 88–91.

22. Tertullian, "To Scapula," 160.

23. See D. M. Olster, "Classical Ethnography and Early Christianity," in *The*

Formulation of Christianity by Conflict Through the Ages, ed. K. B. Free, (Lewiston, N. Y., 1995), 9–32, for a discussion of the implications of the term "third race."

24. E. R. Dodds, *Pagan and Christian in an Age of Anxiety* (Cambridge, 1985), 136–38.

25. Ibid., 135.

26. R. MacMullen, "Two Types of Conversion to Early Christianity," in *Conversion, Catechumenate, and Baptism in the Early Church*, ed. E. Ferguson (New York, 1993), 37.

27. Augustine, "On the Cathechising of the Uninstructed," in *Augustine: On the Holy Trinity, Doctrinal Treatises, Moral Treatises*, vol. 3 of *Nicene and Post-Nicene Fathers* (Peabody, Mass., 1995), 288.

28. Eusebius, *The History of the Church*, trans. G. A. Williamson (Harmondsworth, 1984), 210.

29. See J. D. C. Dunn, *Jesus and the Spirit* (London, 1975), 302–4.

30. R. P. Vande Kappelle, "Prophets and Mantics," in *Pagan and Christian Anxiety: A Response to E. R. Dodds*, ed. R. C. Smith and J. Lounibos (New York, 1984), 92–93.

31. Burtchaell, 191.

32. Eusebius, 210. Dunn, 172, notes both prophetic functions by saying that prophets offer premonitions, guidance from the Spirit, and exhortations to the community.

33. Acts 11:5.

34. Here I follow generally D. E. Aune, *Prophecy in Early Christianity and the Ancient Mediterranean World* (Grand Rapids, Mich., 1983), 23–79, who offers an excellent discussion.

35. Eusebius, 210.

36. Dunn, 189, argues convincingly that glossolalia was the particular sign of the Spirit's presence. For excellent discussions and summaries of the understanding of the importance and nature of prophecy including glossolalia, see P. Esler, *The First Christians in Their Social Worlds* (New York, 1994), and T. W. Gillespie, *The First Theologians: A Study in Early Christian Prophecy* (Grand Rapids, Mich., 1994).

37. Acts 2:1–13.

38. Acts 10:45–47.

39. Acts 19:6.

40. Dunn, 6.

41. 1 Cor.14.

42. 1 Cor. 14:2.

43. Gillespie, 130–39.

44. Esler, 43.

45. Eusebius, 180.

46. Irenaeus, "Against Heresies," in *Ante-Nicene Fathers*, vol 1, ed. A. Roberts et al. (Peabody, Mass., 1995), 334.

47. See, for example, Tertullian, "On the Soul," in *Apologetical Works*, 197. Rives, 283, argues that Tertullian conceived of church authority largely in charismatic terms.

48. Celsus, *Celsus: On the True Doctrine*, trans. R. J. Hoffmann (Oxford, 1987), 106.

49. Tertullian, "On the Soul," 197.

50. Cyprian, *Saint Cyprian: Letters*, trans. Rose Bernard Donna, (Washington, D. C., 1964), 48–49, 302.

51. Dunn, 188, 238.

52. Ibid., 182. See also R. S. Kraemer, *Her Share of the Blessings* (Oxford, 1992), 147.

53. 1 Cor. 12:28.

54. One of the best works is E. S. Fiorenza, *In Memory of Her: A Feminist Theological Reconstruction of Christian Origins* (New York, 1983). For a shorter summary, see Kraemer, 174–209.

55. 1 Cor. 11:2–16. See Kraemer, 146.

56. Kraemer, 181–83.

57. Ibid., 179.

58. M. A. Rossi, "The Passion of Perpetua, Everywoman of Late Antiquity," in *Pagan and Christian Anxiety: A Response to E. R. Dodds*, ed. R. C. Smith and J. Lounibos (New York, 1984), 68.

59. See Esler, 37–51, for a clear correlation of studies of modern glossolalia with Paul's community.

60. I should note that this analysis omits the seeking of the divine by hermits escaping from the social worlds of community. But in Christianity, solitary holy men and women appear after the mid third century. The early Christians were social beings.

61. 1 Cor. 14:5.

62. See 1 Thess. 5:19–20: "Do not quench the Spirit, do not despise prophesying."

63. 1 Cor. 12:27–31. See also Dunn, 265. For a full discussion, see R. Banks, *Paul's Idea of Community* (Peabody, Mass., 1994).

64. See Burtchaell, 349, who argues persuasively that church officers existed as part of the traditional order, but the vitality of the young church existed in the charismatics.

65. Dunn, 348.

66. Tertullian, "Apology," in *Apologetical Works* , 98.

67. Tertullian,"On Baptism," in *Latin Christianity: Its Founder, Tertullian*, vol. 3 of *Ante-Nicene Fathers* (Peabody, Mass., 1995), 677.

68. See, R. A. Campbell, *The Elders: Seniority within Earliest Christianity* (Edinburgh, 1994), for an excellent discussion of this development.

69. For the dating and setting of this work, see A. Milavec, "Distinguishing True and False Prophets: The Protective Wisdom of the *Didache*," *Journal of Early Christian Studies* 2, no. 2 (1994): 117–36.

70. "Didache," in M. Staniforth, trans., *Early Christian Writings: The Apostolic Fathers* (New York, 1968), 232–34.

71. 2 Peter 2:3, 2:10.

72. "Shepherd of Hermas," in *The Apostolic Fathers*, trans. F. X. Glimm et al. (New York, 1948), 281.

73. Dunn, 234.

74. 1 Thess. 5:19.

75. 1 Cor. 1:11.

76. 1 Cor. 13:8.

77. Clement, "First Epistle to the Corinthians," in Staniforth, 51.

78. Ignatius of Antioch, "Epistle to the Magnesians," in Staniforth, 88.

79. Ibid., 76, 113.

80. See J. E. Salisbury, "The Bond of a Common Mind: A Study of Collective Salvation from Cyprian to Augustine," *Journal of Religious History*, 11 (1985), 235–47.

81. See B. Shaw, "The Passion of Perpetua." *Past and Present* 139 (1993): 20–21, for an excellent discussion of "the modes by which this unmediated self-perception, her [Perpetua's] reality[,] was subsequently appropriated by a male editor, and then greatly distorted by subsequent male interpreters."

82. "Perpetua," in Musurillo, 106–9. ©Oxford University Press, 1972. This and all subsequent quotations are reprinted from *The Acts of the Christian Martyrs*, translated by Herbert Musurillo (1972) by permission of Oxford University Press.

83. W. Meeks, *The Origins of Christian Morality: The First Two Centuries* (New Haven, 1993), 26.

84. Augustine, *City of God*, trans. H. Bettenson (Harmondsworth, 1972), 171.

85. Tertullian, "Apology," 106.

86. "Epistle to Diognatus," in Staniforth, 176ff.

87. Justin Martyr, "Apology," in *Writings of Saint Justin Martyr* trans. T. B. Falls (New York, 1948), 43.

88. Tertullian, "To His Wife," in *Fathers of the Third Century: Tertullian, Part Fourth*, vol. 4 of *Ante-Nicene Fathers* (Peabody, Mass.: 1995), 46.

89. Thess. 4:9. See also Meeks, 12.

90. Tertullian, "Apology," 99.

91. M. A. Tilley, "One Woman's Body: Repression and Expression in the *Passio Perpetuae*," in *Ethnicity, Nationality and Religious Experience*, ed. Peter C. Phan (New York, 1991), analyzes the language of the text and shows how Perpetua increasingly refers to members of the community as a fictive family.

92. Rives, 278.

93. Meeks, 2.

94. Tertullian, "Apology," 111.

95. Tertullian, "Spectacles," in *Disciplinary, Moral and Ascetical Works*, trans. R. Arbesmann et al. (New York, 1959), 83–84, and Justin Martyr, "Discourse," 436.

96. Justin Martyr, "Apology," 47.

97. Tertullian, "Apology," 99–100, 106.

98. Ibid., 99.

99. Justin Martyr, "Apology," 107.

100. Meeks, 108.

101. Justin Martyr, "Apology," 63. See also Minucius Felix, "Octavius," in *Apologetical Works and Minucius Felix*, 385.

102. Stark, 127.

103. Tertullian, "Apology," 94.

104. Justin Martyr, "Apology," 75.

105. Ferguson, 244–45, 276.

106. Ignatius of Antioch, in Staniforth, 79.

107. Justin Martyr, "Apology," 107.

108. Ibid., 106–7.

109. Tertullian, "Prayer," in *Disciplinary, Moral and Ascetical Works*, trans. R. Arbesmann et al. (New York, 1959), 168.

110. Justin Martyr, "Apology," 106–7.

111. W. H. C. Frend, "Blandina and Perpetua: Two Early Christian Heroines," in *Women in Early Christianity*, ed. D. M. Scholer (New York, 1993), 172–73; Frend, *Rise of Christianity*, 291; T. J. Heffernan, *Sacred Biography: Saints and Their Biographers in the Middle Ages* (Oxford, 1988), 201. See also "Scillitan Martyrs," in Musurillo, 89, who claimed to have "books and letters of a just man named Paul."

112. Tertullian, "Apology," 101.

113. 1 Cor. 14:26.

114. Tertullian, "Prayer," 186–87.

115. Ibid., 172–74, 182–88.

116. Tertullian, "The Chaplet," in *Disciplinary, Moral and Ascetical Works*, 237.

117. *Didache*, 178–79. See Frend, *Rise of Christianity*, 141–42, for a summary of what little we know about this early rite.

118. P. Cramer, *Baptism and Change in the Early Middle Ages, c. 200–c. 1150* (Cambridge, 1993), 11–14. This book's discussion of baptism is not likely to be superseded soon.

119. Ibid., 9. For "living water," see also *Didache*, 177.

120. See M. R. Miles, *Carnal Knowing*, (Boston, 1989), 33–34, for a fine discussion of the ritual meaning of nakedness in this context.

121. Ibid., 28.

122. See O. Kiefer, *Sexual Life in Ancient Rome* (New York, 1993), 148–49.

123. "Constitutions of the Holy Apostles," in *Ante-Nicene Fathers*, vol. 7 (Peabody, Mass., 1995), 477. See also Cramer, 13, and Miles, 45–46, regarding the problem described in fifth-century texts of men anointing women with oil.

124. Tertullian, "The Chaplet," in *Disciplinary, Moral and Ascetical Works*, trans. R. Arbesmann et al. (New York, 1959), 237.

125. Cramer, 75.

126. Heffernan, 209.

127. Minucius Felix, "Octavius," 334–39.

128. See, for example, Justin Martyr, "Apology," 63, and Tertullian, "Apology," 11.

129. Tertullian, "Ad Nationes," in *Latin Christianity: Its Founder, Tertullian*, vol. 3 of *Ante-Nicene Fathers* (Peabody, Mass., 1995), 115.

130. Ibid.

131. G. E. M. de St. Croix, "Why Were the Early Christians Persecuted?" *Past and Present* 26 (1963): 16, suggests that the perceived threat to peace was a major factor in the persecutions.

132. Tertullian, "Apology," 10–12.
133. de St. Croix, 24, argues that this "monotheistic exclusiveness" was why Christians were persecuted. See also Rives, 249.
134. Tertullian, "Apology," 10.
135. "Scillitan Martyrs," in Musurillo, 86–89.
136. Rives, 243, and de St. Croix, 15.
137. Tertullian, "To Scapula," 157.
138. See Tertullian, "Flight in Time of Persecution," in *Disciplinary, Moral and Ascetical Works*, 276–77.
139. Tertullian, "Flight," 306.
140. Ibid., 299, 305.
141. Tertullian, "To Scapula," 151.
142. A. J. Droge and James D. Tabor, *A Noble Death: Suicide and Martyrdom among Christians and Jews in Antiquity* (Harper, 1992), 156. See also William Tabbernee. "Early Montanism and Voluntary Martyrdom," *Colloquium: The Australian and New Zealand Theological Review* (1985): 33–44. The classic work on the subject remains W. H. C. Frend, *Martyrdom and Persecution in the Early Church: A Study of Conflict from the Maccabees to Donatus* (Oxford, 1965).
143. Frend, *Martyrdom*, 258.
144. Tertullian, "Ad Nationes," 115.
145. Shaw, 14.
146. T. Barnes, *Tertullian. A Historical and Literary Study* (Oxford, 1971), 88.
147. Scriptores Historiae Augustae, *Historia Augusta*, trans. D. Magie. (Cambridge, 1967), 1:409. K. H. Schwarte, "Das angebliche Christengesetz des Sep. Sev.," *Historia* 12 (1963): 185–208, argues against the historical accuracy of this reported edict, but I agree with Frend that the evidence for the edict is much more compelling than the contrary. See W. H. C. Frend, "A Severan Persecution? Evidence of the 'Historia Augusta'" in *Forma Futuri: Studi in Onore del Cardinale Michele Pellegrino* (Torino, 1975), 470–80.
148. J. G. Davies, "Was the Devotion of Septimius Severus to Serapis the Cause of the Persecution of 202–23?" *Journal of Theological Studies* (1954): 73–76.
149. Eusebius, 239.
150. J. B. Rives, "The Piety of a Persecutor," *Journal of Early Christian Studies* 4.1 (1996): 1–26.
151. Tertullian, "To Scapula," 154.
152. "Perpetua," in Musurillo, 108–9.
153. Cramer, 48. See also Ferguson, 358, 360.
154. Tertullian, "On Baptism," 677.

FOUR: PRISON

1. T. Barnes, *Tertullian. A Historical and Literary Study* (Oxford, 1971), 72.
2. "Pionius," in H. Musurillo, comp. and trans., *The Acts of the Christian Martyrs* (Oxford, 1972), 139.
3. "Passion of Perpetua," in Musurillo, 109.

4. "Montanus," in Musurillo, 217.

5. "Perpetua," in Musurillo, 221.

6. Ibid., 109.

7. Tertullian "To the Martyrs," in *Disciplinary, Moral and Ascetical Works*, trans. R. Arbesmann et al. (New York, 1959), 17. Tertullian would later denounce the practice of feeding confessors while in prison because he feared their resolve would be weakened. (See his tract "On Fasting" in *Fathers of the Third Century: Tertullian, Part Fourth*. Vol. 4 of *Ante-Nicene Fathers*. [Peabody, Mass., 1995], 102–115.) However, during the time of Perpetua's imprisonment, he still supported the practice.

8. Tertullian, "To the Martyrs," 17–18.

9. G. D. Schlegel, "The Ad Martyras of Tertullian and the Circumstances of Its Composition," *Downside Review* 63 (1945): 127, argues for this date.

10. Barnes, *Tertullian*, 55, argues for a date of A.D. 197.

11. Tertullian, "To the Martyrs," 24–25.

12. "Perpetua," in Musurillo, 109, 111.

13. Ibid., 111.

14. See T. J. Heffernan, *Sacred Biography: Saints and their Biographers in the Middle Ages* (Oxford, 1988), 210, for an observation of an "echo of the thoughts of the Maccabean mother" in Perpetua's narrative.

15. See W. H. C. Frend, *Martyrdom and Persecution in the Early Church: A Study of Conflict from the Maccabees to Donatus* (Oxford, 1965), for a convincing demonstration of the influence of this text.

16. 4 Macc. 14:13; 15:6–7.

17. 4 Macc. 15:10; 15:12.

18. 2 Macc. 7:21.

19. 4 Macc. 15:29.

20. Tertullian, "To the Martyrs," 20.

21. "Perpetua," in Musurillo, 113.

22. Tertullian, "To the Martyrs," 19.

23. "Perpetua," in Musurillo, 113.

24. Tertullian "Patience," in *Disciplinary, Moral and Ascetical Works* (New York, 1959), 208–9.

25. B. Shaw, "The Passion of Perpetua." *Past and Present* 139 (1993): 25, offers a different explanation of the reference that it was only her father of her whole family who grieved. He suggests that the reference to "family" refers to her unnamed husband's family, all of whom would rejoice in her death. Only her father would mourn her. We cannot know which of these interpretations is closest to Perpetua's meaning.

26. "Montanus," in Musurillo, 219.

27. "Perpetua," in Musurillo, 113.

28. "Scillitan Martyrs," in Musurillo, 89.

29. See Patricia Cox Miller, "The Devil's Gateway: An Eros of Difference in the Dreams of Perpetua," *Dreaming* 2, no. 1 (1992): 48, for the importance of Perpetua's renaming. See also, Peter Dronke, *Women Writers of the Middle Ages: A Critical Study of Texts from Perpetua to Marguerite Porete* (Cambridge, 1984), 5.

30. "Perpetua," in Musurillo, 113, 115.

31. J. B. Rives, "The Piety of a Persecutor," *Journal of Early Christian Studies* 4.1 (1996): 22.

32. "Perpetua," in Musurillo, 115.

33. See Barbara Newman, *From Virile Woman to WomanChrist* (Philadelphia, 1995), 81: "Maternal love must be crushed underfoot in the name of faith."

34. Shaw, "Passion," 35.

35. Jacobus de Voragine, *The Golden Legend*, trans. G. Ryan (New York, 1969), 736.

36. Tertullian, "On the Soul," in *Apologetical Works and Minucius Felix*, trans. R. Arbesmann et al. (New York, 1950), 197.

37. For two excellent brief summaries of modern dream theories, see Kelly Bulkeley, *The Wilderness of Dreams: Exploring the Religious Meanings of Dreams in Modern Western Culture* (Albany, 1994), and Gayle Delaney, ed., *New Directions in Dream Interpretation* (Albany, 1993).

38. Sigmund Freud, *Interpretation of Dreams*, trans. J. Strachey (New York, 1965), 659–60.

39. Bulkeley, 43–44.

40. Ibid., 20.

41. Harry Hunt, in positing multiple kinds of dreams, claims that prophetic dreaming is one possibility, although he is willing to say only that such dreams *may* come true. Bulkeley, 73.

42. Virgil, *Aeneid*, trans. A. Mandelbaum (New York, 1981), 162.

43. S. R. F. Price, "The Future of Dreams: From Freud to Artemidorus," in *Before Sexuality: The Construction of Erotic Experience in the Ancient Greek World*, ed. D. M. Halperin et al. (Princeton, 1990), 372.

44. Ibid., 377.

45. J. LeGoff, "Christianity and Dreams," in *The Medieval Imagination*, trans. A. Goldhammer (Chicago, 1988), 199.

46. L. H. Martin, *Hellenistic Religions* (Oxford, 1987), 80.

47. Apuleius, *Golden Ass*, trans. J. Lindsay (Bloomington, 1960), 236.

48. Gen. 27:12.

49. Job 33:14–19.

50. Gen. 41.

51. See LeGoff, 193–94, 229–31, for examples of dreams in Scripture.

52. See ibid., 212–14, for an excellent summary of Christian mistrust of dreams.

53. Steven F. Kruger, *Dreaming in the Middle Ages* (Cambridge, 1992), offers a detailed summary of medieval dream lore and attitudes.

54. Tertullian, "On the Soul," 280.

55. Ibid., 285–86.

56. Delaney offers a explanation of modern techniques of interpretation, and shows the modern stress on dream interpretation. See Bulkeley, 81–132, for a model of dream interpretation.

57. Gen. 41.

58. LeGoff, 200.

59. Ibid., 201.

60. T. J. Heffernan, *Sacred Biography: Saints and Their Biographers in the Middle Ages* (Oxford, 1988), 201.

61. 2 Esdras, in *New Oxford Annotated Bible* (1977).

62. "Shepherd of Hermas," in *The Apostolic Fathers*. trans. F. X. Glimm et al. (New York, 1948), 230.

63. For an analysis of the dream travels of Hermas, see Patricia Cox Miller, "'All the Words Were Frightful': Salvation by Dreams in the Shepherd of Hermas," *Vigiliae Christianae* 42 (1988): 327–38. Hermas's experience is similar to the phenomenon of "lucid dreaming" in which the dreamer is aware he or she is dreaming. See Stephen LaBerge, *Lucid Dreaming* (Los Angeles, 1985) for an explanation of this kind of dream.

64. "Shepherd of Hermas," 259.

65. Miller, "'All the Words Were Frightful,'" 335.

66. "Shepherd of Hermas," 280.

67. Augustine, *Confessions*, trans. R. S. Pine-Coffin (New York, 1980), 68–69.

68. See W. C. Weinrich, *Spirit and Martyrdom: A Study of the Work of the Holy Spirit in Contexts of Persecution and Martyrdom in the New Testament and Early Christianity* (Washington, D. C., 1981), 43–63, for the link between suffering and the presence of the Spirit. This made a natural association between martyrs and the Spirit of prophecy.

69. Weinrich, xi: "Martyr became a prophet by virtue of a special gift of the Spirit which enabled the martyr to view the invisible world."

70. Eusebius, *The History of the Church*, trans. G. A. Williamson. (Harmondsworth, 1984), 170.

71. "Montanus," in Musurillo, 217.

72. See Musurillo, 219, 221, 223, 235.

73. R. Rousselle, "The Dreams of Vibia Perpetua: Analysis of a Female Christian Martyr," *Journal Psychohistory* 14 (1987): 193–206, represents perhaps the most extreme form of such interpretation.

74. For a Jungian approach to this text, see Marie-Louise von Franz, *The Passion of Perpetua*, Jungian Classics Series, 2 (Irving, Tex., 1980). See also Mary Ann Rossi, "The Passion of Perpetua, Everywoman of Late Antiquity," in *Pagan and Christian Anxiety: A Response to E. R. Dodds*, ed. R. C. Smith and J. Lounibos (New York, 1984), 53–86.

75. This is essentially the approach of the influential twentieth-century psychologist Calvin Hall, who studied dreams. He wrote, "[D]reams are continuous with waking life; the world of dreaming and the world of waking are one." Bulkeley, 51.

76. Cicero, "Dream of Scipio," in *Ancient Roman Religion*, ed. F. C. Grant (New York, 1957), 148.

77. "Perpetua," in Musurillo, 111. M. A. Tilley, "One Woman's Body: Repression and Expression in the *Passio Perpetuae*," in *Ethnicity, Nationality and Religious Experience*, ed. P. C. Phan (New York, 1991), 59, observes quite rightly that the "brother" probably was not a sibling but a "brother in Christ."

78. "Perpetua," in Musurillo, 111.

79. Tertullian, "To the Martyrs," 21.
80. "Perpetua," in Musurillo, 111–13.
81. Gen. 3:15; Gen. 28:12.
82. Tertullian, "To the Martyrs," 18.
83. Artemidorus, *The Interpretation of Dreams*, trans. R. J. White. (Park Ridge, N. J.: 1975) 4. 55, 1. 35.
84. See E. Castelli, "'I Will Make Mary Male': Pieties of the Body and Gender Transformation of Christian Women in Late Antiquity," in *Body Guards: The Cultural Politics of Gender Ambiguity*. ed. J. Epstein and K. Straub (New York, 1991), 37.
85. Peter Dronke, *Women Writers of the Middle Ages: A Critical Study of Texts from Perpetua to Marguerite Porete* (Cambridge, 1984), 7–8.
86. Artemidorus, 2. 42. See also Castelli, 37, and Rousselle, 195.
87. Bulkeley, 13.
88. "Perpetua," in Musurillo, 110.
89. Dronke, 8.
90. Rev. 7.
91. C. McDannell and B. Lang, *Heaven: A History* (New Haven, 1988), 40–42.
92. E. Gardner, ed. *Visions of Heaven and Hell Before Dante* (New York, 1989), 238.
93. "St. Peter's Apocalypse," in Gardner, 11.
94. Most scholars have identified the shepherd as a father figure to Perpetua. See Miller, "The Devil's Gateway," 54; A. Pettersen, "Perpetua—Prisoner of Conscience," *Vigiliae Christianae* 41 (1987): 144; Dronke, 9.
95. "Shepherd of Hermas," 259–60.
96. Pettersen, 148, for example.
97. Heffernan, 209–10.
98. "Perpetua," in Musurillo, 113.
99. Ibid.
100. Ibid., 115.
101. Tertullian, "To the Martyrs," 19.
102. Eusebius, 200.
103. Ibid., 204–05.
104. "Perpetua," in Musurillo, 115.
105. See Newman, 111: "The care she [Perpetua] withdraws from the living, she bestows upon the dead, and what she denies in the flesh she is prepared to grant in the spirit."
106. Dronke, 11. See, J. LeGoff, *The Birth of Purgatory*, trans. A. Goldhammer (Chicago, 1984), 50–51, for a contrast of this vision with later Christian views of Purgatory, but also for a notation of the importance of Perpetua's intercessory powers in shaping later ideas.
107. Virgil, *Aeneid*, 147. For other associations and an excellent discussion of the literary precedents of this vision, see Dronke, 11–12.
108. Dronke, 11.
109. "Perpetua," in Musurillo, 117.
110. See Giselle de Nie, "Consciousness Fecund through God," in *Sanctity and Motherhood*, ed. A. Mulder-Bakker (New York, 1995), 119, for a discussion

of Dinocrates being fed through her prayers.

111. "Perpetua," in Musurillo, 117.
112. See Miller, "The Devil's Gateway," 58, for an analysis of the water as a feminized image of breasts and nurturing.
113. Artemidorus, *Oneirocritica*, 1. 66, in Rousselle, 199.
114. Dronke, 12.
115. "Perpetua," in Musurillo, 117.
116. Ibid., 117, 119.
117. Rossi, 60–61.
118. Miller, "Dreams of Perpetua," 61. See also Dronke, 14, who sees her wanting to "strip herself of all that is weak, or womanish, in her nature." M. R. Miles, *Carnal Knowing* (Boston, 1989), 62: Perpetua's "assumption [is] that her spirituality, like her social identity, will take form in relation to a male-defined reality."
119. Rossi, 61, 65. See also J. E. Salisbury, *Church Fathers, Independent Virgins* (London, 1991), 96–110, for a discussion of transvestite saints who renounce their gender.
120. See Rousselle, 204, for example.
121. L. Robert, "Une vision de Perpétue, martyre à Carthage en 203," *Comptes rendus de l'Académie des Inscriptions et Belles-Lettres*, 1982, 256–58. Shaw, "Passion of Perpetua," 29, disagrees with such a practical explanation in a dream world.
122. Dio Cassius, *Dio's Roman History*, trans. E. Cary (Cambridge, 1961), 235.
123. See Rossi, 65, who also notes, "For Thecla and Perpetua the male disguise represented union with Christ. It effected a transformation of self and the birth of a new identity." See also Castelli, 42: "shifting gender identity as the major signifier for a woman's journey toward . . . victory [in spiritual struggle].
124. Dronke, 14. See also Shaw, "Passion," 29.
125. Lucian, *Lucian*, trans. M. D. Macleod (Cambridge, 1967), 8:65–67. See also Shaw, "Passion," 29 n. 66.
126. See Dronke, 285 n. 58, for parallels between the two texts.
127. Tertullian, "To the Martyrs," 23.
128. Ibid.
129. This is Dronke's opinion, 14.
130. Juvenal, *The Satires of Juvenal*, trans. R. Humphries. (Bloomington, Ind., 1958), 175–81. Shaw, 28 n. 62, sees the use of the image of the Egyptian as "a simple reflection of racism." I agree.
131. See Robert, 228–76, for a discussion of the contest.
132. J. B. Rives, *Religion and Authority in Roman Carthage from Augustus to Constantine* (Oxford, 1995), 64.
133. So argues Robert, "Une vision de Perpétue," but it is disputed by J. Aronen, *"Pythia Carthaginis* o immagini cristiane nella visione di Perpetua," in *L'Africa romana: Atti dei convegni di studio*, 6:645–48. See also Shaw, 28 n. 63.
134. Shaw, 28 n. 63.
135. M. R. Lefkowitz, "The Motivations for St. Perpetua's Martyrdom" *Journal of the American Academy of Religion* 44 (1976): 419.

136. Dronke, 8. I do not concur with Rousselle's analysis of the importance of feet as a sexual symbol in this context. Rousselle, 201–2.

137. J. E. Salisbury, *Iberian Popular Religion, 600 B.C. to 700 A.D.* (New York, 1985), 243–45, for a discussion on ritual magic associated with bare feet.

138. Ibid., 244.

139. See A. R. Littlewood, "The Symbolism of the Apple in Greek and Roman Literature," Harvard Studies in Classical Philology 72, 147–81, for a full discussion of the symbolism. See Miller, "Dreams of Perpetua," 61–63. for an analysis of this symbol in the dream of Perpetua.

140. Artemidorus, *Oneirocritica*, 1. 73, in Rousselle, 203.

141. Rossi, 62, sees in this document a "unique example of the mingling of pagan and Christian symbols in dreams."

142. Dronke, 14.

143. "Perpetua," in Musurillo, 119.

144. Ibid., 119–23.

145. E. R. Dodds, *Pagan and Christian in an Age of Anxiety* (Cambridge, 1985), 49 n. 2, argues that for these reasons the dream is not authentic. Shaw, "Passion of Perpetua," 32, expresses doubts that it is an authentic dream but leaves open the possibility for strong differences among dreams of martyrs.

146. See W. H. C. Frend, *Martyrdom and Persecution in the Early Church: A Study of Conflict from the Maccabees to Donatus* (Oxford, 1965), 365.

147. Ibid.: Frend notes the emphasis on martyrdom in these visions. The church leaders did not enter paradise in Saturus's vision, and Perpetua saw only martyrs in heaven.

148. "Perpetua," in Musurillo, 119.

149. Ibid., 123.

150. Ibid.

151. Musurillo, 22.

152. S. B. Pomeroy, *Goddesses, Whores, Wives and Slaves: Women in Classical Antiquity* (New York, 1975), 193.

153. "Perpetua," in Musurillo, 123, 125.

154. See Heffernan, 222–29, for a detailed analysis of the significance of the depiction of Felicity's pregnancy.

155. Ibid., 229.

FIVE: THE ARENA

1. T. Wiedemann, *Emperors and Gladiators* (New York, 1992), 23. For the best description of this arena, see David L. Bomgardner, "The Carthage Amphitheater: A Reappraisal," *American Journal of Archaeology* 93 (1989): 85–103.

2. Wiedemann, 21.

3. Ibid., 23.

4. Bomgardner, 100–102.

5. Ibid., 89, 100.

6. Ibid., 96.

7. My thanks to the archaeologists who have worked in Carthage for years, and who helped me see and understand the spaces. The help of Professors JoAnn Freed, M. Garrison, R. Hitchner, and Colin Wells was invaluable.

8. Carlin A. Barton, *The Sorrows of the Ancient Romans: The Gladiator and the Monster* (Princeton, 1993), 187, argues that these spectacles were for the Romans "a necessary precondition of the sacred, of a person's most essential being."

9. Lactantius, in Tertullian, "To Scapula," in *Apologetical Works and Minucius Felix*. trans. R. Arbesmann et al. (New York, 1950), 153 n. 3.

10. Wiedemann, 46.

11. Ibid., 34–35.

12. Ibid., 15.

13. J. B. Rives, *Religion and Authority in Roman Carthage from Augustus to Constantine* (Oxford, 1995), 62–64.

14. René Girard, *Violence and the Sacred*, trans. P. Gregory. (Baltimore, 1977), 8.

15. Tertullian, "Spectacles," in *Disciplinary, Moral and Ascetical Works*, trans. R. Arbesmann et al. (New York, 1959), 70.

16. Ibid., 65.

17. Barton, 19.

18. R. Auguet, *Cruelty and Civilization: The Roman Games* (New York, 1994), 43, notes further that the costuming recalled "the religious origin of the games," and thus, he further observes, the relationship between costumed processions and religious observances.

19. Tertullian, "Spectacles," 73.

20. Auguet, 49.

21. A. Rouselle, *Porneia: On Desire and the Body in Antiquity*. trans. F. Pheasant (New York, 1988), 116–19.

22. Ibid., 119–20.

23. Barton, 22.

24. See Eusebius, *History of the Church* (New York, 1965), 202.

25. Barton, 63.

26. Pliny, *Panegyricus*, 33. 1, in Barton, 21.

27. Weidemann, 38.

28. Ibid., 39.

29. Scriptores Historiae Augustae, *Historiae Augustae*, trans. D. Magie (Cambridge, 1967), 3.

30. Weidemann, 138–39.

31. Justin Martyr, "2nd Apology," in *Writings of Saint Justin Martyr*, trans. T. B. Falls (New York, 1948), 132.

32. Tertullian, "Spectacles," 100.

33. Ibid., 101.

34. Seneca,"Ep. VII," *Ad Lucilium Epistulae Morales*, trans. R. M. Gummere (Cambridge, 1967), 31.

35. Tertullian "Spectacles" 84.

36. Ibid.

37. Ibid., 83.

38. Wiedemann, 141–42.

39. Prudentius, "Against Symmachus, Book Two," in *The Poems of Prudentius*, trans. M. C. Eagan (Washington, D. C., 1965), 175.
40. Tertullian, "Spectacles," 95.
41. Juvenal, *The Satires of Juvenal*, trans. R. Humphries (Bloomington, Ind., 1958), 66–67.
42. Seneca, "Ep. VII," 31.
43. Ibid., 33.
44. Herodian, *History*, trans. C. R. Whittaker (Cambridge, 1969), III, 13, 349.
45. Augustine, *Confessions*, trans. R. S. Pine-Coffin (New York, 1980), 124.
46. Weidemann, 141.
47. Ibid., 61.
48. Ibid., 60–61.
49. See K. M. Coleman, "Fatal Charades: Roman Executions Staged as Mythological Enactments," *Journal of Roman Studies* 80 (1990): 44–73, for a good summary of this practice.
50. Eusebius, 201.
51. Tertullian, "Apology," in *Apologetical Works and Minucius Felix*, trans. R. Arbesmann et al. (New York, 1950), 48.
52. Ibid.
53. Coleman, 62.
54. Ibid., 70.
55. Auguet, 93.
56. Eusebius, 172.
57. "Montanus," in H. Musurillo, *The Acts of the Christian Martyrs* (Oxford, 1972), 225–27.
58. Ibid., 227.
59. Tertullian "To the Martyrs," in *Disciplinary, Moral and Ascetical Works*, trans. R. Arbesmann et al. (New York, 1959), 24–27.
60. "Scillitan Martyrs," in Musurillo, 89.
61. "Perpetua," in Musurillo, 121.
62. "Marian and James," in Musurillo, 195.
63. Eusebius, 195.
64. "Martyrdom of Polycarp," in *Early Christian Writings: The Apostolic Fathers*, trans. M. Staniforth (New York, 1968), 156.
65. Eusebius, 169.
66. Justin, "Apology," 34.
67. "Perpetua," in Musurillo, 125.
68. Ibid.
69. Ibid.
70. Ibid.
71. Ibid.
72. Ibid.
73. Ibid.
74. Auguet, 95.
75. Ignatius of Antioch, "Epistle to the Romans," in Staniforth, 105.
76. There is controversy about whether the martyrs died in the main amphitheater at Carthage or in another military amphitheater. This dispute is

based on phrases in the *Passio* like *munus castrense* and the emphasis on the military's role in these games. There has not been another amphitheater found in Carthage, but the military ones elsewhere in the empire tended to be temporary affairs. We cannot at this time completely resolve this controversy. In absence of more information, I find it more compelling that so public an event, so attended by the people who were directly involved in the proceedings, would have been held in the main amphitheater of Carthage. The military could well have played an important role in producing the executions, because, particularly under Septimius Severus, they were an important force.

77. Auguet, 62.
78. "Perpetua," in Musurillo, 126–27.
79. Ibid., 127.
80. Ibid.
81. "Flavian," in Musurillo, 237.
82. See Rouselle, *Porneia*, 116.
83. "Perpetua," in Musurillo, 127.
84. Ibid.
85. Ibid.
86. Eusebius, 194.
87. Auguet, 94.
88. Tertullian, "Spectacles," 97.
89. J. E. Salisbury, *Church Fathers, Independent Virgins* (London, 1991), 37.
90. Jacobus de Voragine, *The Golden Legend*, trans. G. Ryan (New York, 1969), 553.
91. Eusebius, 200.
92. "Perpetua," in Musurillo, 127.
93. Ibid., 129.
94. Brent Shaw, "The Passion of Perpetua," *Past and Present* 139 (1993): 7.
95. Ibid., 8.
96. Auguet, 95.
97. Eusebius, 202.
98. "Perpetua," in Musurillo, 129.
99. Auguet, 103.
100. See Francine Cardman, "Acts of the Women Martyrs," in *Women in Early Christianity*, ed. D. M. Scholer (New York, 1993), 150: "In both the maternal and the social body, the demands of mothering exert a pull away from martyrdom, and so must be denied in order for women to enact their final confession of faith."
101. See Clarissa W. Atkinson, *The Oldest Vocation: Christian Motherhood in the Middle Ages* (Ithaca, 1991), 58, and Danielle Jacquart and Claude Thomasset, *Sexuality and Medicine in the Middle Ages* (Princeton, 1988), 72.
102. Atkinson, 59.
103. "Perpetua," in Musurillo, 129.
104. Ibid.
105. Ibid.
106. Ibid.

107. Eusebius, 202.
108. "Perpetua," in Musurillo, 129.
109. Jean Laporte, *The Role of Women in Early Christianity* (New York, 1982), 10, notes, "The confessors are charismatics by their very confession, and it seems that they endure physical suffering in a state of partial ecstasy."
110. "Perpetua," in Musurillo, 129.
111. Ibid., 129–31.
112. Ibid., 131, n. 21.
113. Rouselle, 119.
114. "Perpetua," in Musurillo, 131.
115. Ibid.
116. Seneca, "Ep. 82," 245.
117. "Perpetua," in Musurillo, 131.
118. Ibid.

SIX: AFTERMATH

1. Herodian, *History*, trans. C. R. Whittaker (Cambridge, 1969), III, 10, 327.
2. Ibid., 13, 351–53.
3. Anthony Birley, *Septimius Severus: The African Emperor* (London, 1971), 244–68, has an excellent summary of this campaign.
4. Herodian, III, 14, 355–57.
5. Ibid., 14, 361.
6. Dio Cassius, *Dio's Roman History*, trans. E. Cary (Cambridge, 1961), 267–69.
7. Birley, 264.
8. Dio Cassius, 271–73.
9. Ibid., 283.
10. Ibid.
11. Scriptores Historiae Augustae, *Historiae Augustae*, "Ant. Geta," trans. D. Magie (Cambridge, 1967), 37–39.
12. My thanks to Professor David MacDonald for calling these facts to my attention. See D. MacDonald, *The Coinage of Aphrodisias* (London, 1992), 41, 133–34.
13. Scriptores Historiae Augustae, "Ant. Caracalla," 25.
14. Dio Cassius, 297.
15. J. B. Rives, *Religion and Authority in Roman Carthage from Augustus to Constantine* (Oxford, 1995), 250–51.
16. Ibid., 259.
17. Ibid.
18. Herodian, VII, q 219.
19. Ibid., 183 n. 1.
20. Ibid., 177–233.
21. Orosius, *Historiae adversum Paganos* IV, 6, 3–5, in A. Rouselle, *Porneia: On desire and the Body in Antiquity*, trans. F. Pheasant (New York, 1988), 128
22. Susan Raven, *Rome in Africa* (New York, 1993), 142–43.
23. D. L. Bomgardner, "The Carthage Amphitheater: A Reappraisal," *Ameri-*

can Journal of Archaeology 93 (1989): 102.

24. W. H. C. Frend, *Martyrdom and Persecution in the Early Church: A Study of Conflict from the Maccabees to Donatus* (Oxford, 1965), 379.

25. Ibid., 399.

26. Ibid., 370.

27. See T. Barnes, "The Chronology of Montanism," *Journal of Theological Studies*, n.s., 21, no. 2 (1970): 403–8; R. J. Heine, *Montanist Oracles and Testimonia*. North American Patristic Society, vol. 14 (Macon, Ga., 1989); P. de Labriolle, *La crise montaniste* (Paris, 1913), for an overview of this movement.

28. D. Powell, "Tertullianists and Cataphrygians," *Vigiliae Christianae* 29 (1975): 43, argues that the New Prophecy shared many of the late-second-century Christian beliefs of martyrdom and expectation of the arrival of the New Jerusalem.

29. Tertullian, "Flight in Time of Persecution," in *Disciplinary, Moral and Ascetical Works*, trans. R. Arbesmann et al. (New York, 1959), 294.

30. See Frend, 367, for a discussion of Tertullian's uncompromising stance with regard to the pagan world.

31. Tertullian, "The Chaplet," in *Disciplinary, Moral and Ascetical Works*, 231–32.

32. Ibid., 233.

33. Ibid., 255.

34. Ibid., 233.

35. Frend, 355.

36. Tertullian, "Flight in Time of Persecution," 307.

37. "Perpetua," in H. Musurillo, *The Acts of the Christian Martyrs* (Oxford, 1972), 121.

38. "Perpetua," in Musurillo, 107. See also, Acts 2:17, paraphrasing the prophet Joel 2:28.

39. See Powell, 35–38, in which he argues that Tertullian and other North Africans in the second century did not split into a schismatic church over the issue of the New Prophecy.

40. See W. H. C. Frend, "Blandina and Perpetua: Two Early Christian Heroines," in *Women in Early Christianity*, ed. D. M. Scholer (New York, 1993), 94, for his view that Montanism and the second century church simply shared convictions. W. C. Weinrich, *Spirit and Martyrdom: A Study of the Work of the Holy Spirit in Contexts of Persecution and Martyrdom in the New Testament and Early Christianity* (Washington, D. C., 1981), 236, also believes the *Passio* of Perpetua does not indicate Montanism directly but instead reveals a state of the Carthaginian church.

41. R. S. Kraemer, *Her Share of the Blessings* (Oxford, 1992), 163.

42. Powell, 47–49.

43. W. H. C. Frend, *Martyrdom and Persecution*, 380. Timothy Barnes, *Tertullian: A Historical and Literary Study* (Oxford, 1971), 258–59, disputes the claim that Tertullian had anything to do with the "Tertullianists."

44. See Rives, 273–85 for an excellent analysis of Tertullian's views on religion and authority, including his view of Montanism.

45. Cyprian, "To Donatus," in *Saint Cyprian: Treatises*, trans. R. J. Deferrari (New York, 1958), 12–18.
46. Ibid., 19–20.
47. Ibid., 7.
48. W. H. C. Frend, *The Rise of Christianity* (Philadelphia, 1984), 313.
49. Cyprian, "Epistle 1," in *Saint Cyprian: Letters*, trans. Rose Bernard Donna (Washington, D. C., 1964), 4.
50. Rives, 290–91.
51. Cyprian, "The Lapsed," in *Saint Cyprian: Treatises*, 58.
52. "Pionius," in Musurillo, 139.
53. Ibid., 143.
54. Ibid., 165.
55. Ibid., 141.
56. Cyprian, "The Lapsed," 63–64.
57. Cyprian, "Epistle 55," in *Cyprian: Letters*, 142.
58. Cyprian, "The Lapsed," 65.
59. Ibid., 86.
60. Ibid., 71. See Rives, 294–300, for a discussion of the way Cyprian increased episcopal power during this time.
61. Cyprian, "Unity of the Catholic Church," in *Cyprian: Treatises*, 95–96.
62. Ibid., 103, 119. See also J. E. Salisbury, "The Bond of a Common Mind: A Study of Collective Salvation from Cyprian to Augustine," *Journal of Religious History*, II 1985, 235–47.
63. "Cyprian," in Musurillo, 175.
64. "Montanus," in Musurillo, 223–25.
65. Frend, *Martyrdom and Persecution*, 455.
66. Ibid., 500.
67. "Felix," in Musurillo, 266–71.
68. W. H. C. Frend, *The Donatist Church* (Oxford, 1952), remains the best analysis of this movement.
69. Augustine, *Confessions*, trans. R. S. Pine-Coffin (New York, 1980), 55–56.
70. Ibid., 68–69.
71. Rives, 310.
72. See Salisbury, 235–47, for a discussion of the change in salvation.
73. Augustine, "Letter 185: On the Treatment of the Donatists," in *Letters*, vol. 4, 165–203, trans. W. Parsons (New York, 1955), 142.
74. Ibid., 144: "They have separated themselves from the Catholic Church, that is, from the unity of all nations."
75. Ibid., 153.
76. Ibid., 173.
77. Peter Brown, *Augustine of Hippo* (Berkeley, 1969), 334.
78. See Frend, *Donatist Church*, for the best analysis of the socioeconomic factors that sustained the movement.
79. "Pionius," in Musurillo, 137.
80. Tertullian, "Apology," in *Apologetical Works and Minucius Felix*, trans. R. Arbesmann et al. (New York, 1950), 125.
81. Peter Brown, *The Cult of the Saints* (Chicago, 1981), 62–68.

82. Celsus, *On the True Doctrine*, trans. R. J. Hoffman (Oxford, 1987), 86. See also Caroline Walker Bynum, *The Resurrection of the Body in Western Christianity, 200–1336* (New York, 1995), 31.

83. Bynum, 47.

84. Ibid., 21–43.

85. Ibid., 35–6.

86. "Phileas," in Musurillo, 231.

87. See Brown, *Cult of Saints*, 79: "The heroism of the martyrs had always been treated as a form of possession, strictly dissociated from normal human courage."

88. "Marian and James," in Musurillo, 201.

89. "Montanus and Lucius," in Musurillo, 235.

90. "Pionius," in Musurillo, 165.

91. "Marian and James," in Musurillo, 213.

92. Bynum, 107.

93. Brown, *Cult of Saints*, 34.

94. Ibid.

95. See "Cyprian," in Musurillo, 175, for the ceremony with which Cyprian was buried.

96. See "Maximilian," in Musurillo, 249, for Pompeiana's efforts to acquire the body of Maximilian for burial near her proposed burial location.

97. Brown, *Cult of Saints*, 88.

98. Eusebius, *The History of the Church*, trans. G. A. Williamson (Harmondsworth: 1984), 203.

99. Joyce E. Salisbury, "Origin of the Power of Vincent the Martyr," in *Proceedings of the PMR Conference* 8 (1983): 97–98.

100. "Cyprian," in Musurillo, 171.

101. J. E. Salisbury, *Iberian Popular Religion, 600 B.C. to 700 A.D.* (New York, 1985), 167.

102. Brown, *Cult of Saints*, 82.

103. Ibid.

104. Augustine, *City of God*, trans H. Bettenson (Harmondsworth, 1972), 1034.

105. Frend, *Martyrdom and Persecution*, 363.

106. Barnes, 79.

107. B. Shaw, "The Passion of Perpetua," *Past and Present* 139 (1993): 42.

108. R. P. Delattre, "Sur l'inscription des martyrs de Carthage, sainte Perpétue, sainte Félicité et leurs compagnons," *Comptes rendus de l'Académie des Inscriptions et Belles-Lettres*, 1907, 193–95.

109. Shaw, 37.

110. See Salisbury, "Power of Vincent," 97–107.

111. Shaw, 35, first observes this gendered nature of the Acta.

112. Ibid., 35–36. See also C. I. M. I van Beek, *Passio Sanctarum Perpetuae et Felicitatis*, vol. I, *Textum Graecum et Latinum ad fidem codicum MSS* (Nijmegen, 1956), 68.

113. At least three sermons are certainly by Augustine, and a fourth has been attributed to him, but it is uncertain whether it was actually written by the bishop. See W. H. Shewring, *The Passion of SS. Perpetua and Felicity* (Lon-

don, 1931), 45–59, for a translation of the four sermons.

114. R. Braun, *Opera Quodvultdeo Carthaginiensi episcopo tributa* (Turnhout, 1976).

115. Augustine, "Sermon 4," in Shewring, 58.

116. Augustine, "Sermon 1," in Shewring, 49, 51.

117. Ibid., 50.

118. Ibid., 46–47.

119. Augustine, "Sermon 2," in Shewring, 53, and "Sermon 4," in Shewring, 57.

120. Augustine, "Letter 262," in *Letters*, vol. 5, trans. W. Parsons (New York, 1956), 261.

121. Augustine, "Sermon 2," in Shewring, 53.

122. Ibid.

123. See J. E. Salisbury, *Church Fathers, Independent Virgins* (London, 1991), 49–54, for Augustine's views on the comportment of religious women.

124. As Shaw, 33, wrote: "[T]he very words she wrote contained an irrefutable self-empowerment."

125. Augustine, "Sermons 2," in Shewring, 46, 52, and "Sermon 4," in Shrewing, 54.

126. Augustine, "Sermon 2," in Shewring, 52.

127. Augustine, *City of God*, 1057–58.

128. Augustine, "Sermon 1," in Shewring, 45–46, and "Sermon 4," in Shrewing, 52.

129. Augustine, *De natura et origine animae*, 4. 18. 26, in Shaw, 41.

130. Shaw, 41, notes that Augustine seems rather taken with the "banal pun . . . given the number of times he repeats it."

131. Augustine, "Sermon 2" and "Sermon 3," in Shewring, 54–55.

132. Augustine, "Sermon 4," in Shewring, 56.

133. Shaw, 43–44.

134. Victor of Vita, *History of the Vandal Persecution*, trans J. Moorhead (Liverpool, 1992), 6.

135. Shaw, 45.

136. R. Rousselle, "The Dreams of Vibia Perpetua: Analysis of a Female Christian Martyr," *Journal Psychohistory* 14 (1987): 193–206.

137. M. R. Miles, *Carnal Knowing* (Boston, 1989), 62.

Bibliography

EDITIONS OF THE "PASSION OF PERPETUA"

Dronke, Peter. *Women Writers of the Middle Ages: A Critical Study of Texts from Perpetua to Marguerite Porete*. Cambridge: Cambridge University Press, 1984.

Muncey, R. Waterville. *The Passion of Perpetua: An English Translation with Introduction and Notes*. London: J. M. Dent, 1927.

Musurillo, H., Comp. and trans. *The Acts of the Christian Martyrs*. Oxford: Oxford University Press, 1972.

Robinson, J. A. *The Passion of St. Perpetua*. Text and Studies, vol. 1, no. 2. Cambridge: Cambridge University Press, 1891.

Shewring, W. H. *The Passion of SS. Perpetua and Felicity*. London: Sheed & Ward, 1931.

Thiébaux, Marcelle. *The Writings of Medieval Women: An Anthology*. New York: Garland, 1994.

van Beek, C. J. M. J. *Passio Sanctarum Perpetuae et Felicitatis*, vol. 1, *Textum Graecum et Latinum ad fidem codicum MSS*. Nijmegen, 1956.

von Franz, Marie-Louise. *The Passion of Perpetua*. Jungian Classics Series, 2, Irving, Tex.: Spring Publications, 1980.

Wilson-Kastner, Patricia, et al. *A Lost Tradition: Women Writers of the Early Church*. Lanham, Md.: University Press of America, 1981.

PRIMARY SOURCES

Appian. *Appian's Roman History*. Trans. H. White. Cambridge: Harvard University Press, 1964.

Apuleius. *The Apologia and Florida of Apuleius of Madaura*. Trans. H. E. Butler. Westport, Conn.: Greenwood Press, 1970.

———. *Golden Ass*. Trans. Jack Lindsay. Bloomington: Indiana University Press, 1960.

Aristides, Aelius. *Aelius Aristides: The Complete Works*. Trans. C. A. Behr. Leiden: Brill, 1981, 1986.

Artemidorus. *The Interpretation of Dreams.* Trans. R. J. White. Park Ridge, N. J.: Noyes Press, 1975.

Augustine. *City of God.* Trans. H. Bettenson. Harmondsworth: Penguin Books, 1972.

———. *Confessions.* Trans. R. S. Pine-Coffin, New York: Penguin Books, 1980.

———. *Letters.* Vol. 4. Trans. W. Parsons. New York: Fathers of the Church, 1955.

———. *Letters:* Vol. 5. Trans. W. Parsons. New York: Fathers of the Church, 1956.

———. "On the Catechising of the Uninstructed." Trans. S. D. F. Salmond. In *Augustine: On the Holy Trinity, Doctrinal Treatises, Moral Treatises.* Vol. 3 of *Nicene and Post-Nicene Fathers.* Peabody, Mass.: Hendrickson, 1995.

———. "On the Soul and Its Origin." Trans. P. Holmes. In *Augustine: Anti-Pelagian Writings.* Vol. 5 of *Nicene and Post-Nicene Fathers.* Peabody, Mass.: Hendrickson, 1994.

Celsus. *Celsus: On the True Doctrine.* Trans. R. J. Hoffmann. Oxford: Oxford University Press, 1987.

Cicero. *De Natura Deorum* Trans. H. Rackham. Cambridge: Harvard University Press, 1967.

"Constitutions of the Holy Apostles." In *Ante-Nicene Fathers.* Vol. 7. Peabody, Mass.: Hendrickson, 1995.

Cyprian. *Saint Cyprian: Letters.* Trans. Rose Bernard Donna, Washington, D. C.: Catholic University of America Press, 1964.

———. *Saint Cyprian: Treatises.* Trans. R. J. Deferrari. New York: Fathers of the Church, 1958.

"Didache or Teaching of the Apostles." In *The Apostolic Fathers.* Trans. F. X. Glimm et al. 167–186. New York: Christian Heritage, 1948.

Dio Cassius. *Dio's Roman History.* Trans. E. Cary. Cambridge: Harvard University Press, 1961.

Diodorus. *Diodorus of Sicily.* Trans. R. M. Geer. Cambridge: Harvard University Press, 1962.

Eusebius. *The History of the Church.* Trans. G. A. Williamson. Harmondsworth: Penguin Books, 1984.

Heliodorus. *Ethiopian Story.* Trans. W. Lamb. London: J. M. Dent & Sons, 1961.

Herodian. *History.* Trans. C. R. Whittaker. Cambridge: Harvard University Press, 1969.

Herodotus. *The History.* Trans. D. Grene. Chicago: University of Chicago Press, 1987.

Irenaeus. "Against Heresies." In *Ante-Nicene Fathers,* vol. 1, Ed. A. Roberts et al. Peabody, Mass.: Hendrickson, 1995.

Jacobus de Voragine. *The Golden Legend.* Trans. G. Ryan. New York: Arno Press, 1969.

Jerome. *Jerome: Letters and Select Works.* Trans. W. H. Fremantle. Vol. 6 of *Nicene and Post-Nicene Fathers.* Peabody, Mass.: Hendrickson, 1995.

Justin Martyr. *Writings of Saint Justin Martyr.* Trans. by T. B. Falls. New York: Christian Heritage, 1948.

Juvenal. *The Satires of Juvenal*, Trans. R. Humphries. Bloomington: Indiana University Press, 1958.

Lewis, Naphtali, et al. *Roman Civilization Sourcebook.*Vol. 2, *The Empire*. New York: Harper & Row, 1966.

Livy. *Livy*. Vol. 5. Trans. B. O. Foster. Cambridge: Harvard University Press, 1963.

Lucian of Samasota. *Lucian*. Trans. M. D. Macleod. 8 vols. Cambridge: Harvard University Press, 1967.

Marcus Aurelius, *Meditations*. Harmondsworth: Penguin Books, 1964.

Meyer, Marvin W., ed. *The Ancient Mysteries: A Sourcebook*. New York: Harper Collins, 1987.

Origen. *Contra Celsum*. Trans. H. Chadwick. Cambridge: Cambridge University Press, 1953.

Pliny. *Natural History*. Vol. 4. Trans. H. Rackham. Cambridge: Harvard University Press, 1960.

Plotinus. "The Six Enneads." In *Great Books of the Western World*, ed. M. J. Adler, 11: 301–678. Chicago: Encyclopedia Britannica, 1991.

Plutarch. *Lives of the Noble Grecians and Romans*. Trans. J. Dryden. New York: Modern Library, n. d.

———. *Moralia*. Trans. F. C. Babbitt. Cambridge: Harvard University Press, 1962.

Prudentius. *The Poems of Prudentius*. Trans. M. C. Eagan. Washington, D. C.: Catholic University of America Press, 1965.

Quodvultdeo. *Opera Quodvultdeo Carthaginiensi episcopo tributa*. Ed. R. Braun. Series latina, no. 60. Turnhout: Corpus Christianorum, 1976.

Scriptores Historiae Augustae. *Historia Augusta*. Trans. D. Magie. Cambridge: Harvard University Press, 1967.

Seneca. *Ad Lucilium Epistulae Morales*. Trans. R. M. Gummere. Cambridge: Harvard University Press, 1967.

"Shepherd of Hermas." In *The Apostolic Fathers*, trans. F. X. Glimm et al. 225–354. New York: Christian Heritage, 1948.

Staniforth, Maxwell, trans. *Early Christian Writings: The Apostolic Fathers*. New York: Dorset Press, 1968.

Stephens, Susan A. and John J. Winkler, eds. *Ancient Greek Novels: The Fragments*. Princeton: Princeton University Press, 1995.

Tacitus. *Complete Works of Tacitus*. Trans. A. J. Church. New York: Random House, 1942.

Tertullian. *Apologetical Works and Minucius Felix*. Trans. R. Arbesmann et al. New York: Fathers of the Church, 1950.

———. *Disciplinary, Moral and Ascetical Works*. Trans. R. Arbesmann et al. New York: Fathers of the Church, 1959.

———. *Fathers of the Third Century: Tertullian, Part Fourth*. Vol. 4 of *Ante-Nicene Fathers*. Peabody, Mass.: Hendrickson, 1995.

———. *Latin Christianity: Its Founder, Tertullian*. Vol. 3 of *Ante-Nicene Fathers*. Peabody, Mass.: Hendrickson, 1995.

Victor of Vita. *History of the Vandal Persecution.* Trans J. Moorhead. Liverpool:
   Liverpool University Press, 1992.
Virgil, *Aeneid.* Trans. A. Mandelbaum. New York: Bantam Books, 1981.

SECONDARY SOURCES

Abrahamsen, Valerie. "Women at Philippi: The Pagan and Christian Evidence."
   Journal of Feminist Studies in Religion 3, no. 2 (1987): 17–30.
Altman, Charles F. "Two Types of Opposition and the Structure of Latin Saints'
   Lives. " *Medievalia et Humanistica* 6 (1975): 1–11.
Amundsen, D. W., and C. J. Diers. "The Age of Menarche in Classical Greece
   and Rome." *Human Biology* 41 (1969): 125–32.
Anderson, Graham. *Ancient Fiction: The Novel in the Graeco-Roman World.* Totowa,
   N. J.: Barnes & Noble, 1984.
———. *Sage, Saint and Sophist.* London: Routledge, 1994.
Aronen, J. "*Pythia Carthaginis* o immagini cristiane nella visione di Perpetua." In
   *L'Africa romana: Atti dei convegni di studio,*6:645–48.
Ash, James L. "The Decline of Ecstatic Prophecy in the Early Church." *Journal
   of Theological Studies,* n.s., 21 (1970): 227–52.
Atkinson, Clarissa W. *The Oldest Vocation: Christian Motherhood in the Middle Ages.*
   Ithaca: Cornell University Press, 1991.
Auguet, R. *Cruelty and Civilization: The Roman Games.* New York: Routledge, 1994.
Aune, David E. *Prophecy in Early Christianity and the Ancient Mediterranean World.*
   Grand Rapids, Mich.: Eerdmans, 1983.
Babelon, Jean. *Impératrices Syriennes.* Paris: Editions Albin Michel, 1957.
Bagnall, Roger S. *Egypt in Late Antiquity.* Princeton: Princeton University Press,
   1993.
Balsdon, J. P. V. D. *Roman Women: Their History and Habits.* London: Bodley
   Head, 1962.
Banks, Robert. *Paul's Idea of Community.* Peabody, Mass.: Hendrickson, 1994.
Barnes, Timothy. "The Chronology of Montanism." *Journal of Theological
   Studies,* n.s., 21 no. 2 (1970): 403–8.
———. "The Family and Career of L. Septimius Severus." *Historia* 16 (1967):
   87–107.
———. *Tertullian. A Historical and Literary Study.* Oxford: Clarendon Press, 1971.
———. "Three Neglected Martyrs." *Journal of Theological Studies,* n.s. 22 (1971):
   159–61.
Barton, Carlin A. "The Scandal of the Arena." *Representations* 27 (1989): 1–36.
———. *The Sorrows of the Ancient Romans: The Gladiator and the Monster.* Prince-
   ton: Princeton University Press, 1993.
Benario, Herbert W. "Amphitheatres of the Roman World." *Classical Journal* 75
   (1980): 255–58.
———. "Julia Domna—Mater Senatus et Patriae." *Phoenix* 12 (summer 1958):
   67–70.

Benko, Stephen. *Pagan Rome and the Early Christians*. Bloomington: Indiana University Press, 1984.

———, and J. J. O'Rourke, eds. *The Catacombs and the Colosseum*. Valley Forge: Judson Press, 1971.

Best, E. E. "Cicero, Livy and Educated Roman Women." *Classical Journal* 65 (1970): 199–204.

Birley, Anthony. *Septimius Severus: The African Emperor*. London: Eyre & Spottiswoode, 1971.

Bisbee, G. A. *Pre-Decian Acts of Martyrs and Commentarii* Philadelphia: Fortress Press, 1988.

Bishop, W. C. "The African Rite." *Journal of Theological Studies* 13 (1911/12): 250–71.

Bomgardner, David L. "The Carthage Amphiteater: A Reappraisal," *American Journal of Archaeology* 93 (1989): 85–103.

Bonner, S. F. "Child Care at Rome: The Role of Men." *Historical Reflections/Réflexions Historiques* 12 (1985): 485–523.

Bowersock, G. W. *Greek Sophists in the Roman Empire*. Oxford: Clarendon Press, 1969.

———. *Hellenism in Late Antiquity*. Ann Arbor: University of Michigan Press, 1990.

Brandon, S. G. F., ed. *The Saviour God*. Manchester: Manchester University Press, 1963.

Brooten, Bernadette J. "Early Christian Women and Their Cultural Context." In *Feminist Perspectives on Biblical Scholarship*, ed. Adela Yarbro Collins, 66–91. Chicago: Scholars Press, 1985.

Brown, Peter. *Augustine of Hippo*. Berkeley: University of California Press, 1969.

———. *The Cult of the Saints*. Chicago: University of Chicago Press, 1981.

———. *The Making of Late Antiquity*. Cambridge: Harvard University Press, 1978.

———. *Power and Persuasion in Late Antiquity: Towards a Christian Empire*. Madison: University of Wisconsin Press, 1992.

———. *Religion and Society in the Age of St. Augustine*. New York: Harper & Row, 1972.

———. *The World of Late Antiquity*. New York: Harcourt Brace Jovanovich, 1971.

Brown, Shelby. *Late Carthaginian Child Sacrifice*. Sheffield: Sheffield Academic Press, 1991.

Brueggemann, Walter. *The Prophetic Imagination*. Philadelphia: Fortress Press, 1978.

Bulkeley, Kelly. *The Wilderness of Dreams: Exploring the Religious Meanings of Dreams in Modern Western Culture*. Albany: SUNY Press, 1994.

Burkert, Walter. *Ancient Mystery Cults*. Cambridge: Harvard University Press, 1987.

Burtchaell, James Tunstead. *From Synagogue to Church: Public Services and Offices*. Cambridge: Cambridge Universtiy Press, 1992.

Bynum, Caroline Walker. *The Resurrection of the Body in Western Christianity, 200–1336*. New York: Columbia University Press, 1995.

Cameron, Averil, and Amelie Kuhrt, eds. *Images of Women in Antiquity*. Detroit: Wayne State University Press, 1985.

Campbell, R. Alastair. *The Elders: Seniority within Earliest Christianity*. Edinburgh: T&T Clark, 1994.

Cantarella, Eva. *Pandora's Daughters: The Role and Status of Women in Greek and Roman Antiquity*. Baltimore: Johns Hopkins University Press, 1987.

Cardman, Francine. "Acts of the Women Martyrs." In *Women in Early Christianity*, ed. D. M. Scholer. 98–104. New York: Garland, 1993.

Castelli, Elizabeth. "'I Will Make Mary Male': Pieties of the Body and Gender Transformation of Christian Women in Late Antiquity." In *Body Guards: The Cultural Politics of Gender Ambiguity*, ed. J. Epstein and K. Straub, 29–49. New York: Routledge, 1991.

Chuvin, Pierre. *A Chronicle of the Last Pagans*. Cambridge: Harvard University Press, 1990.

Clark, Gillian. *Women in Late Antiquity*. Oxford: Clarendon Press, 1993.

Coleman, K. M. "Fatal Charades: Roman Executions Staged as Mythological Enactments." *Journal of Roman Studies* 80 (1990), 44–73.

Cooper, Kate. *The Virgin and the Bride: Idealized Womanhood in Late Antiquity*. Cambridge: Harvard University Press, 1996.

Corley, Kathleen E. *Private Women, Public Meals: Social Conflict in the Synoptic Tradition*. Peabody, Mass.: Hendrickson, 1993.

Cramer, Peter. *Baptism and Change in the Early Middle Ages, c. 200–c. 1150*. Cambridge: Cambridge University Press, 1993.

Daube, David. *Civil Disobedience in Antiquity*. Edinburgh: University Press, 1972.

Davies, J. G. "Was the Devotion of Septimius Severus to Serapis the Cause of the Persecution of 202–3?" *Journal of Theological Studies* n.s. 6 (1954): 73–76.

Davies, Stevan. *The Revolt of the Widows*. Carbondale: Southern Illinois University Press, 1980.

Davis, Nathan. *Carthage and Her Remains*. New York: Harper, 1861.

de Nie, Giselle. "Consciousness Fecund through God." In *Sanctity and Motherhood*, ed. A. Mulder-Bakker, 101–61. New York: Garland, 1995.

de St. Croix, G. E. M "Why Were the Early Christians Persecuted?" *Past and Present* 26 (1963): 6–38.

Delaney, Gayle, ed. *New Directions in Dream Interpretation*. Albany: SUNY Press, 1993.

Delattre, A. L. "Inscriptions Chrétiennes de Carthage 1906–1907," *Revue Tunisienne*, 1907, 405–19, 536–44; 1908, 37–45, 169–78, 225–31, 435–44, 521–32.

———. "Quelques Nouvelles Découvertes D'Archéologie Chrétienne à Carthage." *Nuovo Bullettino di Archeologia Cristiana*, 1909, 45–55.

Delattre, R. P. "L'Area Chrétienne et la Basilique de MCIDFA, A Carthage." *Comptes Rendus de Sciences—Academie des Inscriptions et Belles Lettres*, 1907, 118–28.

———. "La Basilica Majorum (puits Rempli de Squelettes)." *Comptes Rendus de Sciences—Academie des Inscriptions et Belles Lettres*, 1908, 59–69.

————. "La Basilica Majorum, Tombeau des Saintes Perpétue et Félicité." *Comptes Rendus de Sciences—Academie des Inscriptions et Belles Lettres*, 1907, 516–32.

————. "Sur l'inscription des martyrs de Carthage, sainte Perpétue, sainte Félicité et leurs compagnons." *Comptes rendus de l'Académie des Inscriptions et Belles-Lettres*, 1907, 193–95.

Dixon, Suzanne. *The Roman Mother*. Norman: Oklahoma University Press, 1988.

Dodds, E. R. *Pagan and Christian in an Age of Anxiety*. Cambridge: Cambridge University Press, 1985.

Droge, A. J., and James D. Tabor. *A Noble Death: Suicide and Martyrdom among Christians and Jews in Antiquity*. San Francisco: Harper, 1992.

Duke, T. T. "Women and Pygmies in the Roman Arena." *Classical Journal* 50 (February 1955): 223–24.

Dumézil, Georges. *Archaic Roman Religion*. Trans. P. Krapp. 2 vols. Chicago: University of Chicago Press, 1966.

Dunbabin, K. M. D. *The Mosaics of Roman North Africa*. Oxford: Clarendon Press, 1978.

Duncan-Jones, R. P. "The Chronology of the Priesthood of Africa Proconsularis under the Principate." *Epigraphische Studien* 5 (1968): 151ff.

Dunn, James D. G. *Jesus and the Spirit*. London: SCM Press, 1975.

Dupont, Florence. *Daily Life in Ancient Rome*. Trans. Christopher Woodall. Oxford: Basil Blackwell, 1993.

Ellis, E. Earle. *Prophecy and Hermeneutic in Early Christianity*. Grand Rapids, Mich.: Eerdmans, 1978.

Esler, Philip. *The First Christians in Their Social Worlds*. New York: Routledge, 1994.

Evans, Arthur. *The God of Ecstasy*. New York: St. Martin's Press, 1988.

Evans, J. K. "Wheat Production and Its Social Consequences in the Roman World." *Classical Quarterly* 31 (1981): 428–42.

Faversham, W. Telfer. "The Origins of Christianity in Africa." *Studia Patristica* 4 (1961): 512–17.

Ferguson, E., ed. *Conversion, Catechumenate, and Baptism in the Early Church*. New York: Garland, 1993.

Ferguson, J. *Greek and Roman Religion*. Park Ridge, N. J.: Noyes Press, 1980.

Fiorenza, Elizabeth Schüssler. *In Memory of Her: A Feminist Theological Reconstruction of Christian Origins*. New York: Crossroad, 1983.

————. "'You are not to be called Father': Early Christian History in a Feminist Perspective." *Cross Currents* 30 (1979): 301–23.

Ford, J. Massignberd. "Was Montanism a Jewish-Christian Heresy?" *Journal of Ecclesiastical History* 17 (1966): 145–58.

Fowden, Garth. *Empire to Commonwealth: Consequences of Monotheism in Late Antiquity*. Princeton: Princeton University Press, 1993.

Fowler, W. Warde. *The Religious Experience of the Roman People*. London: Macmillan, 1911.

Fox, Robin Lane. *Pagans and Christians*. New York: Knopf, 1987.

Free, K. B., ed. *The Formulation of Christianity by Conflict through the Ages*. Lewiston, N. Y.: Edwin Mellen Press, 1995.

Frend, W. H. C. "A Note on Jews and Christians in Third Century North Africa" *Journal of Theological Studies*, n.s., 21 (1970): 92–96.

———. "A Severan Persecution? Evidence of the 'Historia Augusta.'" In *Forma Futuri: Studi in Onore del Cardinale Michele Pellegrino*. Torino: Bottega d'Erasmo, 1975.

———. *The Archaeology of Early Christianity: A History*. Minneapolis: Fortress Press, 1996.

———. "Blandina and Perpetua: Two Early Christian Heroines." In *Women in Early Christianity*, ed. D. M. Scholer, 87–97. New York: Garland, 1993.

———. *The Donatist Church*. Oxford: Basil Blackwell, 1952.

———. *Martyrdom and Persecution in the Early Church: A Study of Conflict from the Maccabees to Donatus*. Oxford: Basil Blackwell, 1965.

———. *The Rise of Christianity*. Philadelphia: Fortress Press, 1984.

———. "The Seniores Laici and the Origins of the Church in North Africa." *Journal of Theological Studies*, n.s., 12 (1961): 280–85.

Freud, Sigmund. *Interpretation of Dreams*. Trans. J. Strachey. New York: Avon Books, 1965.

Gager, John G. "Body-Symbols and Social Reality: Resurrection, Incarnation and Asceticism in Early Christianity." *Religion* 12 (1982): 345–63.

———. *Kingdom and Community: The Social World of Early Christianity*. Englewood Cliffs, N. J.: Prentice-Hall, 1975.

Gardner, Eileen, ed. *Visions of Heaven and Hell before Dante*. New York: Italica Press, 1989.

Gardner, Jane. *Women in Roman Law and Society*. Bloomington: Indiana University Press, 1986.

Garnsey, Peter. "Child Rearing in Ancient Italy." In *The Family in Italy from Antiquity to the Present*, ed. D. Kertzer et al., 48–65. New Haven: Yale University Press, 1991.

Gillespie, Thomas W. *The First Theologians: A Study in Early Christian Prophecy*. Grand Rapids, Mich.: Eerdmans, 1994.

Girard, René. *Violence and the Sacred*. Trans. P. Gregory. Baltimore: Johns Hopkins University Press, 1977.

Gleason, Maud W. "The Semiotics of Gender: Physiognomy and Self-Fashioning in the Second Century C.E." In *Before Sexuality: The Construction of Erotic Experience in the Ancient Greek World*, ed. D. M. Halperin et al., 389–416. Princeton: Princeton University Press, 1990.

Golvin, Jean-Claude. *L'Amphithéâtre Romain*. Paris: Boccard, 1988.

Goodman, Martin. *State and Society in Roman Galilee, A.D. 132–212*. Totowa, N. J.: Rowman & Allanheld, 1983.

Grant, F. C., ed. *Ancient Roman Religion*. New York: Library of Religion, 1957.

Greer, Rowan A. *The Fear of Freedom: A Study of Miracles in the Roman Imperial Church*. University Park: Pennsylvania State University Press, 1989.

Guterman, S. L. *Religious Toleration and Persecution in Ancient Rome*. London: Aiglon Press, 1951.

Hallett, Judith. *Fathers and Daughters in Roman Society*. Princeton: Princeton University Press, 1984.

Heffernan, Thomas J. *Sacred Biography: Saints and Their Biographers in the Middle Ages*. Oxford: Oxford University Press, 1988.

Heine, Ronald J. *Montanist Oracles and Testimonia*. North American Patristic Society, vol. 14. Macon, Ga.: Mercer University Press, 1989.

————. "The Role of the Gospel of John in the Montanist Controversy." *The Second Century* 6 (1987/88): 1–19.

Herrin, Judith. *The Formation of Christendom*. Princeton: Princeton University Press, 1987.

Hiesinger, Ulrich S. "Julia Domna: Two Portraits in Bronze." *American Journal of Archaeology* 73 (January 1969): 39–44.

Hillard, T. "*Materna Auctoritas:* The Political Influence of Roman *Matronae*." *Classicum* 22 (1972): 10–13.

Hoffsten, Ruth. *Roman Women of Rank in the Early Empire as Portrayed by Dio, Paterculus, Suetonius, and Tacitus*. Philadelphia: University of Pennsylvania Press, 1939.

Hopkins, Keith. "On the Probable Age Structure of the Roman Population." *Population Studies* 20 (1966): 245–64.

Ide, Arthur Frederick. *Martyrdom of Women: A Study of Death Psychology in the Early Christian Church to 301 C.E.* Garland, Tex.: Tangelwüld Press, 1985.

Jacquart, Danielle, and Claude Thomasset. *Sexuality and Medicine in the Middle Ages*. Princeton: Princeton University Press, 1988.

Jones, A. H. M. *The Later Roman Empire, 284–602*. Baltimore: Johns Hopkins University Press, 1986.

Kee, H. C. *Medicine, Miracle, and Magic in New Testament Times*. Cambridge: Cambridge University Press, 1986.

————. *Miracle in the Early Christian World*. New Haven: Yale University Press, 1983.

Kertzer, David I. and R. P. Seller, eds. *The Family in Italy from Antiquity to the Present*. New Haven: Yale University Press, 1991.

Kiefer, Otto. *Sexual Life in Ancient Rome*. New York: Dorset Press, 1993.

Klawiter, Frederick C. "The Role of Martyrdom and Persecution in Developing the Priestly Authority of Women in Early Christianity: A Case Study of Montanism." In *Women in Early Christianity*, ed. D. M. Scholer, 105–16. New York: Garland, 1993.

Kraemer, Ross Shepard. *Her Share of the Blessings*. Oxford: Oxford University Press, 1992.

Kruger, Steven F. *Dreaming in the Middle Ages*. Cambridge: Cambridge University Press, 1992.

LaBerge, Stephen. *Lucid Dreaming*. Los Angeles: Jeremy Tarcher, 1985.

Labriolle, Pierre de. *La Crise Montaniste*. Paris: Ernest Leroux, 1913.

Lancel, Serge. *Carthage: A History*. Oxford: Basil Blackwell, 1995.

la Piana, G. "The Roman Church at the End of the Second Century," *Harvard Theological Review* 18 (1925): 201–77.

Laporte, Jean. *The Role of Women in Early Christianity*. Lewsiton, N. Y.: Edwin Mellen Press, 1982.

Lefkowitz, Mary R. "The Motivations for St. Perpetua's Martyrdom." *Journal of the American Academy of Religion* 44 (1976): 417–21.

————, and M. B. Fant. *Women's Lives in Greece and Rome*. Baltimore: Johns Hopkins University Press, 1982.

LeGoff, Jacques. *The Birth of Purgatory*. Trans. A. Goldhammer. Chicago: University of Chicago Press, 1984.

————. "Christianity and Dreams." In *The Medieval Imagination*, trans. A. Goldhammer. Chicago: University of Chicago Press, 1988.

Levenson, Jon D. *The Death and Resurrection of the Beloved Son*. New Haven: Yale University Press, 1993.

Lewis, I. M. *Ecstatic Religion*. New York: Routledge, 1989.

Liebeschuetz, J. H. W. G. *Continuity and Change in Roman Religion*. Oxford: Clarendon Press, 1979.

Lietzmann, H., ed. *Die drei ältesten Martyrologien*. Kleine Texte für theologische und philologische Vorlesungen und Übungen, vol. 2. Bonn: A. Marcus & E. Weber, 1911.

Lightman, M., and W. Zeisel. "Univira: An Example of Continuity and Change in Roman Society." *Church History* 46 (1977): 19–32.

Lincoln, Bruce. *Emerging from the Chrysalis*. Oxford: Oxford University Press, 1991.

Littlewood, A. R. "The Symbolism of the Apple in Greek and Roman Literature." Harvard Studies in Classical Philology 72 (1968), 147–81.

Lucian of Samosata. *Lucian*, vol. 1–8. Trans. M. D. MacLeod. Cambridge: Harvard University Press, 1967.

Lyttleton, M., and W. Forman. *The Romans: Their Gods and Their Beliefs*. London: Orbis, 1984.

MacDonald, David J. *The Coinage of Aphrodisias*. London: Royal Numismatic Society, 1992.

MacMullen, Ramsay. *Christianizing the Roman Empire (A.D. 100–400)*. New Haven: Yale University Press, 1984.

————. *Paganism in the Roman Empire*. New Haven: Yale University Press, 1981.

Marshall, A. S. "Roman Women and the Provinces." *Ancient Society* (1976) 6: 109–27.

Martin, Luther H. *Hellenistic Religions*. Oxford: Oxford University Press, 1987.

Mattingly, D. J., and R. B. Hitchner. "Roman North Africa: An Archaeological Survey." *Journal of Roman Studies* 85 (1995): 165–213.

McCabe, Joseph. *The Empresses of Rome*. New York: Holt, 1911.

McDannell, Colleen and B. Lang. *Heaven: A History*. New Haven: Yale University Press, 1988.

Meeks, Wayne. *The First Urban Christians: The Social World of the Apostle Paul.* New Haven: Yale University Press, 1983.

———. *The Origins of Christian Morality: The First Two Centuries.* New Haven: Yale University Press, 1993.

Merrill, Elmer Truesdell. "Tertullian on Pliny's Persecution of the Christians." *American Journal of Theology,* 52 (1918): 124–35.

Milavec, Aaron. "Distinguishing True and False Prophets: The Protective Wisdom of the *Didache.*" *Journal of Early Christian Studies* 2, no. 2 (1994): 117–36.

Miles, Margaret R. *Carnal Knowing.* Boston: Beacon Press, 1989.

Millar, Fergus. *The Emperor in the Roman World.* Ithaca: Cornell University Press, 1977.

Miller, Patricia Cox. "'All the Words Were Frightful': Salvation by Dreams in the Shepherd of Hermas." *Vigiliae Christianae* 42 (1988): 327–38.

———. "The Devil's Gateway: An Eros of Difference in the Dreams of Perpetua." *Dreaming* 2, no. 1 (1992): 45–63.

Newman, Barbara. *From Virile Woman to WomanChrist.* Philadelphia: University of Pennsylvania Press, 1995.

Neyrey, Jerome H. "Body Language in 1 Corinthians." *Semeia* 35 (1986): 129–70.

Nock, A. D. "Alexander of Abonuteichos." *Classical Quarterly* 22 (1928): 160–62.

———. *Conversion: The Old and the New in Religion from Alexander the Great to Augustine of Hippo.* Oxford: Oxford University Press, 1961.

Oliver, J. H. "Julia Domna as Athena Polias." In *Athenian Studies Presented to William Scott Ferguson,* 521–30. Cambridge: Harvard University Press, 1973.

Olseon, H. "The Five Julias of the Severan Emperors." *Voice of the Turtle* 4 (1965): 197.

Oppenheim, A. L. "The Interpretation of Dreams in the Ancient Near East." *Transactions of the American Philosophical Society* 46 (1956): 179–255.

Pagels, Elaine. *The Origin of Satan.* New York: Random House, 1995.

Pedley, John Griffiths. *New Light on Ancient Carthage.* Ann Arbor: University of Michigan Press, 1980.

Perowne, Stewart. *Caesars and Saints: The Rise of the Christian State, A.D. 180–313.* New York: Barnes & Noble, 1962.

Pettersen, Alvyn. "Perpetua—Prisoner of Conscience." *Vigiliae Christianae* 41 (1987): 139–53.

Phillips, J. E. "Roman Mothers and the Lives of Their Adult Daughters," *Helios,* n.s., 6 (1990): 69–80.

Platnauer, Maurice. *The Life and Reign of the Emperor Lucius Septimius Severus.* 1918. Reprint, Westport, Conn.: Greenwood Press, 1970.

Pomeroy, Sarah B. *Goddesses, Whores, Wives and Slaves: Women in Classical Antiquity.* New York: Schocken, 1975.

Poque, S. "Spectacles et festins offerts par Augustin d'Hippone pour les fêtes de martyrs." *Pallas* 15 (1968): 103–25.

Potter, David. *Prophets and Emperors: Human and Divine Authority from Augustus to Theodosius.* Cambridge: Harvard University Press, 1994.

Powell, Douglas. "Tertullianists and Cataphrygians." *Vigiliae Christianae* 29 (1975): 33–54.

Price, S. R. F. "The Future of Dreams: From Freud to Artemidorus." In *Before Sexuality: The Construction of Erotic Experience in the Ancient Greek World,* ed. D. M. Halperin et al., 365–88. Princeton: Princeton University Press, 1990.

———. *Rituals and Power: The Roman Imperial Cult in Asia Minor.* Cambridge: Cambridge University Press, 1984.

Raven, Susan. *Rome in Africa.* New York: Routledge, 1993.

Rawson, Beryl, ed. *The Family in Ancient Rome: New Perspectives.* Ithaca: Cornell University Press, 1986.

Reitzenstein, Richard. *Hellenistic Mystery-Religions: Their Basic Ideas and Significance.* Trans. J. E. Steely. Pittsburgh: Pickwick Press, 1978.

Rives, J. B. "The Piety of a Persecutor." *Journal of Early Christian Studies* 4, 1 (1996): 1–26.

———. *Religion and Authority in Roman Carthage from Augustus to Constantine.* Oxford: Clarendon Press, 1995.

Robert, Louis. "Une vision de Perpétue, martyre à Carthage en 203." *Comptes rendus de l'Académie des Inscriptions et Belles-Lettres,* 1982, 228–76.

Rossi, Mary Ann. "The Passion of Perpetua, Everywoman of Late Antiquity." In *Pagan and Christian Anxiety: A Response to E. R. Dodds,* ed. R. C. Smith and J. Lounibos, 53–86. New York: University Press of America, 1984.

Rouselle, Aline. *Porneia: On Desire and the Body in Antiquity.* Trans. F. Pheasant. New York: Basil Blackwell, 1988.

Rousselle, R. "The Dreams of Vibia Perpetua: Analysis of a Female Christian Martyr," *Journal Psychohistory* 14 (1987): 193–206.

Rupprecht, Carol Schreier. *The Dream and the Text: Essays on Literature and Language.* Albany: SUNY Press, 1993.

Salisbury, Joyce E. "The Bond of a Common Mind: A Study of Collective Salvation from Cyprian to Augustine." *Journal of Religious History* 11 (1985): 235–47.

———. *Church Fathers, Independent Virgins.* London: Verso, 1991.

———. *Iberian Popular Religion, 600 B.C. to 700 A.D.* Lewiston, N. Y.: Edwin Mellen Press, 1985.

———. "Origin of the Power of Vincent the Martyr." *Proceedings of the PMR Conference* 8 (1983): 97–107.

Saxer, V. *Morts, martyrs, reliques en Afrique Chrétienne aux premiers siècles.* Paris: Beauchesne, 1980.

Schlegel, G. D. "The *Ad Martyras* of Tertullian and the Circumstances of Its Composition." *Downside Review* 63 (1945): 125.

Schwarte, K. H. "Das angebliche Christengesetz des Sep. Sev." *Historia* 12 (1963): 185–208.

Scobie, Alex. "Spectator Security and Comfort at Gladiatorial Games." In *Nikephoros: Zeitschrift für Sport und Kultur im Altertum,* 1988, 191–243.

Segal, Alan F. *Rebecca's Children: Judaism and Christianity in the Roman World.* Cambridge: Harvard University Press, 1986.

Seltzer, Robert M., ed. *Religions of Antiquity*. New York: Macmillan, 1989.

Shafton, Anthony. *Dream Reader: Contemporary Approaches to the Understanding of Dreams*. Albany: SUNY Press, 1995.

Shaw, Brent. "The Age of Roman Girls at Marriage: Some Reconsiderations." *Journal of Roman Studies* 77 (1987): 30–46.

———. "Body/Power/Identity: Passions of the Martyrs." *Journal of Early Christian Studies* 4 (fall 1996): 269–312.

———. "The Passion of Perpetua." *Past and Present* 139 (1993): 3–45.

Shewring, W. H. "Prose Rhythm in the Passio S. Perpetuae." *Journal of Theological Studies* 30 (1928/29): 56–57.

Smith, J. Z. *Drudgery Divine: On the Comparison of Early Christianities and the Religions of Late Antiquity*. Chicago: University of Chicago Press, 1990.

Snyder, Jane McIntosh. *The Woman and the Lyre: Women Writers in Classical Greece and Rome*. Carbondale: Southern Illinois University Press, 1989.

Soren, David, et al. *Carthage*. New York: Simon & Schuster, 1990.

Sprague de Camp, L. *Great Cities of the Ancient World*. New York: Dorset Press, 1972.

Stager, Lawrence E., and Samuel R. Wolff, "Child Sacrifice at Carthage—Religious Rite or Population Control?" *Biblical Archeology Review* 10, no. 1 (January–February 1984): 31–51.

Stark, Rodney. *The Rise of Christianity: A Sociologist Reconsiders History*. Princeton: Princeton University Press, 1996.

Starr, Raymond J. "The Circulation of Literary Texts in the Roman World." *Classical Quarterly* 37 (1987): 213–23.

Tabbernee, William. "Early Montanism and Voluntary Martyrdom." *Colloquium: The Australian and New Zealand Theological Review* 19 (1985): 33–44.

Telfer, W. "The Origins of Christianity in Africa." Studie Patristica, vol. 4: *Texte u. Unters* 79 (1960): 512–17.

Tilley, Maureen A. "One Woman's Body: Repression and Expression in the *Passio Perpetuae*." In *Ethnicity, Nationality and Religious Experience*, ed. Peter C. Phan. New York: University Press of America, 1991.

Vande Kappelle, Robert P. "Prophets and Mantics." In *Pagan and Christian Anxiety: A Response to E. R. Dodds*, ed. R. C. Smith and J. Lounibos, 87–111. New York: University Press of America, 1984.

Veyne, Paul. *Bread and Circuses*. Trans. B. Pearce. London: Penguin Press, 1990.

Walsh, P. G. *The Roman Novel*. Cambridge: Cambridge University Press, 1970.

Warmington, B. H. *Carthage: A History*, New York: Barnes & Noble, 1993.

Weinrich, William C. *Spirit and Martyrdom: A Study of the Work of the Holy Spirit in Contexts of Persecution and Martyrdom in the New Testament and Early Christianity*. Washington, D. C.: University Press of America, 1981.

White, Robert J. *The Interpretation of Dreams: Oneirocritica by Artemidorus*. Noyes Classical Studies. Park Ridge, N. J.: Noyes Press, 1975.

Wiedemann, Thomas. *Emperors and Gladiators*. New York: Routledge, 1992.

Wild, Payson S. "Two Julias." *Classical Journal* 12 (October 1917): 14–24.

Wilken, Robert L. *The Christians as the Romans Saw Them*. New Haven: Yale University Press, 1984.

Wilkins, P. J. "Amphitheatres and Private Munificence in Roman Africa." *Zeitschrift für Papyrologie und Epigraphik* 75 (1988): 215–21.

Williams, Mary Gilmore. "Studies in the Lives of Roman Empresses, I: Julia Domna." *American Journal of Archaeology* 6, no. 3 (1902): 259–305.

Witt, R. E. *Isis in the Graeco-Roman World*. Ithaca: Cornell University Press, 1971.

Index